Elementary Logic

Robert Lover

Elementary Logic

For Software Development

 Springer

Dr. Robert Lover, PhD

ISBN 978-1-84800-081-0   ISBN 978-1-84800-082-7 (eBook)
DOI 10.1007/978-1-84800-082-7

Library of Congress Control Number: 2008928865

Printed on acid-free paper

9 8 7 6 5 4 3 2 1

springer.com

Preface

Goals

Keeping up with new developments in most areas of computing requires familiarity with basic logical concepts. In particular, your success in most aspects of software development significantly depends on your ability to reason correctly, to communicate your reasoning, and to understand and evaluate the reasoning of others. These abilities are critical for anyone who does feasibility analysis, systems analysis, problem specification, database design or management, program design, coding, testing, verification, problem diagnosis, documentation, software maintenance, or research in any of these areas.

If you know little about how logic can be used in software development and if you want to know more, then this book may be of use to you. After reading it you should be better able to reason about software development, to communicate your reasoning, to distinguish between good and bad reasoning, and to read professional literature, which presumes knowledge of elementary logic.

On the other hand, if you think that your own logical abilities are good enough, but that many other people are sadly deficient in these abilities, then please give copies of this book to those who need it.

Overview and Features

Applications of logic to software development are emphasized throughout. Examples involving program instructions are expressed in pseudocode so that the book makes no use of any particular programming language. It is divided into three parts. Part I is about language and logical form. It explains how to find and represent the logical forms of statements expressed in English. It shows how to use a subset of English, here called *logical English*, to represent both the meanings and logical forms of statements. Logical English is intermediate between informal but meaningful English and the largely meaningless and severely abstract notations commonly used in formal logic, and used here in Part III. This intermediate role resembles the role of pseudocode. Like pseudocode, logical English is still recognizable English. And like pseudocode, it is a helpful bridge between informal English and a highly formal notation. They differ in that logical English is used to express statements and conditions while pseudocode is used to express instructions. Part I ends by describing how to use logical English to clarify and express data structure definitions, problem specifications, and conditions in instructions.

Part II is about truth in the ordinary "material" sense of that term. It shows how to use truth tables to determine the truth or falsity of a complex statement built using connectives such as "not", "and", "or", and "if...then..." if you know the truth or falsity of its component statements. Truth conditions for statements involving the quantifiers "all" and "some" are also described. Following that, several computer-related applications of this material are discussed. The final chapter shows how to apply truth value calculations to forward and backward tracing of program execution.

Part III is about "logical" truth. Logical truth is a generalization of material truth. It involves ignoring the meanings and material truth values of individual statements and focusing only on their logical forms. Much of what is known about how to reason correctly can best be stated in terms of logical forms. For example, the statement form "P or not P" is logically true. As a result, no matter what statement is used in place of P, the resulting statement of the form "P or not P" is materially true.

This part also explains and shows how to test statements for logical equivalence, logical implication, and logical redundancy, and how to test arguments for validity and soundness. It also explains how to use rules of inference to make proofs. It then describes how to apply these concepts to problem specifications. This is followed by a proof that no computer program that solves the problem of determining whether any arbitrarily selected program will halt with any arbitrarily selected input can be written. That bad news is followed by the good news that it is possible, though difficult, to prove that a program is correct relative to a problem specification, without doing any testing. Examples showing how to do this in simple cases are given. The last chapter briefly discusses some topics not covered here, e.g. logic testing and quantum computing. It includes a few pointers to additional sources of information about these topics.

Suggested Uses

This book is designed to be used by computer professionals and students who want to study on their own without an instructor. It is also suitable as the primary text for instructor led introductory courses on logic for students who are studying any of the computing disciplines. Earlier versions of much of this material were class tested in a college level course I teach on logic and its applications to computing. In addition, the three parts of the book can be the basis for three or more short professional development courses.

Target Audiences

Students and professionals who expect to be involved with any aspect of software development are the target audiences for this book. No prior knowledge of formal logic is assumed. Some knowledge of software development is assumed.

Audience Resources

Many examples as well as many practice exercises, along with solutions to half of them, are included here. Solutions to all the exercises can be had by instructors at http://www.springer.com/978-1-84800-081-0

Readers can contact me at http://www.logicforsoftwaredevelopment.com. I intend to post corrections to newly discovered errors, pointers to additional resources, logic jokes, and other related information there.

Readers are also urged to use the email link there to send error reports and constructive suggestions for improving this book.

Acknowledgements

I am grateful to the monks, administrators, staff, and faculty at Belmont Abbey College for providing me an environment in which it was possible to write this book. Special thanks, and some commiseration, are due to my students in CS325 who suffered through earlier drafts of much of this material.

Gene Lauver and Bill Seltzer, who have many years of experience in real-world computing, found numerous errors, made many helpful suggestions, and even worked many of the exercises "for fun". Without their help, this book would have been noticeably less useful.

Finally, several anonymous reviewers made helpful suggestions. Wayne Wheeler and Catherine Brett at Springer, UK, provided enthusiastic, cheerful, patient, and professional editorial support.

Robert Lover
Charlotte, NC

Contents

Solutions to Selected Exercises 241

Sources and Bibliography 305

Index 309

Part I
Language and Logical Form

Part I explains how to determine the logical forms of statements and how to use "logical English" to represent those forms without losing touch with their meaning. Logical English consists of abbreviations for logically important parts of statements along with rules for organizing those abbreviations. Its purpose is to help people communicate and reason better. It plays a role in logic similar to the role played by pseudocode in programming. Various examples of its use are described in Chaps. 4–7.

Chapter 1
Atomic Statements

In this chapter the logical structure of the simplest kind of statements, called atomic statements, is described. Logical English is introduced and used to represent this structure. After studying this chapter you should be able to identify names, predicates, and descriptions in atomic statements and express the logical structure of atomic statements using logical English.

Outline

1.1   Vagueness and Ambiguity

Vagueness and ambiguity often cause ineffective communication and bad reasoning. It is best to eliminate much of it before representing the logical structure of (ordinary) English in logical English.

Definition 1. An instance of a word, phrase, statement, or set of statements is said to be *vague* if and only if, in its context, it is unclear whether the expression does or does not apply to some relevant cases and this lack of clarity is not due to ignorance about the facts of the situation.

Example 1. A specification that requires classifying people into those who are tall and those who are not tall would be vague. The specification could be clarified by stipulating that in this specification someone is tall if and only if they are 6 feet tall or taller.

R. Lover, *Elementary Logic: For Software Development*,
DOI: 10.2007/978-1-84800-082-7, © Springer 2008

Example 2. A specification that requires an "appropriately worded error message" at a certain point would be vague. Various levels of clarification could be had by spelling out what would count as an "appropriately worded error message" with various levels of specificity.

Most expressions are vague to some extent. Often this does no harm and greatly simplifies communication. For example, the context may make clear what is meant or cases involving vagueness are not under consideration. Vagueness should be reduced if it makes an important difference in how an expression will be understood.

Definition 2. An instance of a word, phrase, statement, or set of statements is said to be *ambiguous* just in case it can reasonably be understood to have two or more different meanings in that context.

Many expressions are ambiguous. Just look at any dictionary and you will see numerous different meanings for many words and phrases. A classic example of an ambiguous statement is "The Greeks the Romans will subdue." Does it mean the Greeks will subdue the Romans or does it mean the Romans will subdue the Greeks?

Vagueness and ambiguity are very different. An expression can be vague without being ambiguous, ambiguous without being vague, or both vague and ambiguous. Ambiguity can be eliminated by specifying which meaning is intended. Vagueness can be reduced or eliminated by being more precise about how to apply the term.

Example 3. A specification that requires output to be sorted is not necessarily vague, but it is ambiguous. Is the output to be sorted in ascending order or descending order?

Example 4. A specification that required adding "long lists of numbers" is at least vague and perhaps ambiguous. The term "long list" is vague. How long? Depending on context "numbers" may be ambiguous. Are the numbers just integers, just rational numbers, all real numbers? What about complex numbers?

1.2 Logical English

Definition 3. A notation, called *Logical English*, will be described in this and the next few chapters. It consists of abbreviations for and slight rearrangements of statements expressed in English.

Understanding logical English will make a wide variety of computing literature available to you. It is found in program specifications, data structure definitions, program designs, software testing literature, proofs of program correctness, documentation, and computer science literature. Knowing how to write logical English can improve the clarity and efficiency of your communication and your reasoning.

Logical English is a bit like pseudocode. Like pseudocode it is English restricted in vocabulary and form. Like pseudocode it is intended to help people clarify their thoughts, communicate clearly, and reason correctly. Like pseudocode, there is no official definition of it, so different authors use different versions of it. And like pseudocode, once you have mastered one version of it, it is easy to understand and use other versions. It differs from pseudocode in that logical English is used to represent statements and conditions while pseudocode is used to represent instructions. The logical English used here will be characterized by a few rules. The most important rule is:

LE Rule 0: The rules of logical English can be bent or broken in a specific context if doing so will help people communicate or reason better.

1.3   Names

In logical English short names, like "Joe" or "3.53", are often left as is. Long names, like "Rumplestiltskin", are usually shortened, e.g. to "Rump", "R", or "r". In logical English names like "George Washington" that have embedded blanks are written without embedded blanks. Two common ways of doing this are to use underscores in place of blanks, e.g. "George_Washington", or to simply omit the blanks, e.g. GeorgeWashington". When extreme brevity is desired, lowercase letters from the beginning of the alphabet are used to represent names, e.g. "gw" or just "g".

Example 5. Names

English	Logical English
Joe	Joe, j, j_3
George Washington	georgeWashington, GeorgeWashington, George_Washington, gw, g,…
3.53	3.53, n_6, n

LE Rule 1. Abbreviations used in logical English are written without embedded blanks, often using *camelback notation*. Camelback notation consists of writing a sequence of words or abbreviations for words without blanks between them and capitalizing the first character of each word or abbreviation, e.g. GeorgeWashington. Sometimes the first character is written in lower case and the notation is called *sad camelback notation*, e.g. georgeWashington. (The sadness of the camel is indicated by its head being lowered.)

There are no rules about which abbreviation to use for what, but there are common practices. For example, it is helpful if an abbreviation reminds the reader of what it abbreviates. For example using 'g' rather than 'x' to abbreviate 'George' or using '7Open' rather than 'X_{33}' to abbreviate 'File 7 is open.'

1.4   Predicates

A predicate is an expression used to refer to a property of individual things or a relation between pairs of things, among triples of things, quadruples of things, and so on.

Definition 4. A *1-place predicate* is a predicate that refers to a property of individual things. A *2-place predicate* is a predicate that refers to relations between pairs of things. A *3-place predicate* is a predicate that refers to relations among triples of things. In general, an *N-place predicate*, where N can be any positive integer, is a predicate that refers to properties of or relations between or among N things.

Note that predicates in this logical sense of the term are not quite the same as predicates as studied in English grammar.

Example 6. Predicates, with places indicated by …

1-place predicates
> … is an open file
> … is an odd integer
> … is taller than Joe
> Joe is taller than…

2-place predicates
> … is taller than…
> … hates…
> … is between Chicago and …
> Kalamazoo is between … and …
> … is between … and Detroit

3-place predicates
> … is between … and …
> has length…width…and depth…

4-place predicates
> …is more like…than… is like…
> …is to…as…is to…

LE Rule 2. In logical English the names and descriptions (discussed below) to which predicates are applied are written to the right of the predicate, separated by commas, the whole list in parentheses. When single letters of the alphabet are used to represent predicates it is customary to use capital letters, with or without numeric subscripts. Where mathematical concepts are involved, mathematical notation is often included in logical English. Which abbreviation to use is up to the user, but the point is to use the shortest abbreviations that still reminds users of the original meaning. Examples of these abbreviations are given below.

Predicates	Logical English
1-place	
... is an open file	OpenFile(...)
... is an odd integer	OddInt(...)
... is taller than Joe	TallerThanJoe(...)
Joe is taller than...	JoeTallerThan(...)
2-place	
... is taller than...	IsTallerThan(..., ...)
... hates...	Hates(..., ...)
... is between Chicago and ...	BtwnChi(..., ...)
Kalamazoo is between ... and ...	KzoBtwn(..., ...)
... is between ... and Detroit	BtwnAndDet(..., ...)
3-place	
... is between ... and ...	IsBtwn(..., ..., ...)
has length...width...and depth...	LWD(..., ..., ...)
4-place	
...is more like...than... is like...	CompareSim(..., ..., ..., ...)
...is to...as...is to...	Proportion(..., ..., ..., ...)

1.5 Descriptions

There are expressions of English that refer to things by describing them rather than naming them. For example, we might say that Henry is the father of Jack. Or we might say that Henry is a parent of Jack. The expression 'the father of Jack' is called a definite description of Jack's father, while the expression 'a parent of Jack' is called an indefinite description of one of Jack's parents.

Definition 5. A *description* of something refers to that thing by describing it rather than naming it. A *definite description* describes in such a way that exactly one thing is supposed to fit the description. An *indefinite description* describes in such a way that at least one thing is supposed to fit the description, without implying that it is the only thing that fits that description.

Example 7. Descriptions

Description type	Informal English
definite	the father of Jack
definite	Jack's father
indefinite	a parent of Jack
definite	the smallest integer greater than 5
indefinite	an integer greater than 5
indefinite	some integer greater than 5

Care must be taken when using descriptions. While a definite description attempts to describe exactly one thing, it may fail to do so either because it describes nothing or because it describes more than one thing. For example, "the present king of France" is a definite description which describes nothing. While "the square root of 16" describes both 4 and -4. If you use a definite description as if it succeeded in describing exactly one thing, and it does not, then your communication or reasoning may be incorrect.

Similarly, care must be taken when using indefinite descriptions. While an indefinite description attempts to describe at least one thing, it may fail to do so because it describes nothing. For example, "a round square" describes nothing. If you use an indefinite description as if it succeeded in describing at least one thing, and it does not, then your communication or reasoning may be incorrect. In this book definite descriptions will be used more than indefinite descriptions.

Example 8. Definite descriptions

English	Logical English
Jill's husband	husbandOf(Jill)
the sum of 3 and 4	3 + 4
	+(3, 4)
the father of Carol	fatherOf(Carol)
the square of 4	squareOf(4)
	4^2
The value returned by subroutine SUB3 with input 7	SUB3(7)

Complex definite descriptions can be constructed out of simpler definite descriptions. For example, 'my father's father's mother's only aunt' or "the output from applying subroutine7 to the output from subroutine3'. Here are some more examples of complex definite descriptions.

Example 9. Complex definite descriptions

Complex definite descriptions in English	In logical English
the result of adding 5 to the result of multiplying 7 by the result of dividing 44 by 2	7*(44 / 2) + 5
the maximum of the square of a and the square of b	max(a^2, b^2)

1.6   Atomic Statements

Definition 6. A *statement* is the sort of sentence which is either true or false. Statements are distinguished from other kinds of sentences such as questions, commands, promises, instructions, and wishes.

Definition 7. An *atomic statement* is a statement consisting of a single predicate and one or more names or descriptions.

Example 10. Statements with 1-place predicates

Grammatical category	English	Logical English
name	Jo	Jo, j
1-place predicate	...is tall	isTall(...) T(...)
atomic statement	Jo is tall	isTall(Jo) isTall(j) T(Jo) T(j) T_1(j)
name	3	3
1-place predicate	...is an odd integer	oddInteger(...) odd(...) O(...)
atomic statement	3 is an odd integer	oddInteger(3) odd(3) O(3)
name	file7	file7, f_7, f
1-place predicate	...is an open file	openFile(...) O(...)
atomic statement	File7 is an open file	openFile(file7)? openFile(f_7) O(f)

Example 11. Statements with 2-place predicates

Grammatical category	English	Logical English
name	Joe	Joe, j
name	Sam	Sam, s
2-place predicate	...is taller than...	isTallerThan(..., ...) T(..., ...)
atomic statement	Joe is taller than Sam	isTallerThan(Joe, Sam) T_2(Joe, Sam) T(j, s)
name	three	3
name	five	5
2-place predicate	...is less than...	lessThan(..., ...) L(..., ...)
	...<...	...<... <(..., ...)
atomic statement	Three is less than five	lessThan(3, 5) L(3, 5) 3 < 5 or <(3, 5)
atomic statement	John is a parent of Carol	aParentOf (John, Carol)
atomic statement	Carol is a parent of John	aParentOf (Carol, John)

Grammatical category	English	Logical English
atomic statement	Carol is a child of John	aChildOf (Carol, John)
atomic statement	3 is greater than 1	isGreaterThan(3, 1) 3 > 1 >(3, 1)

Exercise 1. For (a)–(d), use the logical English abbreviations described below to transform the English statements into logical English

Grammatical category	English	Logical English
name	Bob	b
name	Alice	a
1-place predicate	...is tall	$T_1(...)$
2-place predicate	...is taller than...	$T_2(..., ...)$
(a) atomic statement	Alice is tall.	
(b) atomic statement	Bob is tall.	
(c) atomic statement	Alice is taller than Bob.	
(d) atomic statement	Bob is taller than Alice.	

The identity predicate is an especially important 2-place predicate. It is applied to pairs of names or definite descriptions. Two names or definite descriptions are said to be identical just in case they are names or descriptions of the same thing. Moreover, we have a special symbol for it, the = symbol. In logical English the mathematical relations <, =, and > are usually written with the symbol between two expressions as with $3 < 5$, $3 = 5$, and $a > b$. This is known as infix notation. Occasionally they are written with the symbol in front of the two expressions as with $< (3, 5)$, $= (3, 5)$, and $> (a, b)$. This is known as prefix notation.

Example 12. Logical English for the identity relation

English	Logical English	
Mark Twain is identical to Samuel Clemens.	MarkTwain = SamualClemens = (MarkTwain, SamualClemens)	
"2" and "two" are names for the same number.	2 = two = (2, two)	(infix) (prefix)
7 is the sum of 3 and 4.	$7 = 3 + 4$	(infix)
16 is the square of 4.	16 = squareOf(4)	(infix)
John is the father of Carol.	John = fatherOf(Carol)	(infix)

Exercise 2. For (a)–(d), use the logical English abbreviations described below to transform the English statements into logical English

Grammatical category	English	Logical English
name	Samuel Clemens	a
name	Mark Twain	b
2-place predicate	...is identical to...	...=... or =(..., ...)

Grammatical category	English	Logical English
(a) atomic statement	Mark Twain is Samuel Clemens.	
(b) atomic statement	Samuel Clemens is Mark Twain.	
(c) atomic statement	Mark Twain is Mark Twain.	
(d) atomic statement	Samuel Clemens is Samuel Clemens.	

Example 13. Statements with 3-place predicates

Grammatical category	English	Logical English
names	3, 5, 7	3, 5, 7
3-place predicate	...is between... and...	isBetween(..., ..., ...)
		btwn(..., ..., ...)
		B(..., ..., ...)
atomic statement	5 is between 3 and 7	isBetween(5, 3, 7)
		btwn(5, 3, 7)
		B(5, 3, 7)
name	Kalamazoo	Kzo, K, k
name	Chicago	Chi, Cgo, C, c
name	Detroit	Det, D. d
atomic statement	Kalamazoo is between Detroit and Chicago	btwn(k, d, c)
		B(Kzo, Det, Chi)
		B(k, d, c)

In English predicates that take more than 3 names are rare. "... is to ... as .... is to ..." is a 4-place predicate used in statements about proportions, e.g. in trigonometry. The expression "is a term of a_1, a_2, ..., a_n" is an N-place predicate.

Example 14. Statements with N-place predicates

Grammatical category	English	Logical English
names	3, a_1, a_2, ..., a_n	3, a_1, a_2, ..., a_n
N-place predicate	is a term of........	termOf(........)
		T(........)
statement	3 is a term of a_1, a_2, ..., a_n	termOf(3, a_1, a_2, ..., a_n)
		T(3, a_1, a_2, ..., a_n)

Exercise 3. For a – h, use the logical English abbreviations described below to transform the English statements into logical English

Grammatical category	English	Logical English
name	Alice	a
name	Bob	b
name	2	c_2
name	3	c_3
name	5	c_5

Grammatical category	English	Logical English
1-place predicate	...is tall	$T_1(...)$
2-place predicate	...is taller than...	$I(..., ...)$
2-place predicate	...is identical to...	...=...
2-place predicate	...is larger than...	$L(..., ...)$
(a) atomic statement	Alice is taller than Bob.	
(b) atomic statement	Alice is identical to Alice.	
(c) atomic statement	2 is larger than 3.	
(d) atomic statement	3 is larger than 5.	
(e) atomic statement	5 is larger than 3.	

Exercise 4. For (a)–(q), use the logical English abbreviations described below to transform the English statements into logical English. When using 'f' and 'g' for addition and multiplication, use prefix notation. When using '+' and '*' for addition and multiplication, use infix notation.

Grammatical category	English	Logical English
name	Bob	b
name	Alice	a
name	Sam	s
name	Mark	d
1-place predicate	...is tall	$T_1(...)$
2-place predicate	...is taller than...	$T_2(..., ...)$
2-place predicate	...is identical to...	=(..., ...) or ... = ...
2-place predicate	...is the father of...	fatherOf(..., ...)
name	2	2
name	3	3
name	5	5
math function name	plus	f
math function name	times	g
(a) atomic statement	Alice is Alice	
(b) atomic statement	Alice is identical to Mark	
(c) atomic statement	Bob is taller than Mark	
(d) atomic statement	Mark is taller than Bob	
(e) atomic statement	Sam is tall	
(f) def. description	2 plus 3	
(g) def. description	3 plus 2	
(h) atomic statement	2 plus 2 = 3 times 2.	
(i) def. description	2 plus (3 plus 5)	
(j) def. desc.	(2 plus 3) plus 5	
(k) atomic statement	2 plus (3 times 3) is identical to (2 plus 3) times 3	
(l) def. description	2 times (3 plus 3)	
(m) def. description	(2 plus 3) times 3	
(n) def. description	5 * 3	
(o) def. description	3 + 5	
(p) atomic statement	(2 + 3) * 5 = (3 + 2) * 5	
(q) atomic statement	2 + (3 * 5) = (3 + 2) * 5	

Chapter 2
Compound Statements

This chapter describes logical English for statements that are made from one or more simpler statements. Such statements are called compound statements. They are formed using words and phrases called statement connectives. Some of those connectives are said to be *truth functional*. Logical English abbreviations for the most important truth functional statement connectives are introduced here. The role of parentheses to reduce ambiguity is also discussed. After studying this material you should be able to transform truth functional compound statements between (ordinary) English and logical English and use parentheses and conventions for dropping them.

Outline

2.1 Truth Functional Connectives

Definition 1. A *statement connective* is a word or phrase used to construct complex statements out of simpler statements.

Example 1. The statement connective "not" and the statement "John is tall." can be used to construct the more complex statement "John is not tall." The connective "and" can be used with the statements "John is tall" and "Carol is thin." to form the statement "John is tall and Carol is thin."

R. Lover, *Elementary Logic: For Software Development*,
DOI: 10.2007/978-1-84800-082-7, © Springer 2008

There are many statement connectives in English. The ones that are important here are said to be 'truth functional'. A statement connective is truth functional if and only if the truth value (true or false) of a compound statement made using it can be determined from knowledge of just the truth values of its component statements, without knowing anything about their meanings. Truth functionality will be discussed in detail in later chapters. In logical English symbols are often used in place of truth functional connectives. Several different sets of symbols for connectives are in common use. The set that will be used here is described below.

Approximate English Meaning	Logic Symbol	Name of Symbol
not	~	tilde
and	∧	up wedge
inclusive or (i.e. and/or)	∨	wedge
if...then...	→	right arrow
if and only if	↔	double arrow

In the following definition L represents the statement on the left, and R represents the statement on the right. Note that L and R can themselves be atomic or compound.

Definition 2. Suppose L and R represent statements. Then: AU1

(a) 'Not R' is called *the negation of R*, abbreviated '(~R)'.
(b) 'L and R' is called *the conjunction of L with R*, abbreviated '(L ∧ R)'. L and R are its *conjuncts*.
(c) 'L or R' is called *the disjunction of L with R*, abbreviated '(L ∨ R)'. L and R are its *disjuncts*.
(d) 'If L then R' is called *the conditional of L with R*, abbreviated '(L → R)'. L is called the *antecedent* of the conditional, and R is called the *consequent* of the conditional.
(e) 'L if and only if R' is called *the biconditional (or the equivalence) of L with R*, abbreviated '(L ↔ R)'. L and R are its *components*.

Recall that in Chapter 1 atomic statements could be represented in logical English by single capital letters followed by a list of names and definite descriptions in parentheses. In this chapter we are not concerned with the names and descriptions. Consequently, here both atomic and compound statements will often be represented by single capital letters of the alphabet, without lists in parentheses. The use of single capital letters without lists in parentheses is not necessary. It is simply a space saving measure. Moreover, it is not necessary to use the abbreviations given above for sentential connectives. In real life, things are usually more complicated than in the examples given here and space saving may be less important than remembering what abbreviation goes with which English statement. In those cases you may be better off using less abbreviated notations.

Example 2. Logical English for connectives

Grammatical category	English	Logical English
atomic statement	John is asleep.	A S(j) JSleep
atomic statement	Today is Monday.	M Mon
atomic statement	d = 7.	D D7
negation	John is not asleep.	(~A) (not A) (~S(j)) (~JSleep)
conjunction	John is asleep and today is Monday.	(A ∧ M) (S(j) ∧ Mon) (A and M) (JSleep ∧ Mon)
conditional	If today is Monday then d = 7.	(M → D) (Mon → D7)
conditional	If John is asleep then today is Monday.	(A → M) (If A then M) (JSleep → Mon)
equivalence	John is asleep if and only if today is Monday.	(A ↔ M) (Jsleep ↔ Mon)

Learning to represent the logical structure of compound English statements using logical English is best done by seeing many examples and then practicing yourself.

Example 3. Logical English for different English statements

Recall that in English there are usually many different ways to say approximately the same thing, i.e. there are many sentences that have approximately the same meaning. Consequently, even if two sentences have slightly different meanings, they may be represented by the same logical English abbreviation, provided that the difference in meaning does not affect truth values. For example, 'It is raining but I am dry.' can be represented by the same abbreviation as 'It is raining and I am dry.' because the slight difference in meaning between the two sentences has no affect on how the truth value of either depends on the truth value of 'It is raining' and the truth value of 'I am dry'.

Suppose that M represents 'Today is Monday.' and T represents 'Taxes are due.' Some sentences that can be represented by '(~M)' are:

(a) Today is not Monday.
(b) It is not the case that today is Monday.
(c) It is false that today is Monday.

Some English statements that can be represented by '(M ∧ T)' are:

(a) Today is Monday and taxes are due.
(b) It is the case that today is Monday and that taxes are due.
(c) Today is Monday even though taxes are due.
(d) Although today is Monday, taxes are due.
(e) Today is Monday but taxes are due.
(f) Today is Monday although taxes are due.

Note that 'Taxes are due and today is Monday' would be represented by (T ∧ M), not by (M ∧ T). The order in which things are said is often important and should be preserved where possible, even when the meaning of two differently ordered abbreviations is the same.

Some English sentences that can be represented by '(M ∨ T)' are:

(a) Today is Monday or taxes are due.
(b) It is the case that today is Monday or that taxes are due.
(c) Either today is Monday or taxes are due or both.

In English there are two logically different uses of 'or', the inclusive use and the exclusive use. Some languages have two separate words for these two meanings. In logical English the word 'or' and the symbol '∨' are used to represents the inclusive use where 'P ∨ Q' means 'P or Q or both P and Q'. The English word 'xor' is sometimes used to represent the exclusive sense of 'or' as in 'P or Q but not both P and Q'. It can also be expressed by '(P ∨ Q) ∧ ~(P ∧ Q)'.

Some English sentences that can be represented by '(M → T)' are:

(a) If today is Monday then taxes are due.
(b) If today is Monday, taxes are due.
(c) Provided that today is Monday, taxes are due.
(d) Taxes are due if today is Monday.
(e) In case today is Monday, taxes are due.

In general, if '(M → T)' is true then we say that M is a sufficient condition for T and that T is a necessary condition for M. Some more English sentences that can be represented by '(M → T)' are:

(f) Today being Monday is a sufficient condition for taxes to be due.
(g) Taxes being due is a necessary condition for today to be Monday.

Some English sentences that can be represented by '(M ↔ T)' are:

(a) Today is Monday if and only if taxes are due
(b) Today's being Monday is a necessary and sufficient condition for taxes being due.
(c) Today is Monday just in case taxes are due.

2.2 Statements with Multiple Connectives

Ambiguity can result when a statement has more than one connective if the scope to which each connective applies is not clear. For example, a statement of the form 'P and Q or R' could be understood as 'P and (Q or R)' or as '(P and Q) or R'. These two forms are not equivalent. Parentheses can be used to disambiguate otherwise ambiguous statement forms. In logic parentheses are used in the same way they are used in mathematics, i.e. work from the inside out.

Example 4. Statements with multiple connectives

English	Logical English
Today is Monday.	M
Taxes are due.	T
Today is Friday.	F
Joe is happy.	H
Joe is broke.	B
(a) Today is Monday or Today is Friday, but not both.	$((M \vee F) \wedge \sim(M \wedge F))$
(b) If today is Monday then today is not Friday.	$M \rightarrow (\sim F))$
(c) If today is not Monday then Joe is not happy.	$((\sim M) \rightarrow (\sim H))$
(d) Joe is happy if and only if taxes are not due.	$(H \leftrightarrow (\sim T))$
(e) If Joe is happy and Joe is broke then taxes are not due.	$((H \wedge B) \rightarrow (\sim T))$
(f) If Joe is broke then Joe is happy just in case today is Friday.	$(B \rightarrow (H \leftrightarrow F))$
(g) If today is neither Monday nor Friday then Joe is neither happy nor broke.	$(((\sim M) \wedge (\sim F)) \rightarrow ((\sim H) \wedge (\sim B)))$

Exercise 1. For each part, identify the missing grammatical category and use the logic notation described below to transform the English statements into logical English.

Grammatical category	English	Logical English
atomic statement	a = 3.	A
atomic statement	b = 5.	B
atomic statement	a + b = 8.	C
(a)	not (a = 3).	
(b)	not (b = 5).	
(c)	a = 3 and b = 5.	
(d)	a = 3 or b = 5.	
(e)	If a = 3 then b = 5.	
(f)	a = 3 if and only if b = 5.	
(g)	If a = 3 or b = 5 then a + b = 8.	
(h)	not not b = 5.	
(i)	If a not = 3 and b not = 5 then a + b not = 8.	

A single statement expressed in English can be represented in logical English in different ways, depending on how much detail is represented. Each of the logical English representations shown below is correct. Which one to use depends upon how much detail is relevant at the time.

Example 5. Alternative representations

English	Logical English representations	
Jack will leave early if and only if the boss is not here.	L	(minimal detail)
	(J ↔ B)	(more detail)
	(J ↔ (~E))	(yet more detail)
	(LeaveEarly(j) ↔ (~Here(b)))	

If transformation from English to logical English is so indeterminate, you might wonder why anyone would do it. The short answer is that it is for the same reason we do accounting with Arabic numerals and mathematical symbols rather than writing it all out longhand in English. Imagine writing "A deposit of thirty seven dollars and eighty two cents added to a previous balance of two hundred forty dollars and seventeen cents gives a new balance of ...." in order to balance your checkbook. The mathematical notation, even though it is not unique and it takes time to learn to use, makes doing mathematics much much easier. Using logical English notation has similar advantages if you want to clearly express and reason correctly about almost anything, including computing related issues.

2.3   Parenthesis Dropping Conventions

Because complex English statements can lead to logical English expressions having confusingly many pairs of parentheses, it is often helpful to use parenthesis dropping conventions similar to those used in mathematics. Recall for example that in mathematics exponentiation has higher precedence than multiplication and division and they have higher precedence than addition and subtraction. In other words, exponentiation is done before multiplication and division which are done before addition and subtraction, so that $3 + 5 * 7$ means $3 + (5 * 7)$ and not $(3 + 5) * 7$. Similarly, $3^2 + 7 * 5^2$ means $(3^2) + (7 * (5^2))$.

LE Rule 3. In addition to the parenthesis dropping conventions of mathematics, the following *parenthesis dropping conventions* (also called *precedence rules*) will be used for logical English.

(a) ~ has the highest precedence of all.
(b) ∧ , ∨ , →, and ↔ have successively lower precedence.
(c) Matching pairs of parentheses can be removed if doing so does not cause ambiguity as to how to restore them. In particular, the outermost pair of parentheses may be removed.

Example 6. Application of LE Rule 3.

Fully parenthesized	With parentheses dropping conventions	Part of LE3 used
(a) (~A)	~A	c
(b) (~(~A))	~~A	c twice
(c) ((~A) ∨ (~B))	(~A) ∨ (~B)	c
	~A ∨ ~B	a
(d) (((~A) ∨ (~B)) → (~C))	((~A) ∨ (~B)) → (~C)	c
	(~A) ∨ (~B) → (~C)	b
	~A ∨ ~B → ~C	a
(e) (~A) ∨ ((~B) → (~C))	~A ∨ (~B → ~C)	a
	but not ~A ∨ ~B → ~C	not allowed!
(f) ((A ∧ B) ∨ C)	(A ∧ B) ∨ C	c
	A ∧ B ∨ C	b
(g) (A ∧ (B ∨ C))	A ∧ (B ∨ C)	c
(h) (A ∨ (B ∨ (C ∨ D)))	A ∨ (B ∨ (C ∨ D))	c
	but not A ∨ B ∨ C ∨ D	not allowed
(i) (((A ∨ B) ∨ C) ∨ D)	((A ∨ B) ∨ C) ∨ D	c
(j) (~(A ∨ (B ↔ C)))	~(A ∨ (B ↔ C))	c
(k) (((((~A) ∧ B) → C) ↔ D)	((((~A) ∧ B) → C) ↔ D	c
	(((~A ∧ B) → C) ↔ D	a
	(~A ∧ B → C) ↔ D	b
	~A ∧ B → C↔D	b
(l) (~(A ∧ (B → (C ↔ D))))	~(A ∧ (B → (C ↔ D)))	c

Exercise 2. Fully restore parentheses to the following logical English notations. Suggestion: work from highest to lowest precedence, in steps.

(a) P ∨ Q ∧ R
(b) P ∧ Q ∨ R
(c) P → Q ∨ R
(d) P ∨ Q → R
(e) (P ∨ Q) ∨ R
(f) P ∨ (Q ∨ R)
(g) ~P → ~Q ∨ R
(h) ~(P → Q) ∨ R
(i) ~P ∧ Q ∨ R → S ↔ T
(j) P ↔ Q → R ∨ S ∧ ~T

Exercise 3. Use the following statement letters to transform each of the English statements below into logical English. Use parenthesis dropping.

English	Logical English
The program compiled correctly.	P
The file was sorted.	S
The file was corrupted.	C
There was an error in the sort routine.	E

English	Logical English
The program ran correctly.	R
The error flag was set at line 4008.	F
a < b	L

(a) If the program ran correctly then the file was sorted.
(b) If there was an error in the sort routine then the file was not sorted.
(c) If the error flag was set at line 4008 then the file was corrupted.
(d) The program compiled correctly and the file was sorted just in case the program ran correctly and there was no error in the sort routine.
(e) A sufficient condition for the file being corrupted is that the error flag was set at line 4008.
(f) A necessary condition for the file being corrupted is that the error flag was set at line 4008.
(g) A necessary and sufficient condition for the file being corrupted is that the error flag was set at line 4008.
(h) The file was sorted unless the program did not run correctly.
(i) If the program compiled correctly and the file was sorted then the program ran correctly or a < b.
(j) a < b if and only if the program did not run correctly or the error flag was not set at line 4008.
(k) If a < b and the file was sorted correctly then the program ran correctly if and only if there was not an error in the sort routine.

Exercise 4. Use the following statement letters to transform each of the Logical English statements below into English.

Logical English	English
P	The program compiled correctly.
S	The file was sorted.
C	The file was corrupted.
E	There was an error in the sort routine.
R	The program ran correctly.
F	The error flag was set at line 4008.
L	a < b.

(a) R → P
(b) ~~R
(c) ~P → ~R
(d) F → L
(e) C ∨ E → ~P
(f) P ∧ ~S → C

Exercise 5. Use the following statement letters to transform each of the English statements below into logical English.

English	Logical English
6 is a domain value of the problem.	S
1 is a domain value of the problem.	O
0 is the solution value of the problem.	N
The domain data is sorted small to large.	A
The domain data is sorted large to small.	D

(a) If 1 is a domain value of the problem then the domain data is not sorted small to large or large to small.

(b) If the domain data is sorted small to large then the domain data is not sorted large to small.

(c) If a domain value of the problem is not 6 and is not 1 then the domain data is not sorted.

(d) If 6 is a domain value of the problem then 1 is not a domain value of the problem.

(e) If the domain data is sorted large to small or small to large then the solution value of the problem is 0.

(f) If the domain data is not sorted large to small and not sorted small to large then the solution value of the problem is 0.

(g) A sufficient condition for the solution value of the problem to be 0 is that a domain value of the problem is 6 if and only if the domain data is sorted small to large.

(h) If a domain value of the problem is 6 then 0 is not the solution value of the problem unless the domain data is sorted small to large.

Exercise 6. Use the following statement letters to transform each of the logical English statements below into English.

Logical English	English
S	6 is a domain value of the problem.
O	1 is a domain value of the problem.
N	0 is the solution value of the problem.
A	The domain data is sorted small to large.
D	The domain data is sorted large to small.

(a) $N \lor \sim N$

(b) $A \leftrightarrow \sim D$

(c) $S \rightarrow \sim O$

(d) $\sim S \land \sim O \rightarrow \sim N$

(e) $N \rightarrow S \lor O$

(f) $\sim(S \land O) \rightarrow \sim S \lor \sim O$

Chapter 3
Quantified Statements

In this chapter logical variables are introduced as placeholders for names. Similarities and differences between logical variables and program variables are discussed. Expressions closely related to statements, called conditions, are described. Expressions indicating quantity, called quantifiers, are also introduced. After studying this material you should be able to:

1. Use variables and quantifiers to express conditions, open descriptions, and quantified statements.
2. Transform conditions, open descriptions, and quantified statements between English and logical English.

Outline

3.1 Logical variables
3.2 Conditions
3.3 Open descriptions
3.4 Quantifiers

3.1 Logical Variables

Unfortunately, the term 'variable' is ambiguous. The kind of variables discussed here are called *logical variables*.

Definition 1. A *logical variable* is a symbol used as a placeholder, where a name or description could otherwise be located.

Lower case letters near the end of the alphabet are commonly used as logical variables, e.g. u, v, w, x, y, z, and letters from this list with subscripts. Recall that lower case letters near the beginning of the alphabet are commonly used as names.

A logical variable stands in place of a name or description; it is not itself a name or description. Logical variables do not refer to or describe anything. Blank spaces in

R. Lover, *Elementary Logic: For Software Development*,
DOI: 10.2007/978-1-84800-082-7, © Springer 2008

forms are paradigm examples of logical variables. Some uses of pronouns in English are logical variables. Mathematics and computer science use them extensively.

Example 1. The blanks in '_____ promises to pay \$500 to _____.' are logical variables because they are placeholders for names or descriptions.

Except for forms that people may fill out, it is usually better to use letters as variables rather than using blanks. This is because we often want the same variable to appear more than once or we want to distinguish one variable from another. With ordinary forms we often indicate these requirements by writing small descriptions in parentheses under or next to blank spaces. Here is an example.

> '_____ (borrower) promises to pay _____ (lender) _____ (amount) no later than _____ (date). If _____ (borrower) does not pay _____ (lender) the amount specified by the date specified then the amount owed to lender will be twice _____ (amount) and will be due thirty days after _____ (date).'

When such a form is filled in, both instances of the variable with a given label are to be replaced by the same name, amount, or date. In most other circumstances, labeled blanks would be less convenient than letters. For example, it is easier to write 'If $x < y$ and $y < z$ then $x < z$' than 'If _____ (first number) < _____ (second number) and _____ (second number) < _____ (third number) then _____ (first number) < _____ (third number).'

Pronouns like 'he', 'she', or 'it' when used in circumstances where no particular individual or thing is represented by the pronoun are logical variables. On the other hand, used in circumstances where they do indirectly refer to specific individuals or things, pronouns are not logical variables. Variables are often used in mathematics the way pronouns are used in ordinary English.

Example 2. In 'If something is > 0 then it is positive.' both 'something' and 'it' are logical variables. But in 'George Washington slept here. He was tired.' the pronoun 'he' is not a logical variable since it refers indirectly to George Washington.

Example 3. The instances of x in 'If $x > 0$ then $x + 1 > 1$' are not logical variables if x is (perhaps implicitly) a name or description of some particular number, otherwise the instances of x are logical variables.

Exercise 1. Identify the variables in the following statements and conditions.

(a) In general, if it looks like a duck and walks like a duck then it is a duck.
(b) Someone was absent from this class at least once.
(c) $3 < 5 + x$.
(d) $3 < = x \wedge x < = 3$.
(e) He who hesitates is lost.
(f) Look before you leap.
(g) $x < 5$.
(h) $x + y = y + x$.

(i) c = a + z.
(j) y = 3 ∨ ~y = 3.

3.2   Conditions

Definition 2. A *condition* or *open statement* is an expression which can be obtained from a statement by replacing one or more names or descriptions in the statement with logical variables. If the term 'open statement' is used in place of 'condition' then a statement is often called a *closed statement*.

Statements are intended to express claims that are either true or false, e.g. $3 > 1$. Conditions are neither true nor false, they are true of some things and false of others, e.g. the condition '$x < 1$' is true of 0 and false of 2. Below are some examples of statements and conditions that can be constructed from them.

Example 4. Conditions from English.

English Statement	Related Conditions
John is tall.	_____ is tall.
	x is tall.
	y is tall.
John is tall and he is tired.	_____ is tall and _____ is tired.
	x is tall and he is tired.
	John is tall and x is tired.
	x is tall and x is tired.
	x is tall and y is tired.
Three is larger than two.	Three is larger than _____.
	Three is larger than x.
	x is larger than two.
	x is larger than y.
	x is larger than x

Example 5. Conditions from logical English.

Logical English Statement	Related Conditions
isTall(John)	isTall(___)
	isTall(x)
	isTall(y)
isTall(John) ∧ isTired(John)	isTall(____) and isTired(_____)
	isTall(x) ∧ isTired(x)
	isTall(John) ∧ isTired(x)
	isTall(x) ∧ isTired(x)
	isTall(x) ∧ isTired(y)
$3 > 2$	3 > _____
	3 > x
	x > 2
	x > y
	x > x

Logical English Statement	Related Conditions
$A(c) \wedge (B(a, b) \wedge b = c)$	$A(x) \wedge (B(a, b) \wedge b = c)$
	$A(x) \wedge (B(x, x) \wedge x = x)$
	$A(x) \wedge (B(a, y) \wedge y = c)$

When a variable is replaced by a name or description, each instance of the variable is to be replaced by the same name or description. For example in '$A(x) \rightarrow B(x, b) \wedge x = c$' if x is replaced by c the result is '$A(c) \rightarrow B(c, b) \wedge c = c$'.

In general, a condition with any number of instances of a single variable is true or false of individual things.

Example 6. The condition $A(x) \rightarrow (B(x, b) \wedge b = x)$ is true or false of individual things. It is true of any thing such that, when a name or definite description of that thing is substituted for each instance of x, the resulting statement is true. It is false of all other things.

A condition with any number of instances of two distinct variables is true or false of pairs of things. In general, a condition with any number of instances of n distinct variables is true or false of n-tuples of things. This issue is discussed again in a later chapter where truth conditions for statements are discussed.

Example 7. $A(x) \rightarrow (B(a, y) \wedge y = c)$ is true or false of pairs of things. It is true of any pair of things, (d, e), such that if d is substituted for each instance of x and e is substituted for each instance of y then the resulting statement is true. It is false of all other pairs of things.

Exercise 2. Determine which of the following are conditions and which are not. Explain why your answer is correct. If an expression is a condition tell whether it is true of single things, pairs of things, triples of things, and so on.

(a) $a = a$
(b) $x = a$
(c) $x = x$
(d) $x = y$
(e) $A(x, x)$
(f) $A(x, y)$
(g) $A(x, b, z)$
(h) $A(x, x) \rightarrow B(c)$
(i) $x > y \wedge y > z$
(j) $maximum(x,y,z) = w$

Exercise 3. For each of the following statements create two different conditions by replacing one or more names or descriptions with variables.

(a) $a < 3 \wedge a = 3 \wedge a > 3$.
(b) If John does not come to work he will be fired.
(c) Jack and Jill went up the hill.
(d) Jack came down and Jill came tumbling after.

(e) $3 + 5 = 5 + 3$.

(f) $3 > a \rightarrow \sim(a = 3)$

Exercise 4. For each of the following conditions, create two different statements by replacing all variables with names or descriptions.

(a) $x = y \land y = x$

(b) $x = y \land y = z$

(c) _____ was absent.

(d) I owe you x.

(e) $x > 99 \land z < 5$.

(f) x is the winner.

3.3   Open Descriptions

Definition 3. An *open description* is the result of replacing one or more name symbols in a description with a variable. An open description can be an *open definite description*, e.g. 'the largest prime number $< x$', or an *open indefinite description*, e.g. 'some prime number $< x$'.

Exercise 5. For each description below, make two different open descriptions.

(a) the present king of France

(b) the result of squaring 4

(c) $3 + 5$

(d) the positive square root of 16

(e) a person in this room

(f) a square root of 16

(g) some record from file 77

(h) some row of table 8

Open definite descriptions are often used to make function notations in mathematics and assignment instructions in programs. Here are some examples, using '$\leftarrow$' to represent assignment.

Example 8. Function notations and assignment instructions.

Open Definite Description	Function Notation	Assignment Instruction
posSqrt(x)	$y = posSqrt(x)$	$y \leftarrow posSqrt(x)$
$x + 2y$	$z = x + 2y$	$z \leftarrow x + 2y$
x^2	$y = x^2$	$y \leftarrow x^2$
min(x, y)	$z = min(x, y)$	$z \leftarrow min(x, y)$

Just as statements can be made from conditions by replacing all variables with names and descriptions, so descriptions can be made from open descriptions by replacing one or more variables with names or descriptions. Some examples are given below.

Example 9. Descriptions from open descriptions.

Open Description	Related Descriptions
the king of _____	the king of France
	the king of England
	the king of nothing
my father's _____	my father's car
	my father's father's car
x^2	3^2
	$(77 * 4)^2$
$x + y - z$	$3 + 5 - (1/3)$

Exercise 6. For each of the following open descriptions, create two different descriptions by replacing all the variables with names or descriptions.

(a) $y + x$
(b) is heavier than x
(c) $(x^2)^3$
(d) subroutine77(x, y, z)

3.4 Quantifiers

Definition 4. A *quantifier* is an expression used to indicate what quantity of something is being discussed.

The term 'quantity' in this definition is to be taken broadly to include not just 'how many' but also quantities such as 'all' and 'some'.

English has many quantifiers, e.g. zero, one, two, ... a few, several, many, more than 3, fewer than 10, an even number of, all, each, every, some, none, etc. Below are some examples of quantifiers used in English statements.

Example 10. Quantifiers in English statements

English Statement	Quantifier
All humans are mortal.	All
Some humans are mortal.	Some
Most crows are black.	Most
A few swans are black.	A few
None of the records were processed.	None
If some of the records were not processed then all of us are in trouble.	Some, all
There is an even prime number.	There is
Three of the programs were tested.	Three

The two most important quantifiers used in logic are 'all' (each, every, any, etc.) and 'some' (there are, there exists, at least one, etc). They are important enough to have special symbols associated with them, $\forall$ for 'all' and $\exists$ for 'some'.

Definition 5. A *universal quantifier* is an expression used to discuss 'all', 'each', or 'every one' of a set of things. An *existential quantifier* is an expression used to discuss 'some' or 'at least one' of some set of things.

The logical English notation used for statements with quantifiers takes a bit of getting used to. It involves introducing variables and rearranging some parts of English. The best way to learn to use quantifier notation is to see many examples and then do many exercises. It may seem confusing at first, but eventually it becomes quite easy, and it is very useful. For example, it is used extensively in mathematics and computer science. It is also used extensively in the rest of this book.

Example 11. Logical English with a universal quantifier

English	Logical English
All humans are mortal	$\forall x$(if human(x) then mortal(x))
	$\forall x$(human(x) $\rightarrow$ mortal(x))
	$\forall x$(H(x) $\rightarrow$ M(x))

One way to think of 'All humans are mortal.' is to think of it as saying of all (each, every) thing that if it is human then it is mortal, or if anything is human then it is mortal. Each step of the transformation of the English statement to the third logical English form either emphasizes logically important details or suppresses logically unimportant details. As a result, the last version is a little shorter than the first, and, more importantly, its logical structure is clearer. Brevity and clear logical structure are both aids to better communication and better reasoning.

Exercise 7. Using P(x) to abbreviate 'x is a program' and B(x) to abbreviate 'x has bugs' go through the transformation process described above starting with 'All programs have bugs.' in place of 'All humans are mortal.'

Example 12. Logical English with an existential quantifier

English	Logical English
Some integers are prime numbers.	$\exists x$(integer(x) and prime(x))
	$\exists x$(I(x) and P(x))
	$\exists x$(I(x) $\wedge$ P(x))

One way to think of 'Some integers are prime numbers.' is to think of it as saying that there is (exists) at least one thing which is both an integer and is a prime number. Again, each step of the transformation of the English statement to the third logical English form either emphasizes logically important details or suppresses logically unimportant details.

Exercise 8. Go through a similar transformation starting with the statement 'Some programs have bugs'.

Example 13. Using quantifiers and variables

English	Logical English
is a program	P
is useful	U
is bigger than	B
A	a (a name)
B	b (another name)
Everything is a program.	
Anything is a program.	
Each thing is a program.	
All things are programs.	$\forall x(P(x))$
Something is a program.	
Programs exist.	
There is something that is a program.	
Some programs exist.	
At least one thing is a program.	
Some things are programs.	$\exists x(P(x))$
All programs are useful.	$\forall x(P(x) \rightarrow U(x))$
Some programs are useful.	$\exists x(P(x) \land U(x))$
Some programs are not useful.	$\exists x(P(x) \land \sim U(x))$
No programs are useful.	$\forall x(P(x) \rightarrow \sim U(x))$
or	$\sim\exists x(Px \land Ux)$
Everything is useful.	$\forall x(U(x)$
Nothing is useful.	$\sim\exists x(U(x))$
or	$\forall x(\sim U(x))$
a is bigger than b.	$B(a, b)$
b is bigger than a.	$B(b, a)$
Everything is bigger than b.	$\forall x(B(x, b))$
b is bigger than everything.	$\forall x(B(b, x))$
Something is bigger than b.	$\exists x(B(x, b))$

Note the difference between the following two examples.

Not everything is bigger than b.	$\sim\forall x(B(x, b))$
(i.e. Something is not bigger than b.)	
Everything is not bigger than b.	$\forall x(\sim B(x, b))$
(i.e. Nothing is bigger than b.)	

Note the use of two quantifiers and two different variables in the following examples.

Everything is bigger than something.	$\forall x\exists y(B(x, y))$
Something is bigger than everything.	$\exists x\forall y(B(x, y))$
Everything is bigger than everything.	$\forall x\forall y(B(x, y)$
Something is bigger than something.	$\exists x\exists y(B(x, y))$
Nothing is bigger than everything.	$\sim\exists x\forall y(B(x, y))$
Nothing is bigger than anything.	$\sim\exists x\exists y(B(x, y))$
or	$\forall x\forall y(\sim B(x, y))$
If something is bigger than b then a is bigger than b.	$\exists x(B(x, b) \rightarrow B(a, b))$
a is bigger than b or b is bigger than a.	$B(a, b) \lor B(b, a)$
If something is bigger than b then b is useful.	$\exists y(B(y, b)) \rightarrow U(b)$

Note the use of parentheses in this statement.

If something is useful then everything is useful	$\exists x(U(x)) \rightarrow \forall x(U(x)) \lor$
or nothing is useful.	$\sim\exists x(U(x))$
If a is a useful program then there are useful things.	$U(a) \land P(a) \rightarrow \exists x(U(x))$

Exercise 9. Using the same abbreviations, write logical English for the following statements.

(a) Something is useful.
(b) Something is not useful.
(c) Something is bigger than a.
(d) a is bigger than something.
(e) Everything is bigger than something.
(f) Something is bigger than everything.
(g) a is bigger than everything or a is bigger than nothing.
(h) If every program is useful then some programs are useful.
(i) If some program is useful then all programs are useful.
(j) If a is a useful program then all programs are useful.
(k) If a is a program and a is not useful then not all programs are useful.

Exercise 10. Using the abbreviations as above transform the following logical English notation into English.

(a) $\sim\exists x(U(x)) \rightarrow \exists x(\sim U(x))$
(b) $\exists x(B(x, b)) \leftrightarrow B(b, a)$
(c) $\exists x(B(x, b)) \wedge B(a, b)$
(d) $\forall x\exists y(B(x, y)) \vee \exists x\forall y(B(x, y))$
(e) $\sim\exists x(U(x)) \rightarrow \forall x(\sim U(x))$

Chapter 4
Expressing Arguments

This chapter discusses how to find and express arguments and their logical structures using logical English. After studying it you should be able to:

1. Determine whether a passage in English is an argument.
2. Find the premises and conclusion of an argument.
3. Determine whether an argument is inductive or deductive.
4. Express the logical structure of an argument using logical English.

Outline

4.1 Arguments

Definition 1. Reasoning is the process of moving from some statements (called premises) to other statements (called conclusions) because the reasoner believes that if the premises were true they would provide support, evidence, or reasons for believing that the conclusions would also be true.

Reasoning is to be contrasted with moving from statement to statement by other means or for other purposes, e.g. by means of free association, or in order to rhyme, to intimidate, to stir emotions, to persuade, to explain, to describe, and so on.

Definition 2. An *argument* is one or more statements used to express, describe, or record reasoning. A *simple argument* is a collection of statements such that all but one of them, called *premises*, are offered as evidence for the other one, called the *conclusion*. A simple argument has exactly one conclusion, although it may have

R. Lover, *Elementary Logic: For Software Development*,
DOI: 10.2007/978-1-84800-082-7, © Springer 2008

many premises. A *compound argument* is a collection of simple arguments organized so that the conclusions of some of its component arguments are premises of other component arguments. Often there is one final grand conclusion that the collection of component arguments is organized to support.

Example 1. Since today is Monday, tomorrow must be Tuesday.

This is a simple argument with only one premise, "today is Monday" and one conclusion, "tomorrow must be Tuesday."

Example 2. Since today is Monday, tomorrow must be Friday.

This example has the same premise as Example 1, but its conclusion is "tomorrow must be Friday." It was chosen to emphasize the fact that an argument does not have to be a good argument to be an argument.

Example 3. It will probably rain here soon, since the sky is dark and it is raining just west of here.

Example 3 has two premises "the sky is dark" and "it is raining just west of here." Its conclusion is "it will probably rain here soon." This example illustrates two points, first that an argument can have several premises and second that the conclusion of an argument is not always stated last.

Example 4. A = 3. B = 5. Therefore A + B = 8.

Example 4 was chosen to emphasize that an argument may be expressed by means of several sentences rather than just one sentence.

Example 5. Since the file is sorted, it must be in ascending or descending order. It is not in ascending order. Hence it is in descending order.

Unlike Examples 1–4, this argument is compound. Its first component argument has "the file is sorted" as premise and "it must be in ascending or descending order" as conclusion. The second has two premises. Its first premise is the conclusion of the first argument. Its second premise is "It is not in ascending order." Its conclusion is "it is in descending order."

We all understand that some arguments are better than others. Examples 1, 4, and 5 above are very good arguments, while Example 3 might be moderately good and Example 2 is a very bad one.

4.2   Deductive and Inductive Arguments

Definition 3. An argument is said to be *deductive* if and only if it expresses the claim that the truth of its premises would guarantee the truth of its conclusion, i.e. that its premises and conclusion are related so that if its premises were true then its conclusion would also have to be true. An argument that is not deductive is said to be *inductive*.

Notice that whether an argument is deductive or inductive does not depend on whether its premises or conclusion are true or false and it does not depend on how good the argument is. It depends on its author's indicated belief about the strength of the connection between the premises and the conclusion. Also, author's beliefs are often difficult to determine. Usually the only clues available are the context of the argument and the way the conclusion is expressed. Examples 1, 2, 4, and 5 are deductive while Example 3 is inductive. This book is concerned only with criteria and methods that work reliably on deductive arguments.

4.3   Some Practical Suggestions

To make practical use of these concepts requires certain abilities. The first is being able to recognize statements and distinguish them from instructions, questions, wishes, etc.

The second is being able to recognize arguments and distinguish them from mere lists of assertions, conditional statements, stories, etc. The task of recognizing arguments is complicated by the fact that some arguments are compound, so the conclusion of one component argument is a premise in some other component argument. As a result, the same statement may be both a premise (of one argument) and a conclusion (of another argument). Fortunately, there are phrases such as "we reason as follows" and "consider the following" which usually indicate the presence of an argument. In other cases the context suggests that arguments are present, as in mathematics, logic, and computer science books. In many cases arguments are recognized by first discovering conclusions.

There are words and phrases such as "since", "is implied by", "because", and "as a result of the fact that", which are usually followed by the premises of an argument. They are called *premise indicators*. There are also *conclusion indicators* such as "therefore", "we infer that", "consequently", "so it must be that", "probably", and "it is likely that" which are usually followed by the conclusion of an argument. In looking for arguments it is also worth knowing that some premises and some conclusions are *implicit*, i.e. understood to be part of the argument but not explicitly stated. Definitions of words and commonly known facts such as the order of days of the week are often implicit premises in ordinary arguments. Example 1 probably has something like "The day after Monday is Tuesday" as an implicit premise. An extreme example is discussed below.

Example 6. If he is telling the truth then I am a monkey's uncle.

Analysis: This is an argument with an implicit premise and an implicit conclusion.

Premise1: If he is telling the truth then I am a monkey's uncle.
Premise2: I am not a monkey's uncle. (implicit)
Conclusion: He is not telling the truth. (implicit)

Being able to distinguish between deductive arguments and inductive arguments is another important skill since the criteria and rules of deductive logic do not work reliably with inductive arguments. Sometimes this can be done by considering the context of the argument. Mathematical arguments are usually deductive while arguments about the weather tomorrow are usually inductive. In addition, some conclusion indicators such as "therefore," "consequently," and "it must be that" are generally followed by the conclusion of a deductive argument. Other conclusion indicators such as "probably" and "it is likely that" are generally followed by the conclusion of an inductive argument.

Examples 7–12 below show uses of the suggestions just discussed. Each passage is analyzed with respect to the following issues:

1. Is the passage an argument or a collection of arguments?
2. If it is an argument or collection of arguments, what are the premises and the conclusion of each argument?
3. If it is an argument, is it deductive or inductive?

Example 7. I have tested this program with hundreds of test cases and it worked correctly in each case. Hence, this program is correct.

Analysis: This is an argument because the first statement is given as a reason for believing the second. Moreover, "hence" is usually used as a conclusion indicator. The premises and conclusion of this argument are:

Premise1: I have tested this program with hundreds of test cases.
Premise2: It worked correctly in each case.
Conclusion: This program is correct.

You could also say that this argument has a single premise consisting of the conjunction of the two listed above, but it is usually clearer if premises that are conjunctions are broken into their component parts. This argument is deductive because there is no uncertainty expressed about the truth of the conclusion.

Example 8. The error is in subroutine X or subroutine Y. If the error were in subroutine Y then someone would probably have reported a problem with it by now. Since no one has reported a problem with subroutine Y yet, the problem must be in subroutine X.

Analysis: This is clearly an argument because some statements are given as reasons for believing another. Using "P" with or without subscripts to indicate premises and using "C" to indicate a conclusion the argument can be expressed thus.

P_1: The error is in subroutine X or subroutine Y.
P_2: If the error were in subroutine Y then someone would probably have reported a problem with subroutine Y.
P_3: No one has reported a problem with subroutine Y.
C: The problem must be in subroutine X.

Despite the word "probably" in one of the premises, the word "must" in the conclusion shows that this argument is deductive. There is no uncertainty expressed about the truth of the conclusion. The use of "probably" in a premise and "must" in the conclusion suggests that this argument is not correct.

Example 9. Since the rest of the program works perfectly, if there is a problem with the program it must be in the new procedure.

Analysis: This is an argument, because "since" is a premise indicator and the first statement is given as a reason to believe the second.

    P: The rest of the program works perfectly.
    C: If there is a problem with the program it must be in the new procedure.

It is deductive.

Example 10. The program used to work perfectly. Then you modified it. Now it doesn't work perfectly. You ought to work on it some more.

Analysis: Clearly an argument.

    P_1: The program used to work perfectly.
    P_2: Then you modified it.
    P_3: Now it doesn't work perfectly.
    C: You ought to work on it some more.

Clearly deductive.

Example 11. FCOUNT must be = 0 or > 0 at line 20. If FCOUNT > 0 at line 20 then FILE5 will be opened or a file-not-found message will be sent just in case the trace flag is set.

Analysis: This is not an argument. It is a mere collection of statements. None of the statements is offered as evidence for any other one.

Example 12. FCOUNT must be = 0 or > 0 at line 20. If FCOUNT > 0 at line 20 then FILE5 will be opened or else a file-not-found message will be sent just in case the trace flag is set. The trace flag cannot be set if FCOUNT = 0 at line 20. So if FCOUNT = 0 at line 20 and FILE5 is not opened and a file-not-found message is not sent then the trace flag is not set.

Analysis: An argument. The word "so" as used here is a conclusion indicator.

    P_1: FCOUNT must be = 0 or > 0 at line 20.
    P_2: If FCOUNT > 0 at line 20 then FILE5 will be opened or else a file-not-found message will be sent just in case the trace flag is set.
    P_3: The trace flag cannot be set if FCOUNT = 0 at line 20.
    C: If FCOUNT = 0 at line 20 and FILE5 is not opened and a file- not-found message is not sent then the trace flag is not set.

Clearly deductive.

Exercise 1. For each passage below, analyze the passage in the way Examples 7–12 were analyzed. Give reasons for your claims.

(a) If today is Friday then today is payday.
(b) If today is Friday then today is payday. Moreover, today is Friday. Hence, today is payday.
(c) If x were 5 at line 2,020 then the program would have crashed, and it did. So probably x was 5 at line 2,020.
(d) If the program was run yesterday then a run log entry for it would have been made. No run log entry for it was made. Moreover, if the program was not run yesterday then the records in it are not current. Hence the records in it are not current.

4.4   Expressing the Logical Structures of Arguments

The overall structure of a simple argument is described by identifying its premises and its conclusion. In the previous examples this was done by prefixing premises with P and conclusions with C. Another commonly used format is to list premises above the conclusion and draw a line between the premises and the conclusion.

Example 13.

> FCOUNT must be = 0 or > 0 at line 20.
> If FCOUNT > 0 at line 20 then FILE5 will be opened or else a
>   file-not-found message will be sent just in case the trace flag is set.
> The trace flag cannot be set if FCOUNT = 0 at line 20.
> _____
> If FCOUNT = 0 at line 20 and FILE5 is not opened and a file-
>   not-found message is not sent then the trace flag is not set.

If the premises are very short, more than one premise may be written on a single line.

Example 14.

> a = 3, b = 4, c = 5
> _____
> c > a + b

If the premises or conclusion are long, as they are in Example 13 then logical English abbreviations may help bring out the logical structure of the argument.

Example 15.

> FC = 0 ∨ FC > 0
> FC > 0 → (F5Open ∨ (NotFoundMsg ↔ TraceSet))

$$FC = 0 \rightarrow \sim\text{TraceSet}$$
$$\overline{((FC = 0) \wedge \sim\text{F5Open} \wedge \sim\text{NotFoundMsg}) \rightarrow \sim\text{TraceSet}}$$

If an argument is compound then more elaborate formats are used. One common style is vertical, as in Example 16. This is the way many proofs in mathematics books are organized except that underlines are replaced by conclusion indicators such as "therefore" and "hence."

Example 16.

Prime(x)	Premise
Even(x)	Premise
x = 2	Conclusion of first argument, premise of third
x = b	Premise
b = a	Premise
x = a	Conclusion of second argument, premise of third
a = 2	Conclusion of third argument

A clearer way to represent this structure resembles a tree.

Example 17.

$$\frac{\dfrac{\text{Prime(x), Even(x)}}{x = 2} \qquad \dfrac{x = b,\ b = a}{x = a}}{a = 2}$$

Notice that the line under "Prime(x), Even(x)" does not extend to "x = b." That is because the argument from x = b and b = a to x = a does not depend on Prime(x) or Even(x). Separate arguments get separate underlines.

Exercise 2. Use logical English to express the structure of each of the arguments below. If the argument is simple then use the format shown in Examples 13 and 14. If the argument is compound then use the tree structure shown in Example 17.

(a) Since today is Monday, tomorrow must be Tuesday.
(b) Since today is Monday, tomorrow must be Friday.
(c) It will probably rain here soon, since the sky is dark and it is raining just west of here.
(d) A = 3. B = 5. Therefore A + B = 8.
(e) Since the file is sorted, it must be in ascending or descending order. It is not in ascending order. Hence it is in descending order.
(f) If he is telling the truth then I am a monkey's uncle.
(g) I have tested this program with hundreds of test cases and it worked correctly in each case. Hence, this program is correct.
(h) The error is in subroutine X or subroutine Y. If the error were in subroutine Y then someone would probably have reported a problem with it by now. Since

no one has reported a problem with subroutine Y yet, the problem must be in
subroutine X.

(i) a*b > 0 because either a > 0 and b > 0 or else a < 0 and b < 0. Since c < 0 and a*b
> 0, it follows that c*a*b < 0. And since d is also < 0, d*c*a*b must be > 0.

(j) Since a = 1 and b = 2, a + b = 3. Moreover, since c = 4 and d = 5, c + d = 9. In
addition, e = 6, so c + d + e = 15, Hence a + b + c + d + e = 18.

Chapter 5
Defining Data Structures

This chapter is about using logical English to define and describe data structures. It begins with a description of the identity relation. This relation is used in defining all data structures. The second part shows how logical English can be used to define and describe sets, bags, sequences, relations, functions, and other data types. These examples also show the way mathematical notation is used with logical English. The presentation in this part is brief because you are assumed to be familiar with much of it. After studying this chapter you should be able to:

1. Describe the identity relation and its more important properties.
2. Use logical English to describe sets, bags, sequences, relations, functions, and other data structures.
3. Read much of the computer science literature that uses logical English and mathematical notation.

Outline

R. Lover, *Elementary Logic: For Software Development*,
DOI: 10.2007/978-1-84800-082-7, © Springer 2008

5.1   Properties of the Identity Relation

5.1.1   Identity is Reflexive, Symmetric, and Transitive

Definition 1. We say that b and c are *identical* if and only b and c refer to (name or describe) the same thing.

For example, 8 is identical to $3 + 5$ because "8" and "$3 + 5$" refer to the same number. While identity is a two place predicate we do not usually represent the claim that b is identical to c using a notation like Iden(b, c). Identity has a special symbol of its own and a different format (called infix notation), so that saying that b is identical to c is usually done using the notation "$b = c$." The terms "equal" and "identical" are often used to mean the same thing. Three important facts about identity are listed below. Here x, y, and z are intended to be place holders for names or legitimate definite descriptions.

1. $\forall x(x = x)$ (= is reflexive)
2. $\forall x \forall y(x = y \rightarrow y = x)$ (= is symmetric)
3. $\forall x \forall y \forall z(((x = y) \wedge (y = z)) \rightarrow x = z)$ (= is transitive)

5.1.2   Leibniz's Law

Another property of the identity relation is that if P is any 1-place predicate then

4. $\forall x \forall y((x = y \wedge P(x)) \rightarrow P(y))$ (Leibniz's law)

It is important to be clear about what this law means. It means that if x and y refer to the same thing and if the thing referred to by x has property P then the thing referred to by y has that same property. Once you understand it, this law may seem obviously true. And as long as the properties involved are true or false of the thing x and y both refer to, independent of how they are named or described, Leibniz's law applies. This is normally the case, for example, in mathematics and computer science. Such contexts are said to be *extensional*. Not all contexts are extensional however. For example, it is a fact that

Mark Twain = Samuel Clemens.

But suppose I did not know this. Then I could perfectly well believe that Mark Twain wrote *The Adventures of Tom Sawyer* and not believe that Samuel Clemens wrote *The Adventures of Tom Sawyer*. Moreover, if my belief that Mark Twain wrote *The Adventures of Tom Sawyer* counts as a property of Mark Twain then, since Mark Twain = Samuel Clemens, Leibniz's law requires that I must also believe that Samuel Clemens wrote *The Adventures of Tom Sawyer.* But I don't. Contexts like this that involve what people believe, hope, fear, etc. all give rise to apparent counterexamples to Leibniz's law. There are various ways around this problem, such as insisting that my belief that Mark Twain wrote *The Adventures of*

Tom Sawyer is not a property of the person sometimes called Mark Twain, it is a property of me. Only extensional contexts, in which such confusing issues do not arise, will be considered here.

5.2 Defining Data Structures

A data structure is defined by specifying the type of data it is composed of, how this data is organized, the basic operations that are allowed to be performed on that data, and the relations that must be maintained when those operations are performed. No operations other than those that can be defined in terms of the basic operations are allowed for that data type.

5.2.1 Sets

Logical English is often used to express facts about sets of things. The notation and concepts of set theory are fundamental to mathematics and computer science. Intuitively, a set is a collection of things. For example, the set of all positive integers or the set of all programs currently running on a particular computer.

A set is determined by its elements. For example, each positive integer is an element of the set of all positive integers. The elements of a set are usually indicated in one of two ways, either by listing all the elements of the set, or by describing a condition which is true of all and only the elements of the set. In either case it is common to use curly brackets (also called set brackets), "{ 'and' }," to indicate the beginning and end of a set description. For example, each of the notations below describes the same set.

{1, 3, 2, 4}	List notation
{x|x is an integer and x > 0 and x < 5}	Condition notation

The symbol "|" in condition notation can be read "such that" or "where."

The elements of the set above are 1, 3, 2, and 4. If S = {1, 3, 2, 4} then the fact that 1 is an element of S would normally be written "1 $\in$ S." The fact that 5 is not an element of S could be written "not 5 $\in$ S" (or "5 $\sim\in$ S"). In logical English it is customary to use uppercase letters to represent sets and lower case letters to represent elements of sets.

Definition 2. If A and B are sets then *A is identical to B* just in case they have the same elements, regardless of the order in which the elements are listed or the number of times an element is listed. In logical English this definition can be expressed thus.

$$A = B \leftrightarrow \forall x(x \in A \leftrightarrow x \in B)$$

Example 1. {1, 2, 3, 4} = {1, 3, 2, 4} = {1, 2, 3, 2, 4, 1} = {1, 1+1, 1+2, 4}

Definition 3. A set which has no elements is called a *null set* or *empty set*. Since all empty sets have exactly the same elements they are all identical, hence there is only one null set. One common notation for the null set is { }, another is ø. In logical English it could be defined thus.

$$ø = \{x | \sim x = x\}$$

Definition 4. If A and B are sets then *A is a subset of B* just in case every element of A is also an element of B. The symbol "⊂" is normally used to represent the subset relation. In logical English this definition can be expressed by:

$$A \subset B \leftrightarrow \forall x(x \in A \rightarrow x \in B)$$

Example 2. $\{1, 3\} \subset \{1, 2, 3\}$, but not $\{1, 2, 3\} \subset \{1, 2\}$.

If $A \subset B$ then B may or may not be a subset of A. For example, $\{1, 3, 5\} \sim \subset \{3, 5\}$. On the other hand $\{1, 5\} \subset (5, 1)$ and $\{5, 1\} \subset \{1, 5\}$. In general, if $A \subset B$ and $B \subset A$ then $A = B$ and *vice versa*.

Various operations on sets are defined. The most useful of them are intersection, union, complement, and product.

Definition 5. If A and B are sets then *the intersection of A and B* is the set of elements they have in common. The symbol "∩" is used for intersection and it is common to express this definition as follows.

$$A \cap B = \{x \mid x \in A \wedge x \in B\}$$

Example 3. $\{3, 5, 7\} \cap \{2, 3, 4, 7\} = \{3, 7\}$

Definition 6. If A and B are sets then *the union of A and B* is the set of all elements that are in one or both of the sets. The symbol "∪" is normally used to represent set union. Hence,

$$A \cup B = \{x \mid x \in A \vee x \in B\}$$
$$\{1, 3, 5\} \cup \{2, 3, 4\} = \{1, 2, 3, 4, 5\}$$

Definition 7. *The complement of B in A* is the set of elements of A that are not in B. The symbol "-" is often used for complement. Hence,

$$A - B = \{x \mid x \in A \wedge \sim x \in B\}$$

Examples 4. $\{1, 3, 5\} - \{2, 3, 4\} = \{1, 5\}$ and $\{2, 3, 4\} - \{1, 3, 5\} = \{2, 4\}$

Definition 8. *The cross product of A and B* is the set of ordered pairs of elements with the first element of the pair in A and the second element of the pair in B. The symbol × is usually used to indicate this operation, so,

$A \times B = \{<x, y> | x \in A \land y \in B\}$

Example 5. $\{2, 4\} \times \{1, 3, 5\} = \{<2, 1>,<2, 3>,<2, 5>,<4, 1>,<4, 3>,<4, 5>\}$

Exercise 1. Suppose $A = \{2, 4, 6, 8\}$, $B = \{1, 3, 5, 7\}$, and $C = \{1, 2. 3\}$. Use list notation to express the result of performing the following operations.

(a) $A \cup B$
(b) $A \cap B$
(c) $A \cap C$
(d) $A - B$
(e) $A - C$
(f) $A \times C$
(g) $C \times A$

Exercise 2. Write each of the following using logical English notation. Use I(x) to abbreviate the condition that x is an integer, P(x) abbreviate the condition that x is a positive integer, and so on.

(a) The set of all integers.
(b) The intersection of the set of all positive integers and the set of all negative integers.
(c) b is an element of C.
(d) x is an element of the intersection of B with C if and only if x is an element of B and x is an element of C.
(e) The ordered pair <b, c> is an element of the product of sets F and G.
(f) If A is a subset of B and B is a subset of a then A is identical with B.

Exercise 3. Use English to express the meanings of the following expressions of set theory.

(a) $b \in G$
(b) $B \in B \cap C$
(c) $B = C \leftrightarrow (B \subset C) \land (C \subset B)$
(d) $((x \in B) \land (B \subset C)) \rightarrow x \in C$
(e) $<a, b> \in B \times C$
(f) $((\sim(B \subset C)) \lor (\sim(C \subset B))) \leftrightarrow (\sim(B = C))$

5.2.2 *Bags*

Bags are like sets except that multiple instances of the same element are counted as many times as they occur, but as with sets, the order in which they are given does not matter. Bags are also called multisets. There is no standard notation for bags. Here set brackets with asterisks, {* and *}, will be used. Recall that two sets are identical just in case they have the same elements. Similarly, two bags are identical just in case they have the same elements and identical elements occur the same number of times. Hence:

$\{*1, 2, 3, 2*\} = \{*2, 2, 1, 3*\} = \{*1, 2, 1+1, 3*\}$ but
not $\{*1, 2, 3, 2*\} = \{*1, 2, 3*\}$.

Bags are often used to represent statistical data such as the ages of people in a sample. In such a case two people of the same age count as two instances of that age, although the order in which age data is represented is irrelevant.

While sets are implemented in a few programming languages, the implementation is usually feeble. Bags are almost never implemented. Most programmers represent sets and bags using arrays. Sets are represented by writing programs that ignore multiple instances of the same value in an array and ignore the order in which they appear. Bags are implemented by writing programs that count the number of instances of each value but ignore the order in which they appear.

5.2.3 Sequences

Sequences are like bags except that with sequences, order also counts. The elements of a sequence are often called *terms* of the sequence. The terms of a sequence are normally "indexed" by positive integers, so that the first term of a sequence is called t_1, the second term is called t_2, and so on. The integer 1 is called the index of t_1, 2 is called the index of t_2, and so on. Most programming languages do not have the ability to express indices as subscripts Instead they write indices in square brackets as with x[1], x[2], and so on.

Definition 9. The shortest sequences are called *null sequences*, they are sequences with zero terms. The next shortest are *singleton sequences*, they have a single term. The next shortest sequences are called *ordered pairs*, they have two terms. Next are ordered triples, quadruples, and so on. A *finite sequence* has n terms, for some nonnegative integer, n. An *infinite sequence* has at least as many terms as the sequence of nonnegative integers.

Definition 10. Two sequences are said to be identical just in case they have the same number of elements and elements in corresponding positions are all identical.

Examples 6.

$<1, 2, 1, 3> = <1, 1+1, 1, 3>$ but
not $(<1, 2, 1, 3> = <1, 2, 3>)$ and
not $(<1, 2, 1, 3> = <1, 1, 2, 3>)$

Ordered pairs are especially important, since they are what relations and functions are made from. In particular notice that

$<a, b> = <c, d> \leftrightarrow a = c \land b = d.$

There are several commonly used notations for sequences in mathematics. Examples of three of the most common are shown below. Each describes the same sequence.

e$_1$, e$_2$, e$_3$, e$_4$ Comma separated notation
<e$_1$, e$_2$, e$_3$, e$_4$>   Angle bracket notation
[e$_1$, e$_2$, e$_3$, e$_4$]   Square bracket notation

Exercise 4. For each pair of sequences below determine whether they are identical considered as sequences, as bags, and as sets.

(a) <1, 1+1, 1+1+1>   <1, 2, 3>
(b) <1, 1+1, 1+1+1>   <1, 3, 2>
(c) <1, 1+1, 1+1+1>   <1, 2, 2, 3>
(d) <1, 2, 1+1+1>   <1, 2, 1, 3>
(e) <1, 2, 3>   <3, 2, 1>
(f) <3, 1, 2, 3>   <1+1, 3, 1, 3>

5.2.4 Relations

Definition 11. In set theory a *relation* is a set whose elements are ordered pairs of things. The things can be of any kind. In logical English this could be expressed by

R is a relation $\leftrightarrow$ R is a set and $\forall x(x \in R \rightarrow \exists y \exists z(x = <y, z>))$

Every 2-place predicate determines a relation, called the extension of that relation. If the extension of a predicate P is called S$_p$ then

S$_p$ = {<x, y> | P(x, y) is true}

However, there are more sets of ordered pairs than there are predicates in any ordinary language. so not every relation is definable in this way. On the other hand, the relations we can easily talk about in a specific language are definable in this way.

Definition 12. The domain of a relation is the set of all things that are first terms of the elements (ordered pairs) of the relation and *the range of a relation* is the set of all things that are second terms of the elements of the relation.

For example, the relation {<1, 2>, <3, 4>, <5, 2>} has {1, 3, 5} as its domain and {2, 4} as its range. If DOM(R) is used to represent the domain of a relation, R, and RNG(R) is used to represent its range then these definitions can be expressed as

DOM(R) = {x | $\exists$y(<x, y> $\in$ R}
RNG(R) = {y | $\exists$x(<x, y> $\in$ R}

Example 7. The identity relation, =, between names in a given language. The = relation is the set of all ordered pairs of names in the language where both names are names of the same thing. In English for example, <Mark Twain, Samuel Clemens> is an element of the = relation, but <Mark Twain, George Washington> is not. The domain and range of = are the same, they are the set of names in the given language.

Example 8. The less than relation, <, among positive integers, using P(x) to represent the condition "x is a positive integer."

> $< \, = \{<x, y> \mid P(x) \wedge P(y) \wedge x < y\}$
> $<3, 4> \, \in \, <$ and $<3, 77> \, \in \, <$. but $<4, 3>$ is not $\in <$.
> $DOM(<) = \{x \mid P(x)\}$
> $RNG(<) = \{x \mid P(x) \wedge x > 1\}$

The reason that $1 \sim\in RNG(<)$ is that no positive integer is less than 1.

Example 9. The relation cityIn defined below.

> cityIn $= \{<x, y> \mid x$ is a city $\wedge$ y is a state $\wedge$ x is a city in state y$\}$
> <Kalamazoo, Michigan> $\in$ cityIn but
> <Boston, Michigan> $\sim\in$ cityIn.

Exercise 5. For each of the following determine whether the statement is true or false, and say why.

(a) $<3, 5> \, \in \, <$
(b) $<3, 3 + 2> \, \in \, <$
(c) $<3, 3> \, \in \, <$
(d) $<1, 2> \, \in \, <$
(e) $<1, 1 + 1> \, \in \, <$
(f) $<1 + 1, 2> \, \in \, <$

Exercise 6. For each of the following, determine the domain and range of the relation, and express each using logical English. Use I(x) to represent the property of being an integer, R(x) to represent the property of being a rational number, and P(x) to represent the property of being a person. Invent and explain your own notation for the less than relation, the parent of relation, and so on.

(a) The less than relation between integers.
(b) The less than relation between rational numbers.
(c) The "is a parent of" relation between people.
(d) The "is a child of" relation between people.
(e) The "likes" relation between people.
(f) The "dislikes" relation between people.
(g) The "is taller than" relation between basketball players.
(h) The "is shorter than" relation between college professors.

5.2.5 Functions

Definition 13. A *function* is a relation with the property that no two ordered pairs of the relation have the same first element and different second elements. Functions are often called *operations*.

Some 2-place predicates determine functional relations, i.e. functions. Those functions are called extensions of the corresponding predicates. If the extension of a functional predicate P is called F_p then

$$F_p = \{<x, y> \mid P(x, y) \text{ is true}\}$$

However, there are more sets of ordered pairs that are functions than there are functional predicates in any ordinary language. So not every function is definable in this way, but the ones we can easily talk about in such a language are.

Definition 14. If F is a function then the *function notation* $y = f(x)$ can be used in place of $<x, y> \in F$, i.e.

$$y = f(x) \leftrightarrow <x, y> \in F$$

If F is a functional relation then $f(x)$ is an open definite description and if $b = f(a)$ then $<a, b> \in F$ and $f(a)$ is a definite description of b.

The use of an upper case letter to denote a functional relation expressed as a set of ordered pairs and the corresponding lower case letter to denote that relation expressed in equational form is just a convention used in this book. Other notations are common in other places.

Example 10.

(a) The < relation is not a functional relation since <1, 2> and <1, 3> are both elements of <.

(b) The relation F(x, y) where y is the (biological) father of x is a functional relation since each person has only one biological father. So $y = f(x)$ could also be used to describe this functional relation.

(c) The relation S(x, y) where y is a son of x is not a functional relation since many different sons could have the same father, so S(x) (son of x) would not uniquely refer to one person.

(d) The relation posSqrt, where $<x, y> \in$ posSqrt if and only if x and y are numbers and y is the positive square root of x, is a function.

(e) The relation sqrt, where $<x, y> \in$ sqrt if and only if y is a square root of x, is not a functional relation, since both <16, 4> and <16, -4> are elements of sqrt.

(f) The "one more than" (successor) relation, S, is a functional relation since $<x, y> \in$ S if and only if y is one more than x, i.e. $y = x + 1$. So $s(x) = x + 1$.

An ordered triple of things can be described as an ordered pair whose first term is an ordered pair, e.g. <1, 3, 5> can be thought of as <<1, 3>, 5>. Similarly, an ordered quadruple can be thought of as an ordered pair whose first term is an ordered triple, e.g. <1, 2, 3, 4> can be thought of as <<<1, 2>, 3>, 4>. In general, an ordered n-tuple can be thought of as an ordered pair whose first term is an ordered (n-1)-tuple. As a result, functions with any number of inputs (also called arguments) are included in the definition above.

Example 11. The addition function, called plus, defined on numbers is the set of ordered pairs <<x, y>, z> such that z is the sum of x and y. so

   plus = {<<x, y>, z> | z = x + y}.

Hence

   plus(<x,y>, z) if and only if z = x + y.

   Since functions are special kinds of relations and each relation has a domain and a range, it follows that each function has a domain and a range.

Examples 12.

(a) The domain of the positive square root function, posSqrt, is the set of all numbers that have positive square roots, i.e. it is the set of all nonnegative numbers. The range of posSqrt is the set of all numbers that are positive square roots of some number, i.e. the set of all nonnegative numbers.
(b) The domain of the addition function, plus, is the set of all ordered pair of numbers, since every ordered pair of numbers has a sum. The range of plus is the set of all numbers that are sums of some pair of numbers, e.g. the set of all numbers.
(c) The domain of the father of relation, F, where F(x, y) if and only if y is the father of x is the set of all people who have fathers, i.e. the set of all people. The range of F is the set of all people who are fathers of someone.

Exercise 7. For each of the following relations, determine its domain and its range. Then determine whether it is a functional relation.

(a) The relation R(x, y) such that x and y are people and y is a (biological) child of x.
(b) The relation R(x, y) such that x and y are people and y is a (biological) parent of x.
(c) The relation R(x, y) such that x and y are people and y is the current husband of x in a monogamous society.
(d) The relation R(x, y) such that x and y are people and y is a current husband of x in a polygamous society.
(e) The relation R(x, y) such that x and y are positive integers and y is a factor of x.
(f) The relation R(x, y) such that x and y are positive integers and x is a factor of y.
(g) The relation R(<x, y>, z) with x, y, and z integers and z = x or z = y.
(h) The relation R(<x, y>, z) with x, y, and z integers and z = x and z = y.

5.2.6 Stacks

Example 13. Stacks

(a) The data of a stack can be data values of any (one) type. For example, a stack of numbers, a stack of memory addresses, a stack of sets, and so on.

(b) The data components are arranged as a sequence.

(c) The basic allowed operations are push, pop, length, and top.

Definition 15. x is a stack $\leftrightarrow$ x =<S, push, pop, length, top> where

(a) S is a sequence of data values of any one type.

(b) The only operations allowed to be performed on S are push, pop, length, and top and operations definable in terms of those operations

(c) The operations push, pop, length, and top are defined below:

let $<e_1, e_2, \ldots e_{n-1}, e_n>$ represent any nonempty sequence, "$<>$" represent the empty sequence, and "val" represent any data value of the same type as the values of S. Here the rightmost element of the sequence is the top of the stack. Then the functions push, pop, top, and length can be defined as follows:

$$\text{push}(<e_1, e_2, \ldots e_{n-1}, e_n>, \text{val}) = <e_1, e_2, \ldots e_{n-1}, e_n, \text{val}>$$
$$\text{push}(<>, \text{val}) = <\text{val}>$$
$$\text{pop}(<e_1, e_2, \ldots e_{n-1}, e_n>) = <e_1, e_2, \ldots e_{n-1}>$$
$$\text{pop}(<>) = <>$$
$$\text{length}(<e_1, e_2, \ldots e_{n-1}, e_n>) = n$$
$$\text{length}(<>) = 0$$
$$\text{top}(<e_1, e_2, \ldots e_{n-1}, e_n>) = e_n$$
$$\text{top}(<>) = \text{error}$$

This is not the only way stacks can be defined. The point here is to show how the notation of logical English can be used.

5.2.7 1-Dimensional Arrays

Example 14. 1-Dimensional arrays

(a) The data can be data values of any (one) type.

(b) The data components are arranged as a fixed length sequence.

(c) The allowed operations are get and put.

Definition 16. x is a 1-dimensional array $\leftrightarrow$ x = <S, n, get, put> where

(a) n is a nonnegative integer

(b) S is a sequence of data values of any (one) type of length n

(c) The operations get and put are defined as follows:

let $<e_1, e_2, \ldots e_{n-1}, e_n>$ represent any nonempty sequence of length n, "$<>$" represent the empty sequence, "val" represent any data value of the same type as the values of S and let i be any positive integer $<= n$, then

$get(<e_1, \ldots e_{i-1}, e_i, e_{i+1}, \ldots e_n>, i) = e_i$

$get(< >, i) = error$

$put(<e_1, \ldots e_{i-1}, e_i, e_{i+1}, \ldots e_n>, i, val) = <e_1, \ldots e_{i-1}, val, e_{i+1}, \ldots e_n>$

$put(< >, i, val) = error$

You may be more familiar with these operations in the context of programming language instructions where "put" is represented by assignment. In such programming languages $put(<e_1, \ldots e_{i-1}, e_i, e_{i+1}, \ldots e_n>, i, val)$ would be written $S[i] \leftarrow val$.

Exercise 8. Try to formulate a similar definition for some other data structure with which you are familiar, e.g. string, 2-dimensional array, queue, circular queue, tree, or graph.

Chapter 6
Expressing Problem Specifications

This chapter is about expressing functional problem specifications using logical English. After studying this material you should be able to:

1. Determine the domain and solution condition of functional problem specifications expressed in English.
2. Identify various defects in problem specifications.
3. Express the logical structure of functional problem specifications using logical English.

Outline

6.1   Functional problem specifications
6.2   What can go wrong with problem specifications
6.3   Expressing problem specifications with logical English

6.1   Functional Problem Specifications

Definition 1. A *functional problem specification* (or *problem definition*) consists of two things, a *domain specification* and a *solution specification*. The domain specification of a problem is a set of conditions, called *domain conditions*, which define the *domain* of that problem, i.e. the set of things the problem is about. The solution specification of a problem is a set of conditions, called *solution conditions*, which describe, for each element of the domain, the conditions that anything would have to satisfy in order to be the solution for that element of the domain. The set of solutions of a problem is sometimes called its *range*. In addition, it must be that for each element of the domain no more than one thing (perhaps nothing) can satisfy the solution conditions of the problem, i.e. for each element of the domain of the problem there is at most one solution.

The kinds of problems defined here are called "functional" because they must have at most one solution for each element of their domain. For example, the problem of finding some number bigger than 7 is not functional, since there are many numbers

R. Lover, *Elementary Logic: For Software Development*,
DOI: 10.2007/978-1-84800-082-7, © Springer 2008

bigger than 7. On the other hand, the problem of finding the smallest integer bigger than 7 is functional, since there is only one such number, 8. Finally, the problem of finding the nth even prime number is functional but has no solution for n > 1 since 2 is the only even prime number.

Normally the term "functional problem specification" will be shortened to just "problem specification" or just "problem." Finally, problem specifications are also called problem definitions.

Example 1. The domain condition of the problem of finding the positive square root of any positive integer is the condition of being a positive integer. The solution condition for each element of the problem domain is the condition of being the positive square root of that domain element.

Example 2. The domain of the function corresponding to the problem of Example 1 is the set of positive integers and the range is the set of numbers that are positive square roots of positive integers.

A problem specification, sometimes called an external specification, describes a problem, it does not describe how that problem can be solved. Describing how a problem can be solved is the job of an algorithm or program design, sometimes called an internal specification. There is, however, a very close relation between functional problem specifications and program designs. As described later, program designs will include preconditions and postconditions, typically as comments. The preconditions of a program design describe what inputs a program is intended to work with and the postconditions describe, for each of those inputs, what conditions the corresponding output should satisfy. If a program design solves a specific problem (and no more general one) then the preconditions of the program design are the same as the domain conditions of the problem and the postconditions of the program design are the same as the solution conditions of the problem. Program designs will be discussed in detail in later chapters.

Example 3. The problem of finding the larger of any ordered pair of numbers. The domain of the problem is the set of all ordered pairs of numbers. For any given ordered pair of numbers, the corresponding solution (range element) is the larger of the two numbers. Note that both the domain and range have infinitely many elements.

If a program solves exactly this problem then its intended inputs are ordered pairs of numbers and, for any given ordered pair of numbers, its output is the larger of the two input numbers. For example, the ordered pair of numbers (3, 5) is an element of the domain of this problem, and the corresponding solution is the number 5. A program which solved this problem would return 5 as its output when given the ordered pair of numbers (3, 5) as inputs.

Example 4. Consider the problem of sorting a specific list of names. The domain of this problem is the set whose only element is that list of names. The solution condition is that any solution must be that list of names in sorted order. The range is the set whose only element is that list of names in sorted order. Note that the domain and range have only a single element each. Moreover, if a program solves exactly this problem then its only intended input is that specific list of names and its only correct output will be that list in sorted order.

Example 5. The more general (and more typical) problem of sorting any list of names. The domain of this problem is the set of all possible lists of names. For a given list of names the solution condition is that the solution must be that list in sorted order. The range of this problem then is the set of all lists of names that are in sorted order. Note that both the domain and the range are infinite. Moreover, if a program solves exactly this problem than its intended input is any list of names and the corresponding output will be that list in sorted order. Note that any program that solves this problem will also solve the previous problem, but not *vice versa*.

Example 6. The problem of finding a customer record from a specific customer file, given the customer's account number. A program which solved this specific problem would take this specific file and an account number from the list of accounts in this file as inputs and would return the corresponding customer record as output.

The domain of this problem is the set of all ordered pairs <file, custno> where "file" is the file in question and "custno" is the customer number of a customer with an account number in that file. For any such pair, the range element (solution) is the corresponding record from that file. The number of elements in the domain of this problem is the number of account numbers of customers whose accounts are in that file. The number of elements in the range of this problem is the number of customer records in the file.

Exercise 1. Describe the domain and range for each of the following problem specifications. Tell how many elements are in the domain and in the range. Say what a program that solved the problem would do.

(a) The problem of alphabetizing a specific list of English words.
(b) The problem of alphabetizing arbitrary lists of English words.
(c) The problem of eliminating duplicates from a specific list of numbers.
(d) The problem of eliminating duplicates from arbitrary lists of numbers.

Exercise 2. Explain how a single program can solve many different problems. Give a simple example of a single program and several different problems that it solves. Note you don't have to write the program, just describe what it does.

6.2 What Can Go Wrong with Problem Specifications

Writing good problem specifications is one of the major tasks of software development. Defective specifications lead to defective programs and dissatisfied customers. Among the problems commonly encountered are vagueness, ambiguity, incompleteness, logical inconsistency, functional ambiguity, and redundancy. This chapter describes the use of logical English and mathematical English to help express problem specifications clearly. Later chapters will describe methods for reasoning about clearly expressed specifications, e.g. to simplify them or to detect and correct defects.

Recall that an expression is vague if and only if there are cases for which it is unclear whether the expression does or does not apply. Such cases are often called "borderline cases." Also, an expression is ambiguous just in case it has two or more different meanings. In real life vagueness and ambiguity are responsible for more program fixes than are caused by errors in programming.

Exercise 3. Look for examples of vagueness and ambiguity in the problem specifications described in Exercise 1 above.

Definition 2. A problem specification is said to be *incomplete* if there are elements of the problem domain for which no solution condition is specified.

Example 7. If a specification mentions four types of domain element but does not specify what counts as a solution in one or more of the cases then the specification is incomplete.

Specification are often incomplete because the specifier believes that certain cases are "obvious." Sometimes they are obvious, but programmers get into a lot of trouble filling in "obvious" cases on their own.

Notice that a specification can be complete even though there is no solution for some domain elements. For example, consider the problem of finding the nth even prime number for any positive integer n. The problem specification has the set of all positive integers as its domain. For any positive integer, n, the solution condition is that the solution value be the nth even prime number. Notice, however, that for $n > 1$ there is no such thing as the nth even prime number since the first and only even prime number is 2. This problem definition cannot be said to be incomplete, since it clearly specifies what condition a solution would have to satisfy for each element of its domain.

Definition 3. A specification is *logically inconsistent* just in case its domain condition or its solution condition is logically inconsistent or if the two are inconsistent with each other.

If the domain condition of a problem is logically inconsistent then the problem would have an empty domain. Logical inconsistency will be discussed in detail in later chapters.

Example 8. A problem specification that defined its domain to include a plane geometric figure which is both round and not round would be logically inconsistent.

Very few specifications are given where logical inconsistency is so obvious. Where inconsistency often becomes a serious problem is with complex problem specifications, where the logically conflicting parts are widely separated. However, inconsistency can happen even with a short specification if parts of it are written at different times or by different people.

Example 9. A problem specification that had the number 3 in its domain and required that the solution in that case should be an even number and also that the solution should not be an even number. Since this is not logically possible such a specification would be logically inconsistent. Again, few people write specifications that are so obviously inconsistent, but many specifications are written which are inconsistent.

Definition 4. A specification is *functionally ambiguous* just in case it specifies two different solution conditions for some element of its domain.

Recall that a specification is supposed to describe a function from domain elements to solutions, with at most one solution for each domain element.

Example 10. A problem specification that had the number 3 in its domain and for which, according to one part of the specification, the corresponding solution is 5 while, according to another part of the specification, the solution is 8 would be functionally ambiguous.

Definition 5. A problem specification is said to be *redundant* just in case some part of the specification can be removed without changing the domain or solution set of the problem. Also, the part that can be removed is said to be *redundant* relative to the rest of it.

The most obvious cause of redundancy is when one part of the specification is repeated. More subtle cases occur when some parts of the specification logically imply other parts of the specification, making the latter redundant.

Example 11. Below are specifications for a sales commission problem. Describe the domain and solution condition of the problem. Also look for vagueness, ambiguity, incompleteness, inconsistency, and redundancy in these problem specifications.

> Everyone gets a base salary no matter what. Trainees get an additional $100 per week. Experienced salespeople in established territories are expected to sell at least $2,000 per week. If they do not then they get only their base salary. Anyone who sells more than $2,000 in a week gets a 10% commission on the amount over $2,000. Anyone selling in a new territory gets an additional 15% commission on the sales amount over $2,000. Experienced salespeople get 25% commission on sales over $2,000 per week in new territories.

First ask what the problem is. It is to find the salaries of salespeople as determined by certain conditions. The domain of the problem, then, is some unspecified set of salespeople as represented by their sales, experience, and territories. For a given salesperson the solution to the problem would be a number representing that person's salary. The solution condition describes how a salesperson's salary depends upon the conditions described in the specification. Here are some conditions involved in the solution condition:

1. Whether the salesperson is experienced or not.
2. Whether the person's territory is established or new.
3. Whether the person sold more than $2,000 per week.

These conditions can be used in problem specifications such as the following:

1. If salesperson is experienced and sales are less than or equal $2,000 then salary is base salary.
2. If salesperson is new and sales are less than or equal to $2,000 then salary is base salary plus $100.
3. If salesperson's sales are greater than $2,000 per week and territory is established then salary is base salary plus 10% of amount above $2,000 plus $100 if salesperson is new.
4. If salesperson's sales are greater than $2,000 per week and territory is new then salary is base salary plus 25% of amount above $2,000 plus $100 if salesperson is new.

Of course, these conditions could have been expressed in many different ways. Note that it took a certain amount of reading between the lines just to get this far. As for vagueness, ambiguity, and so on, there is much to complain about.

1. *Vagueness.* The terms "trainee" and "established territory" may be vague, depending on the context. If there are clear designations, e.g. by management, as to which salespeople are trainees and which territories are established then there may be no vagueness.
2. *Ambiguity.* In most contexts there would be no ambiguity issues with this specification.
3. *Incompleteness.* What are new salespeople expected to sell? What do they get if they don't sell at least $2,000 per week?
4. *Logical inconsistency.* Not much to complain about here.
5. *Functional ambiguity.* Nothing ambiguous here.
6. *Redundancy.* The last condition "Experienced salespeople get 25% commission on sales over $2,000 per week." is redundant given the previous conditions.

Exercise 4. The Multiple Adaptive Digital Diagnostically Organized Computer, MADDOC, is the computer based medical diagnosis system on the Intergalactic Starship Belmont. A small part of it is to be reprogrammed according to new specifications given by its new Medical Officer, Zarg. Rumor has it that Zarg was not properly reassembled during his last Teleporter use. As a result you feel the need to be very careful about the specifications. Here they are:

> The part of the program to be reprogrammed is to calculate the number of aspirin tablets to give to crew who show certain symptoms (not discussed here). Zarg tells you that everyone gets at least one tablet, so that they do not go away feeling untreated. Martian crew who are new to the ship get an additional tablet. Crew who work in the nuclear boiler room get four additional tablets. Crew who have had more than five tablets in the last 24 hours get no more.

Describe the problem, its domain and its solution condition(s). Also look for vagueness, ambiguity, incompleteness, inconsistency, and redundancy in this problem specification.

6.3   Expressing Problem Specifications with Logical English

One thing you can do to help reduce defects is to try to transform specifications from ordinary English into logical English. This process focuses your attention on relevant issues, such as vagueness, ambiguity, and incompleteness. Moreover, the attempt can be helpful even if you don't finish it. Fortunately, formalization can be done at various levels of detail. A top down approach to formalization is often useful and avoids wasting time on irrelevant details. Once specifications are clearly expressed, the machinery of logic can be applied to test them for various flaws. However, with a few exceptions discussed briefly at the end of part III, the process of expressing problem specifications in logical English is most useful when restricted to simple problem specifications, those parts of large specifications that need clarification, or the higher level iterations of complex problem specifications. Otherwise it is easy to get lost in logical notation.

Example 12. Using the following abbreviations, express the following problem using logical English. Given any two integers, find the smaller of them.

English	Logical English
x is an integer	$I(x)$
The ordered pair <x, y>	$\langle x, y \rangle$ or (x, y)
x is in the domain of the problem	$DOM(x)$
The smaller of x and y	$MIN(x, y)$
y is the solution for domain element x	$SOL(x, y)$

The domain condition of this problem can be expressed by

$$DOM(x) \leftrightarrow x = \langle x_1, x_2 \rangle \wedge I(x_1) \wedge I(x_2)$$

and the solution condition can be expressed by

$$SOL(x, y) \leftrightarrow y = MIN(x_1, x_2)$$

Different situations call for different levels of formal detail. For example, if we wanted to spell out the meaning of MIN we could write

$$y = MIN(x_1, x_2) \leftrightarrow (x_1 < x_2 \wedge y = x_1) \vee (\sim(x_1 < x_2) \wedge y = x_2).$$

So the solution condition could be expressed in more detail by

$$SOL(x, y) \leftrightarrow ((x_1 < x_2 \wedge y = x_1) \vee (\sim(x_1 < x_2) \wedge y = x_2)).$$

There is no one level of detail which is always best. A good rule of thumb is not to express any more detail than is useful for what you are trying to do at the time.

There is almost always more than one correct way to translate English into logical English. For example, "y is the minimum of x_1 and x_2" was expressed above by

$$(x_1 < x_2 \wedge y = x_1) \vee (\sim(x_1 < x_2) \wedge y = x_2)$$

but it could also be expressed as

$$(x_1 < x_2 \rightarrow y = x_1) \wedge (\sim(x_1 < x_2) \rightarrow y = x_2).$$

The reason either expression would work is that they are logically equivalent, i.e. they are both true or both false no matter what the values of the variables are. Logical equivalence will be discussed in detail in a later chapter.

This next example shows, again, that specifications can be done at more than one level of detail. Normally it is a good idea to use a "top down" approach to formalization. This amounts to formalizing the overall specification first, using high level abbreviations, i.e. abbreviations that leave out low level details. Then, if it is useful, make the lower level details explicit.

Example 13. Express the following problem using logical English. Given a finite sequence of integers in any order, find the corresponding sequence of integers arranged in ascending order.

For this problem, the domain condition, DOM(x), is that x is a finite sequence of integers with no restrictions on its order. The domain therefore is the set of all finite sequences of integers. The solution condition, SOL(x, y), is that y is the finite sequence with the same terms as x, but arranged in ascending order.

Using the following abbreviations:

> PERM(x, y)   For y is a permutation of x,
> INTSEQ(x)   For x is a finite sequence of integers, and
> ASORT(y)   For y is sorted in ascending order,

the specification for this problem can be written

> DOM(x) $\leftrightarrow$ INTSEQ(x)
> SOL(x, y) $\leftrightarrow$ PERM(x, y) $\wedge$ ASORT(y).

In some circumstances it would be helpful to give more details about the meanings of PERM, INTSEQ, and ASORT. For example, if the following abbreviations are used

> PI(x)   For x is a positive integer,
> x[i]   For the ith element of sequence x, and
> LEN(x)   For the length of the sequence x,

then the meaning of ASORT(y) can be expressed as

> $(\forall i)((PI(i) \wedge i < LEN(y)) \rightarrow (y[i] <= y[i + 1]))$

and the problem specification above can be written

> DOM(x) $\leftrightarrow$ INTSEQ(x)
> SOL(x, y) $\leftrightarrow$ PERM(x, y) $\wedge$ $(\forall i)((PI(i) \wedge i < LEN(y)) \rightarrow (y[i] <= y[I + 1]))$.

This version clearly describes what ASORT means, at the expense of using a much more complex expression. (A similar analysis could be done for PERM and INTSEQ.) Which representation of the solution condition is best would depend upon how much detail about ASORT (or PERM or INTSEQ) needs to be made explicit. Too much detail wastes time with irrelevant details. Too little detail leads to ignoring relevant issues. When used with the right level of detail logical English is a great help, although initially it does require some getting used to.

Example 14. Express the following problem using logical English. Find the minimum and the maximum of any ordered triple of not necessarily distinct integers. Stop at the first level of detail.

Using the following abbreviations

$I(x)$	x is an integer,
$<x_1, x_2>$	The ordered pair $<x_1, x_2>$,
$<x_1, x_2, x_3>$	The ordered triple $<x_1, x_2, x_3>$,
$MIN3(x_1, x_2, x_3)$	The minimum of $<x_1, x_2, x_3>$,
$MAX3(x_1, x_2, x_3)$	The maximum of $<x_1, x_2, x_3>$,
$DOM(x)$	x is in the domain of the problem, and
$SOL(x, y)$	y is the solution for domain element x

we can express the problem as follows.

$$DOM(x) \leftrightarrow x = <x_1, x_2, x_3> \wedge I(x_1) \wedge I(x_2) \wedge I(x_3)$$
$$SOL(x, y) \leftrightarrow y = <y_1, y_2> \wedge I(y_1) \wedge I(y_2) \wedge y_1 = MIN3(x_1, x_2, x_3)$$
$$\wedge y_2 = MAX3(x_1, x_2, x_3)$$

The meaning of MIN3 could be express by

$$w = MIN3(x, y, z) \leftrightarrow (w = x \vee w = y \vee w = z)$$
$$\wedge w <= x \wedge w <= y \wedge w <= z$$

Exercise 5. Write the corresponding expression for MAX3.

Exercise 6. Express the following problem using logical English. Find the positive square root of any positive number. Use the following abbreviations.

$SQRT(x, y)$	y is the positive square root of x
$DOM(x)$	x is in the domain of the problem, and
$SOL(x, y)$	y is the solution for domain element x

All the examples above were numeric. But of course many problems have solution values that are not numbers. For example, classification problems are about finding the class in which something belongs.

Example 15. Express the following problem using logical English notation. Find the grade to be assigned any test where scores of >=90 get "A," 80–89 get "B," 70–79 get "C," 60–69 get "D," and < 60 get "F" and all test scores are integers between 0 and 100. Using the obvious abbreviations.

DOM(x) ↔ I(x) ∧ 0 <= x ∧ x <= 100
SOL(x, y) ↔ ((x >= 90 ∧ y = "A") ∨ (80 <= x ∧ x <= 89 ∧ y = "B")
              ∨ (70 <= x ∧ x <= 79 ∧ y = "C") ∨ (60 <= x ∧ x <= 69 ∧ y =
              "D") ∨ (x < 60 ∧ y = "F"))

Exercise 7. Express the following problem using logical English. Determine what class a student belongs to as a function of the number of semester hours of credit earned where a student with <= 30 credits is a freshman, 31–60 credits is a sophomore, 61–90 credits is a junior, and >90 credits is a senior. There is no upper limit on the number of credits a student can earn. Use the abbreviations from the previous examples.

Many problems are *table lookup problems*. The simplest problems of this kind require finding an item in a single list or table. More complicated problems of this kind include SQL queries of relational data bases.

Example 16. Find the population of any city in some table of cities and their populations. Assume that the table has two columns, city names in column 1 and populations in column 2. Then, using the following abbreviations

c   The city population table being used
ISCITY(x)   x is a city name

The specifications for this problem can be written

DOM(x) ↔ ISCITY(x) and ∃r(I(r) ∧ x = c[r, 1])
SOL(x, y) ↔ y = c[r, 2]

This expresses the fact that the domain of the problem is the set of cities in column 1 of the city population table and that what is wanted is the corresponding population in column 2. Notice the use of an existential quantifier.

Other table look up problems include:

(a) Find the cosine of any angle from a table of cosines.
(b) Find the name of an employee given the employee's social security number.
(c) Find the price of a book given its ISBN.
(d) Find the name of a city given the ZIP code of an address in that city.
(e) Find the rate per $1,000 of life insurance for a person with specified age, sex, medical history, etc.

Decision problems are another common type of problem. These problems involve determining whether some condition is or is not true of some thing. Examples include:

(a) In some list of cities and their populations, are there any cities with populations > one million?
(b) Are there any duplicates in a certain list?
(c) Is this file sorted?
(d) Did the program compile?

Example 17. Does list L of integers have any duplicates in it? Note that the domain of this problem is not L but the set whose only element is L. Using the previously introduced abbreviations along with

____ ∈ L abbreviates ____ is an element of list L

the problem can be expressed

$$\text{DOM}(x) \leftrightarrow x = L \text{ (not } x \in L)$$
$$\text{SOL}(x, y) \leftrightarrow (y = \text{"yes"} \land \exists u \exists v(I(u) \land I(v) \land \sim(u = v) \land x_u = x_v)$$
$$\lor (y = \text{"no"} \land \sim(\exists u \exists v(I(u) \land I(v) \land \sim(u = v) \land x_u = x_v)$$

Exercise 8. Express the following problem specifications using logic notation. Use the following abbreviations. Invent others if you need them.

DOM(x)	x is in the domain of the problem
SOL(x, y)	y is the solution of the problem for domain element x
NUMSEQ(z)	z is a finite sequence of numbers
MIN(z, y)	y is the minimum of the elements of sequence of numbers z
ASORT(y)	y is sorted in ascending order
DSORT(y)	y is sorted in descending order

(a) The problem of finding the minimum of a finite sequence of numbers.
(b) The problem of determining whether an arbitrary finite sequence of numbers is sorted (in ascending order or descending order).
(c) The problem of determining whether one finite sequence of numbers is longer than another finite sequence of numbers.

Exercise 9. The problem is to check a student record and classify it as "OK" or "NG." Each student record has many fields. Among those fields are the TIME field, the CODE field, and the AGE field. The specification details are described below. The TIME field has values "day" and "night," the CODE field has values "trad" and "adp," and the AGE field has values that are integers between 0 and 100.

If the TIME field is "day" and the AGE field has a value less than 24 then if the CODE field is "trad" then the record is "OK." Under these same conditions if the CODE field is not "trad" then the record is "NG." If the time field is not "day" then the record is "NG" unless the AGE field has a value greater than or equal to 24, in which case it is "OK."

Use the following abbreviations, and others if needed.

STUREC(x)	x is a student record
TIME.x	The time field of student record x
CODE.x	The code field of student record x
AGE.x	The age field of student record x
CLASS(x)	The classification of student record x

Finish expressing this problem using logical English.

DOM(x) ↔ STUREC(x)
SOL(x, y) ↔ (y = "OK" ∧... ...) ∨ (y = "NG" ∧ ... ...)

Exercise 10. Recall the problem of determining sales commissions that was discussed earlier.

Everyone gets a base salary no matter what. Trainees get an additional $100 per week. Experienced salespeople in established territories are expected to sell at least $2,000 per week. If they do not then they get only their base salary. Anyone who sells more than $2,000 in a week gets a 10% commission on the amount over $2,000. Anyone selling in a new territory gets an additional 15% commission on the amount over $2,000.

Use the following abbreviations, and others if needed.

SP(x)	x is a salesperson
EXP(x)	x is experienced
EST(x)	x sells in an established territory
SOLDAMT(x)	The amount of x's sales in $

Express this problem using logical English.

Exercise 11. At one time the consumer loan laws of one state allowed lenders to charge insurance origination fees for the life insurance and for the accident and health insurance they may offer borrowers. Borrowers are not required to buy either kind of insurance. For each of the two kinds of insurance the origination fee is: $0 if the amount of indebtedness is less than $250, $1 if the amount is between $250 and $500, and $2 if the amount is greater than $500. Borrowers occasionally renew their loans, i.e. borrow more before the original loan is completely repaid. In that case they can again choose none, one, or both kinds of insurance and another loan origination fee can be charged for each kind of insurance except that no more than two origination fees for each type of insurance can be charged in any one year period.

Use the following abbreviations, and others if needed.

B(x)	x is a borrower
WANTSINS(x)	x wants life insurance
PRIORFEES(x)	Number of life insurance fees charged x within the previous year

DEBTAMT(x)   Amount of indebtedness of x's loan
FEE(x)   Amount of life insurance origination fee x can be charged

Express this problem using logical English.

Exercise 12. The problem is to determine what type of bill (polite, nasty, or none) and what kind of advertisement to send (flyer, catalog, or none) to a customer as a function of whether the customer is rich, paid up, and high volume. Here are the details.

Everyone gets a printed sales flyer except those who are not rich, not paid up, and not high volume. Rich customers get a long catalog unless they are not paid up and not high volume. Poor customers get a long catalog just in case they are high volume. The only people who get nasty bills are those who are poor, not paid up, and not high volume. Others get a polite bill if and only if they are not paid up.

Use the following abbreviations, and others if needed.

CUST(x)   x is a customer
RICH(x)   x is rich
PAIDUP(x)   x is paid up
HIVOL(x)   x is high volume customer
PBILL(x)   x is a polite bill
NBILL(x)   x is a nasty bill
FLYER(x)   x is a flyer
CTLG(x)   x is a catalog

Express this problem using logical English.

Exercise 13. The problem is to determine a diagnosis (ill or well) for patients given three possible symptoms (dizzy, congested, fever). Here are some details.

If a patient is dizzy and congested then patient is ill. If patient has fever and is congested then also ill. If no fever and not congested then patient is well. If no fever and not dizzy then patient is well. If dizzy, fevered, and congested then patient is ill. In all other cases, patient is well.

Use the following abbreviations, and others if needed.

P(x)   x is a patient
D(x)   x is dizzy
C(x)   x is congested
F(x)   x has a fever

Express this problem using logical English.

Example 18. The parity of a sequence of 0s and 1s is said to be even if the number of 1 bits in the sequence is even, and odd if the number of 1 bits in the sequence is odd. A parity checking scheme is a procedure for trying to detect errors in the storage or transmission of data. An even parity checking scheme for use with eight bit character codes, e.g. ASCII or EBCDIC codes, involves the following. Before each character is saved to memory or transmitted its parity is determined. If its parity is even then a ninth parity bit of 0 is added to the character code, otherwise a ninth parity bit of 1 is added. As a result, the parity of the nine bit sequence will always be even. Then the nine bit sequence is saved to memory or transmitted. Later, when the corresponding nine bit sequence is retrieved from memory or received, its parity is checked. If the received nine bit sequence has odd parity then an error is detected. If it has even parity then no error is detected, which is not to say that no error exists.

Two problems associated with parity checking are the problem of generating the parity bit for any eight bit character code and the problem of checking the parity of a nine bit code with parity bit. Using the following abbreviations

BINSEQ(x)	x is a sequence of 0s and 1s
NUMONES(x)	the number of 1s in sequence x
LEN(x)	the length of x, e.g. LENx=9
BIT(n, x)	the nth bit of x, e.g. BIT(5,x) = 1
EVENPARITY(x)	x has even parity

The problem of determining the parity bit (bit 9) of any nine bit sequence of 0s and 1s can be expressed as follows.

$$DOM(x) \leftrightarrow BINSEQ(x) \text{ and } LEN(x) = 9$$

$$SOL(x, y) \leftrightarrow (y = \text{`OK'} \land EVENPARITY(x))$$
$$\lor (y = \text{`ERROR'} \land \sim EVENPARITY(x))$$

Exercise 14. Using the same abbreviations as in the example above, and others if needed, express the problem of determining the parity bit (0 or 1) of any 8 bit sequence of 0s and 1s.

Chapter 7
Expressing Program Designs

In this book the terms "algorithm" and "program design" will often be used interchangeably. When they are distinguished, algorithms are more abstract than program designs. In this abstract sense a single algorithm might be implemented by many different program designs. Such program designs might take account of specific features of particular programming languages, while abstract algorithms would be indifferent to details of specific languages. In any case the difference between abstract algorithms and more concrete program designs is not usually of interest here.

Readers of this book are assumed to have some programming experience. The discussion below is not intended to teach anyone how to design or write programs. Instead, it is intended to show a bit about the role that logical English plays in expressing algorithms by means of pseudocode. It is also intended to describe the specific version of pseudocode used here. After studying this material you should be able to translate algorithms expressed in ordinary English into the pseudocode described below.

Outline

7.1   Pseudocode for Instructions

Definition 1. Pseudocode is a restricted subset of English formatted to resemble a programming language.

R. Lover, *Elementary Logic: For Software Development*,
DOI: 10.2007/978-1-84800-082-7, © Springer 2008

While there is no standard pseudocode, once you understand one version, it is easy to understand other versions. Many programmers use pseudocode. Abstract versions of it are used to express abstract algorithms. More language specific versions of it are used to express designs for programs in those languages. Pseudocode is supposed to be clear enough that a human being can execute it "by hand," without using a computer and with little or no knowledge of programming languages.

7.1.1 Atomic Instructions

Assignment statements are the simplest kind of instruction. The simplest assignment statements assign a literal value to a program variable, e.g.

   $x \leftarrow 3.14$

In this instruction, "x" is a program variable, "$\leftarrow$" represents assignment, and "3.14" is a literal value.

Program constants and variables play a dual role. When a program is written they are logical variables, i.e. they are placeholder symbols which do not represent any particular values. When a program is executed, a program constant is given a fixed value for the duration of that run of the program. It is like a name in English. A program variable is like a pronoun in English, it may have one value at one time and a different value at a different time during a single run of a program.

The general form of an assignment statement is

   var $\leftarrow$ expression

where "var" is a program constant or variable, "$\leftarrow$" represents assignment, and "expression" is a program constant, a program variable, or a definite description constructed from program constants, program variables, and function symbols in ways the reader is surely familiar with. For example,

   $x \leftarrow 3 + 5/2 - PI$

7.1.2 Compound Instructions

A compound instruction consists of two or more instructions and a control structure. The control structure is a specification of the order in which the instructions are to be executed.

7.1.2.1 Sequential Control Structure

The simplest control structure is to execute instructions in the order in which they are written. For example, the instructions

$x \leftarrow 3$
$y \leftarrow 5$
$z \leftarrow x + y$

would be executed by first assigning 3 to x, then assigning 5 to y, and then assigning $3 + 5$ to z.

7.1.2.2 Alternation (or Selection) Control Structure

Alternation is accomplished by first determining the truth value of a condition and then executing one instruction if the condition is true and executing some other instruction (or no instruction at all) if the condition is false. In most programming languages this is represented by "if ...then...," "if... then... else...," and "case" instructions. For example,

If $(x > 3)$ then print x endif

This same instruction can also be written vertically as

If $(x > 3)$ then
       print x
endif

Here is another example.

If $(x > 3)$ then print x else print 3 endif

The vertical form of this is

If $(x > 3)$ then
       print x
else
       print 3
endif

The expression "$(x > 3)$" is a condition, in the logical sense, when it is written, i.e. it would be true of some values that could be assigned to x and false for others. When instructions involving this condition are executed, x is given a specific value, so the condition becomes a statement, which is either true or false.

7.1.2.3 Repetition (or Looping) Control Structure

Repetition consists of executing instruction(s) 0 or more times. In most programming languages it is implemented by means of loops or iterators. The number of times the instruction(s) is repeated depends on the values of various variables just before the loop is entered. For example, the instructions

print x
$x \leftarrow x + 1$

which form the body of the following while loop

While (x > 3) do
      print x
      x ← x −1
endwhile

would be executed 0 times if x were less than or equal to 3 when the loop statement was executed. They would be executed 1 time if x were greater than 3 and less than or equal to 4 when the loop was executed, twice if x were greater than 4 and less than or equal to 5, and so on.

The indented part of the while loop is called the loop body. In the version of pseudocode used here the body of a loop should always be indented. Notice that "endwhile" is written directly below "While." "endwhile" should always be written directly below the corresponding "While."

The while loop above is called a pretest loop because the condition is tested before the body of the loop can be executed even once. There are also posttest loops, such as the following.

Do
      print x
      x ← x + 1
until (x > 3)

This loop will execute the loop body once and then check the truth value of the condition. As long as the condition is false, the loop body will be repeated. For example, if x = 0 initially then the loop body will be executed three times. If x = 2 initially the loop body will be executed twice. If x = 3 or more initially then the loop body will be executed just once. Again notice the indentation used.

7.1.2.4   Nested Control Structures

The instructions that are parts of compound instructions may themselves be compound instructions. For example

If (x > 3) then
      print x
      If (y < 0) then
            print y
      endif

and

While (x > 3) do
      If (y < 0) then
            print y
      endif
endwhile

```
        While (z = 4) do
             If (x > z) then
                       print 'This is a mess.'
             else
                       print 'This is also a mess.'
             endif
        endwhile
```

Such instructions are called "nested" instructions. Notice again how indentation shows level of nesting and shows where an instruction begins and ends. While most programming languages are indifferent to indentation, pseudocode is written for humans to read, and humans are greatly helped by following the indentation rules illustrated above.

7.1.2.5 Parallel Control Structures

Some programming languages allow parallel execution of instructions. These languages are intended to be used on computers that have more than one processor. There are interesting, and very hard, logical issues involving parallel computing. These issues will not be addressed here.

7.2 Pseudocode for Algorithms

An algorithm expressed in pseudocode consists of one or more instructions and some additional lines of text, as shown in the example below. The numbers at the left are not part of the pseudocode. The are there to make it easier to refer to lines of the pseudocode.

Example 1

```
 0  Algorithm findMin(x, y)
 1  # Preconditions: x and y are integers.
 2  # Postconditions: Returns the smaller of x and y or their common
 3  #  value if x = y.
 4
 5      If (x < y) then
 6              Return x
 7      else
 8              Return y    # Here x = y or x > y
 9      endif
10
11  endAlgorithm
```

Line 0 is called the header line. It consists of the word "Algorithm," a space, the name of the algorithm, and a list of zero of more input parameters separated by commas and enclosed in parentheses. In this example the name of the algorithm is "findMin" and the two input parameters are "x" and "y."

Lines 1–3 are called comment lines. The symbol "#" is used to indicate a comment. Everything to the right of "#" to the end of the line is a comment. A comment can begin anywhere in a line. Line 8 has a comment in it but is not a comment line. Comments are used to communicate information to human beings, but they are not instructions and they do not influence the execution of the algorithm.

Recall the discussion of problem specifications in Chap. 5. An algorithm is normally created to solve a problem. The preconditions and postconditions in lines 1–3 specify the problem this algorithm was intended to solve.

Lines 4 and 10 are blank. Blank lines are used to provide visual separation between major parts of an algorithm. A long algorithm might have several blank lines separating several major parts of the algorithm.

Lines 5–9 are a typical if…then…else… instruction. Note that they are indented to the right of lines 0–3, and 11.

Finally, line 11 marks the physical end of the pseudocode. Note that line 11 is directly below line 0.

Below are more examples of simple algorithms expressed first in English and then in pseudocode. In all the following, "Pre:" is used to abbreviate "Precondition": and "Post": to abbreviate "Postcondition":

Example 2. To find the smaller of two real numbers, compare them. If the first is smaller than the second then it is the smaller, otherwise the other one is the smaller. If they are equal then either one can be considered the smaller one.

```
Algorithm findSmaller(a, b)
# Pre: a and b are two real numbers.
# Post: Returns the smaller of a and b, or their common value if they are equal.

    If (a < b) then
            Return a
    else
            Return b
    endif

endAlgorithm
```

Example 3. To determine the parity bit of a sequence of 8 bits, using even parity, count the number of 1 bits in the sequence. Then if that number is odd then the parity bit is 1 otherwise the parity bit is 0.

```
Algorithm findEvenParityBit(S)
# Pre: S is a sequence of 8 binary digits, $d_0$, $d_1$, $d_2$, … $d_7$.
# Post: Returns 1 if the number of 1 bits in S is odd and returns # 0 otherwise.
```

```
    count ← 0
    I ← 0
    While (I < 8) do
            If (d_I = 1) then
                        count ← count + 1
            endif
            I ← I + 1
    endwhile
    If (count mod 2 = 0) then        # i.e. if count is even
            Return 0
    else
            Return 1
    endif
endAlgorithm
```

Example 4. To determine whether a specific number is an element of a 2-dimensional table of numbers, examine the first row, then the second row, etc. Within each row examine the columns in order. If the value is found then return true else return false.

```
Algorithm search2Dtable(T, k)
# Pre: T is a 2-dimensional table of numbers and k is a number.
# Post: Returns true if k is in T and returns false otherwise.

    nrows ← the number of rows of T
    ncols ← the number of columns of T
    r ← 0
    While (r < nrows) do
            c ← 0
            While (c < ncols) do
                        If (T[r, c] = k) then
                                    Return true
                        endif
                        c ← c + 1
            endwhile
            r ← r + 1
    endwhile
    Return false

endAlgorithm
```

Notice that the English leaves out some details that are made explicit in the pseudocode. Also, pseudocode, while it resembles a programming language, is still English. It can include large fragments of English such as "the number of rows of T." You could "test" a pseudocode algorithm by executing it by hand. Finally, it would be much easier to convert the pseudocode into a program in a programming language then it would be to convert the corresponding English.

Example 5. To determine whether two intervals of real numbers overlap, e.g. have a nonempty intersection, first determine whether the smaller ends or the larger ends of the intervals coincide. If they do then the intervals overlap. Otherwise determine which interval starts to the left of the left end of the other, then determine whether the larger end of that interval is at or to the right of the smaller end of the other. If both those conditions are true then the intervals overlap, otherwise they do not.

Algorithm overlap(a, b, c, d)
Pre: [a, b] and [c, d] are endpoints of intervals of real numbers.
Post: Returns true if [a, b] and [c, d] overlap and false otherwise.

```
    If ((a = c) or (b = d)) then
            Return true
    else                              # a not = c and b not = d
            if ((a < c) and (b > = c)) then
                        Return true          # a < c < = b, so overlap
                    else
                        Return false
                    endif
            else                          # c < a, since the other two cases are
                                          # covered above
                    If (d > = a) then          # c < a < = d, so overlap
                        Return true
                    else
                        Return false
                    endif
            endif
    endif

endAlgorithm
```

Exercise 1. Write pseudocode for each of the following algorithms. Note your solutions do not have to be exactly the same as the given solutions, but they should be similar and equivalent.

(a) To find the smallest of three integers first find the smaller of the first two then find the smaller of that and the third.
(b) To determine whether an integer is even, divide it by 2 and examine the remainder. If the remainder is 0 then the integer is even, otherwise it is odd.
(c) To find the smallest of a nonempty list of integers, examine the integers in order from beginning to end, keeping track of the smallest integer examined so far. At the end it will be the smallest in the list.
(d) To count the number of elements of a list of integers which are 7, examine the list from beginning to end keeping track of how many 7s have been encountered so far.
(e) To determine whether a nonempty list of numbers is sorted small to large look for pairs of numbers in the list which are out of order, i.e. larger first and smaller second. If no such pairs are found then the list is sorted from small to large.

(f) To determine whether every element of one nonempty list of numbers is less than every element of another nonempty list of numbers, find the largest element of the first list, find the smallest element of the second list, and if the former is less than the latter then the condition is true, otherwise it is false.

(g) To determine whether x is in the interval [a, b] or in [c, d] but not in the intersection of the two intervals, first determine whether x is in [a, b] then determine whether x is in [c, d]. If x is in neither or both intervals then the condition is false, otherwise the condition is true.

(h) To determine whether two intervals of real numbers overlap, e.g. have a nonempty intersection, first determine whether the smaller ends or the larger ends of the intervals coincide. If they do then the intervals overlap. Otherwise determine which interval starts to the left of the left end of the other, then determine whether the larger end of that interval is at or to the right of the smaller end of the other. If both those conditions are true then the intervals overlap, otherwise they do not.

Part II
Material Truth

Part II describes rules and criteria for combining knowledge of the factual truth or falsity of some statements, along with knowledge of logical forms, to determine the factual truth or falsity of other statements.

Chapter 8
Truth for Statements with at Most One Connective

This chapter describes truth conditions for atomic statements, quantified statements, and compound statements with one connective. It concludes with several computing related applications. After studying this chapter you should be able to:

1. Use the truth conditions for the basic truth functional connectives to determine the truth value of a statement involving at most a single truth functional connective, given the truth values of its component parts.
2. Understand the effect of short cut evaluation of "and" and "or" in programs, and determine when they are being used.
3. Calculate using bitwise extensions of "not," "and," "or," and "xor."
4. Apply bitwise extensions of truth functions to make and use masks and simple codes.

Outline

R. Lover, *Elementary Logic: For Software Development*,
DOI: 10.2007/978-1-84800-082-7, © Springer 2008

8.1   The Laws of Excluded Middle and Noncontradiction

The logic described in this book is based on two assumptions about truth and falsity. They are:

The Law of Excluded Middle: Every statement is either true or false.
The Law of Noncontradiction: No statement is both true and false.

The exact status of these "laws" has been the subject of debate among students of logic for at least 24 centuries. Here these laws are used as constraints on what logic can be applied to. The logic discussed here applies to closed statements that are either true or false but not both and it applies indirectly to open statements (conditions) that are true or false, but not both, of things. Most statements that are relevant to computing are of these types.

8.2   Atomic Statements

In the following definitions, the terms "materially true" and "materially false" will be used to in place of "true" and "false" in the ordinary sense of those terms The prefix "material" is used to emphasize that ordinary truth and falsehood are being discussed rather than "logical truth" and "logical falsehood." Logical truth and logical falsehood are discussed in a later chapter. Outside of definitions, "true" and "false" are used without the prefix to represent the ordinary "material" kind of truth and falsity.

Definition 1. An *identifier* is any name or definite description.

The purpose of this definition is to avoid using the phrase "name or definite description" repeatedly.

Recall that an atomic statement consists of a predicate, P, and one or more identifiers, n_1, n_2, ... n_k. The simplest predicates are true or false of individual things, e.g. the predicate "had wooden false teeth." is often said to be true of George Washington. More complex predicates are true of ordered pairs of things, ordered triples of things, and so on.

Definition 2. If P is a predicate and n is an identifier then an atomic statement of the form P(n) is *materially true* just in case the thing named or described by n has the property P.

Example 1. For example, "Snow is white." is true if and only if the thing named by "Snow" has the property of being white. This can also be expressed by saying that "Snow is white." is true if and only if snow is white. The reason this sounds so trivial is that the truth of an English statement is being explained in English. If truth in German were the issue then it would not seem trivial to say: "Der himmel ist blau."

is true (in German) because the thing named by "Der himmel" has the property of being blue.

Definition 2 continued. Similarly, an atomic statement of the form $P(n_1, n_2)$ where P is a predicate and n_1 and n_2 are identifiers, is *materially true* just in case the ordered pair of things named or described by n_1 and n_2 have the property P. An atomic statement of the form $P(n_1, n_2, n_3)$ is *materially true* just in case the ordered triple of things named or described by n_1, n_2, and n_3 have the property P, and so on.

Example 1 continued. Similarly, "Three is larger than two" is materially true because the number named by "three" is larger than the number named by "two." Moreover, "Kalamazoo is between Detroit and Chicago." is materially true because the city named by "Kalamazoo" is between the city named by "Detroit" and the city named by "Chicago".

8.3   Truth Functional Connectives

Recall that words or phrases used to form compound statements from one or more simpler statements are called *statement connectives*, or just *connectives*. For example, the connective "and" can be used with the statement "Today is Tuesday" and the statement "3 > 2" to form the compound statement "Today is Tuesday and 3 > 2." Similarly "because" can be used to make a compound statement out of simpler ones, as in "John did not come to work today because he was on vacation."

Definition 3. A statement connective which has the property that the truth value of a compound statement made using it is determined solely by the truth values its component parts, without regard to their meanings, is said to be a *truth functional connective*. For example, if you know that "Today is Tuesday" is true then, since "3 > 2" is also true, you can infer that "Today is Tuesday and 3 > 2" is true. Moreover, if today is not Tuesday then you can infer that "Today is Tuesday and 3 > 2" is false. On the other hand, knowing that the sidewalk is wet and that it rained this morning does not determine the truth value of "The sidewalk is wet because it rained this morning." Connectives like "because" are said to be *non truth functional connectives*.

Definition 4. Associated with each truth functional connective is a function that describes how the truth values of component parts of a statement determine the truth value of a compound statement formed using that connective. Such a function is called a *truth function*. The truth functions associated with "not", "and". "or", "if and only if", and "if then" are defined in the next sections.

In these definitions L and R can be replaced by any statements. L is to the left of the connective and R is to the right of the connective.

8.3.1 *Negation*

Recall that one statement is said to be the *negation* of another just in case the former expresses the claim that the latter is not the case. For example, if P represents the statement "Today is Tuesday." then the negation of P is "It is not the case that today is Tuesday." This is normally written "Today is not Tuesday."

Definition 5. If R is any statement then "not R" is materially true (false) just in case R is materially false (true).

This definition can also be expressed in the form of a function definition table, called a truth table. In these tables "T" and "F" represent "true" and "false." This table defines the negation function.

R	not R
T	F
F	T

Reading left to right, the last two rows of the table represent the fact that if R is true then "not R" must be false, while if R is false than "not R" must be true.

8.3.2 *Conjunction*

Recall that a statement of the form "L and R" is called a conjunction.

Definition 6. If L and R are any two statements then "L and R" is materially true just in case L is materially true and R is materially true.

This definition can also be expressed in the form of the following function definition table.

L	R	L and R
T	T	T
T	F	F
F	T	F
F	F	F

On the lower left, each of the last four rows of this table describe some combination of truth values for L and R. On the right the corresponding truth value of "L and R" is given.

8.3.3   Disjunction: Inclusive and Exclusive

Recall that a statement of the form "L or R" is called a disjunction. Disjunction is a bit trickier than conjunction because there are two kinds, inclusive and exclusive.

Definition 7. If L and R are any two statements then "L or R," in the inclusive sense of "or," is materially true just in case at least one of them is materially true.

For example, if you are eating at home, your spouse might say "You can have pie for dessert or you can have ice cream for dessert." and you might reply with "I think I will have both." Moreover, in mathematics and computing the inclusive sense of disjunction is what is normally used. The corresponding function definition table is:

L	R	L or R
T	T	T
T	F	T
F	T	T
F	F	F

Definition 8. If L and R are any two statements then "L or R," in the exclusive sense of "or," is materially true just in case one of them is materially true and the other is materially false.

Exclusive disjunction is sometimes indicated by adding "but not both" at the end of a statement. In most cases exclusivity is implicit, as on a restaurant menu which says that for $5 you can have a sandwich and a beverage or dessert. For $5 you expect to get a sandwich and either a beverage or dessert, but not both a beverage and a dessert. In contexts where it is desirable to have a separate word for the exclusive sense of or, the word "xor" is used. Since exclusive disjunction is used so rarely here, no symbolic abbreviation for it will be use.

The truth table for exclusive disjunction is:

L	R	L x or R
T	T	F
T	F	T
F	T	T
F	F	F

8.3.4   Material Equivalence

Recall that statements of the form "L if and only if R" are called biconditional statements or just biconditionals.

Definition 9. If L and R are any two statements then "L if and only if R" is materially true just in case both L and R have the same truth value. Moreover, if "L if and only if R" is materially true than L and R are said to be *materially equivalent,* otherwise they are *materially inequivalent.*

In English the connective used to express equivalence is the phrase "if and only if" (sometimes abbreviated "iff"), as used for example, in "Today is pay-day if and only if today is Friday." The phrase "just in case" is also used to express equivalence, as in "You win the prize just in case your number is the first one drawn."

The truth function associated with material equivalence is shown in the following table.

L	R	L if and only if R
T	T	T
T	F	F
F	T	F
F	F	T

Material equivalence is normally used to express interesting facts about the world. While "All people are animals if and only if $3 < 5$" is materially true, because both parts of it are true, it is such an uninteresting fact that it sounds odd even to mention it. On the other hand, if "Today is payday if and only if today is Friday" were true then that would be an interesting fact and is likely to be mentioned.

Exercise 1. Determine which of the statements below are materially equivalent. Explain your answers. Assume the numbers referred to here are all nonnegative integers. Hint: first determine which statements are true and which are false.

(a) There are odd numbers.
(b) There are numbers which are both even and odd.
(c) If a number is even and prime than it is not odd.
(d) If a number is prime and not even than it is odd.
(e) Every number is odd.
(f) Every number is either odd or even.
(g) Every number identical to 3 is prime.
(h) There is a number identical to 3 which is prime.
(i) The smallest prime number is 2.
(j) The smallest even prime number is 2.

Exercise 2. Assume that P is true and Q is false. For each pair of statements below determine whether the one on the left is materially equivalent to the one on the right. Note that in each case this requires only a simple truth value calculation, not the construction of a whole truth table.

(a) P   Q
(b) P or Q   Q
(c) P and Q   Q
(d) P and not Q   Q

8.3.5 *Material Implication*

Recall that statements of the form "If L then R" are sometimes called conditional statements or just conditionals.

Definition 10. If L and R are any two statements then *"If L then R" is materially true* if and only if it is not the case that L is materially true and R is materially false. Moreover if "If L then R" is materially true then we say that *L materially implies R.*

This may seem like an odd concept at first, but it turns out to be very useful and very important. The connective "implies" is also commonly used to express material implication, as in "L implies R." Unfortunately, this use of "implies" is often confused with logical implication, discussed later.

The truth function associated with material implication is described in the following table.

L	R	If L then R
T	T	T
T	F	F
F	T	T
F	F	T

This truth table represents only one way in which people use the term "implies." For example, it does not represent the causal sense in which "thunder implies lightening." However, the truth function defined by this table does represent most uses of "if then" in mathematics and computer science.

Exercise 3. Determine which of the statements below materially imply which others. Explain your solution.

(a) There are odd numbers.
(b) There are numbers which are both even and odd.
(c) If a number is even and prime than it is not odd.
(d) If a number is prime and not even than it is odd.
(e) Every number is odd.
(f) Every number is either odd or even.
(g) Every number identical to 3 is prime.

(h) There is a number identical to 3 which is prime.
(i)   The smallest prime number is 2.
(j)   The smallest even prime number is 2.

Exercise 4. Assume that P is true and Q is false. For each pair of statements below
determine whether the one on the left materially implies the one on the right. Then
determine whether the one on the right materially implies the one on the left. Note
that in each case this requires only a simple truth value calculation, not the
construction of a whole truth table.

(a) P   Q
(b) P and Q   Q
(c) P or Q   Q
(d) If P then Q   Q

Statements which express material implication are sometimes called *hypothetical statements*. If "P implies Q" is such a statement then the P part is called the
hypothesis or *antecedent* and the Q part is called its *consequent*. Statements of this
form are also called *conditional statements*. In that case P is called the condition of
the statement.

This may give rise to some confusion because there are "conditional statements"
in most programming languages. In this book what you have in programming
languages are called "*conditional instructions*" to distinguish them from conditional
statements in the logical sense. Conditional statements are either true or false while
conditional instructions are either executed or not executed. You may agree or disagree with a conditional statement, but it would be silly to agree or disagree with a
conditional instruction. For example, "If you have a toothache then your blood
pressure will be elevated." is a conditional statement while "If you have a toothache
then take two aspirin and call me in the morning." is a conditional instruction. Both
conditional statements and conditional instructions have conditions, but the second
part of a conditional statement is a statement while the second part of a conditional
instruction is an instruction.

8.4   Conditions

Definition 11. If P is a 1-place predicate and x is a variable or open definite
description with one variable then the condition P(x) is true of all and only those
things which have property P. Similarly, a condition P(x, y) is materially true of those
ordered pairs of things that have property P. A condition P(x, y, z) is materially true
of those ordered triples of things that have property P, and so on for any finite number
of variables. A condition that is not materially true of something is materially false of
that thing.

For example, the condition "x is red" is true of all and only red things. The condition "x is taller than y" is true of exactly those ordered pairs of things such that the

first is taller than the second. The condition "x is between y and z" is true of just those ordered triples of things such that the first is between the second and the third.

8.5   Quantified Statements

Definition 12. A universally quantified statement, $\forall xP(x)$, is materially true just in case the condition $P(x)$ is materially true of everything. An existentially quantified statement, $\exists xP(x)$, is materially true just in case the condition $P(x)$ is materially true of something.

For example, the statement "Everything is identical to itself.," expressed "$\forall x(x = x)$" is true because the condition "$x = x$" is true of everything. Similarly "Something is equal to 3.," expressed "$\exists x(x = 3)$", is true because the condition "$x = 3$" is true of something, namely 3.

Exercise 5. Use the definitions above to determine which of the statements below are materially true and which are materially false.

(a) There are odd numbers.
(b) There are numbers which are both even and odd.
(c) If a number is even and prime than it is not odd.
(d) If a number is prime and not even than it is odd.
(e) Every number is odd.
(f) Every number is either odd or even.
(g) Every number identical to 3 is prime.
(h) There is a number identical to 3 which is prime.
(i) The smallest prime number is 2.
(j) The smallest even prime number is 2.

If the intended interpretation of a statement has a finite domain then universally quantified statements are equivalent to conjunctions. For example, consider "All odd numbers greater than 1 and less than 9 are prime." The domain of the intended interpretation is the set of odd numbers greater than 1 and less than 9, i.e. $\{3, 5, 7\}$. So "All odd numbers greater than 1 and less than 9 are prime" is equivalent to "(3 is an odd number greater than 1 and less than 9 and 3 is prime) and (5 is an odd number greater than 1 and less than 9 and 5 is prime) and (7 is an odd number greater than 1 and less than 9 and 7 is prime)."

Similarly, if the intended interpretation of a statement has a finite domain then existentially quantified statements are equivalent to disjunctions. For example, consider again "Some odd numbers greater than 1 and less than 9 are prime." The domain of the intended interpretation is the set of odd numbers greater than 1 and less than 9, i.e. $\{3, 5, 7\}$. So "Some odd numbers greater than 1 and less than 9 are prime" is equivalent to "(3 is an odd number greater than 1 and less than 9 and 3 is prime) or (5 is an odd number greater than 1 and less than 9 and 5 is prime) or (7 is an odd number greater than 1 and less than 9 and 7 is prime)."

Exercise 6. Identify the domain of the intended interpretation for each of the following statements, say whether it is finite or infinite, and if it is finite then write the statement as a conjunction or disjunction. Let S = {2, 3, 4, 5}

(a) All prime numbers are odd.
(b) All prime numbers are even.
(c) Some prime numbers are odd.
(d) Some prime numbers are even.
(e) All elements of S are prime numbers.
(f) All elements of S are even numbers.
(g) All prime numbers in S are odd.
(h) All prime numbers in S are even.
(i) All even numbers in S are prime.
(j) All odd numbers in S are prime.

8.6   Summary of Material Truth Conditions

Definition MT (for Material Truth) and MTC (for Material Truth Condition) summarize the definitions given earlier in the chapter.

Definition MT. If S is a statement then S is materially true if and only if

(a) S is an atomic statement, i.e. S is of the form "$P(n_1, n_2, ..., n_k)$" and P is a k-place predicate symbol, $n_1, n_2, ..., n_k$ are identifiers, and the things named or described by by $n_1, n_2, ...n_k$ (in that order) have the property P
(b) S is a statement of the form "not P" and P is materially false
(c) S is a statement of the form "P and Q" and both P and Q are materially true
(d) S is of the form "P or Q" and P is materially true or Q is materially true
(e) S is of the form "P if" and "only if Q" and both P and Q are materially true or both are materially false
(f) S is of the form "If P then Q" and P is materially false or Q is materially true
(g) S is of the form "$\forall x P(x)$" and the condition P(x) is materially true of everything
(h) S is of the form "$\exists x P(x)$" and the condition P(x) is materially true of something
(i) S is materially false if and only if it is not materially true

Definition MTC.

(a) A condition P(x) is materially true of those things that have property P.
(b) A condition P(x, y)is materially true of those ordered pairs of things that have property P.
(c) In general, a condition $P(v_1, v_2, ...v_n)$ is materially true of those n- tuples of things that have property P.
(d) A condition is materially false of those things of which it is not materially true.

Truth tables can be used to determine how the truth value of a compound statement depends on the truth values of its component statements. While making them might be tedious if the number of atomic statements is large, the procedure of making a truth table, if properly done, is guaranteed to come to an end after a finite number of steps and is guaranteed to determine which category a statement belongs to. Moreover there are decision procedures for various special classes of quantified statements, e.g. for statements having only a single quantifier. Unfortunately there is no such "mechanical decision procedure" for determining the material truth value of quantified statements in general.

8.7 Some Applications

8.7.1 Short Cut Evaluation: "cand" and "cor"

Some programming language compilers and interpreters use what is called "short cut evaluation" of conjunctions and disjunctions. For example, notice that in order to determine that "L and R" is false it is sufficient to know that L is false, without bothering to determine the truth value of R. Some program implementations do just that, i.e. if they determine that L is false they do not bother to evaluate the truth value of R. This saves a bit of time so that programs execute faster. The shortcut version of "and" is sometimes called "cand," which is short for "conditional and." The truth table for "cand" is given below, where "-" in the column under R indicates that the truth of R is not evaluated.

L	R	L cand R
True	True	True
True	False	False
False	–	False

A similar trick can be done with disjunction based on the fact that in order to determine that "L or R" is true, it is sufficient to determine that L is true, without bothering to determine the truth value of R. This shortcut version of "or" is sometimes called "cor," which is short for "conditional or." The truth table for "cor" is:

L	R	L cor R
True	–	True
False	True	True
False	False	False

In most cases using "cand" and "cor" speeds things up and does no harm. Occasionally, however, it creates confusion, especially when trying to revise or debug a program. For example, you would expect the truth value of "L and R" to be the same as the truth value of "R and L." For example, consider instructions I_1 and I_2 below.

I_1: If ((z = x/y) and (x < y)) then print "Hello world"
I_2: If ((x < y) and (z = x/y)) then print "Hello world"

If normal evaluation of "and" is used then executing these two instructions should give the same result for all possible values of x, y, and z. Even if y = 0 they should both result in a divide by zero error. But if short cut evaluation is used and if y = 0 and if "x < y" is false then I_2 will cause control to be passed to the next instruction without generating an error message, while I_1 will generate a divide by zero error message.

More generally, expecting "and" and "or" to be evaluated normally can lead to confusion about what happens when your programs are executed. For example, when testing or debugging a program, the confusion caused by not taking into account the difference between normal and short cut evaluation of "and" and "or" can be very frustrating. In some cases, you can turn short cut evaluation on or off, as a compiler option. Unless small amounts of time are very important, it is simpler to use normal evaluation, if you can.

A few programming languages such as Ruby have separate symbols for normal and shortcut evaluation of "and" and "or."

In most cases you have no control over which evaluation method is used. Some compilers and interpreters use one and some use the other. In that case it would be helpful to know which one is being used so that you are not mislead about how instructions will be executed. You can easily tell whether short cut evaluation is being used by constructing and executing a simple program. For example:

```
         #Line 02 generates error message if ordinary evaluation of "and" is
         #used. Prints "Shortcut used" and does not generate error
         #message if shortcut evaluation is used.
01       x ← 1
02       If ((x > 1) and (x/0 = 5))
03               Print 'x/0 = 5 should generate error message'
04       Else
05               Print 'Shortcut used'
06       Endif
```

Exercise 7. Write a program to detect shortcut evaluation of "or."

Exercise 8. Explain why your solution to Exercise 7 works.

8.7.2 Bitwise Extensions of Truth Functions

8.7.2.1 Bit Functions that Correspond to Truth Functions

Recall that the fundamental unit of digital information is the *bit*, short for *binary digit*. The binary digits are 0 and 1. One bit of information is represented by a single binary digit. Larger units of digital information are represented by sequences of 0s and 1s. For example, a sequence of eight 0s and 1s represents eight bits of information, usually called a *byte*.

If 1 is identified with "true" and 0 with "false" then many important operations on digital information are essentially the same as truth functions. They are so similar that they are given the same names as the corresponding truth functions. For example, *inversion*, i.e. converting 1 to 0 and 0 to 1, is often called "negation," and is described below. Note its similarity to the truth table for negation.

L	Not L
1	0
0	1

Similarly there are bit versions of "and," "or," and "xor."

L	R	L and R	L or R	L xor R
1	1	1	1	0
1	0	0	1	1
0	1	0	1	1
0	0	0	0	0

8.7.2.2 Extensions to Sequences of Bits

Operations on one or two bits of information at a time do not get you much in the way of information processing. These operations can be extended to sequences of bits by applying them repeatedly to the bits of successive columns. In the example for "not" below the first column applies the fact that the negation of "1" is "0," the second column applies the fact that the negation of "0" is "1," and so on. In the "and" example, the first column applies the fact that "1 and 0" = "0", the second that "0 and 0" = 0, the third that "1 and 1" = "1", and so on.

```
not  10110010   initial bit sequence
     01001101   bitwise negation of initial sequence

     10110010        10110010          10110010
and  00101101    or  00101101     xor  00101101
     00100000        10111111          10011111
```

Exercise 9. Do the following bitwise calculations.

(a) not 11010110

(b)   11010110
    and 01100101

(c)   11010110
    or 01100101

(d)   11010110
    xor 01100101

8.7.2.3   Computing Applications

Masks

Definition 4. A *bit mask* is a pattern of bits used to modify selected bits of other patterns of bits. For example, using bitwise conjunction, the bit pattern 11110000 can be used to set the rightmost four bits of any other eight bit pattern to zero, leaving the leftmost four bits unchanged, as is shown below.

> 10010101 initial bit pattern
> and 11110000 bit mask
> 10010000 result of bitwise "and" operation

Similarly, the mask 10101010 would preserve the values of the odd numbered bits of an eight bit sequence while setting the values of the even numbered bits to zero.

Bit masks can be used to control what happens during the execution of a program. For example, the mask 11110000 could be used to indicate that a particular user is allowed to modify the first four fields but is not allowed to modify the second four fields of a data entry screen. Similarly, a user with mask 10101010 can modify fields in the odd numbered positions but not those in the even numbered positions.

Encryption and Decryption

Bitwise extensions of "xor" can be used to *encrypt* and *decrypt* information. The basic idea behind this coding scheme is that the information to be encrypted is first transformed into digital form, i.e. into a sequence of bits. An example would be eight bit per character ASCII encoding of ordinary texts, or bitmaps of images. The original sequence of bits is called the *plaintext*. Another sequence of bits, called the *encryption key*, is used to transform the plaintext into a sequence of bits different from the plaintext. The transformed plaintext is called the *cyphertext*. The cyphertext is supposed to be difficult to decrypt unless you have a sequence of bits called the *decryption key* and you know what to do with it. The decryption key is used with the cyphertext to reconstruct the plaintext. The method described here uses the same key for encryption and decryption. Some more sophisticated methods, such as public key cryptography, use different keys.

The method described here is based on the following four equations, which you can verify by examining the bit function tables for "xor."

> (1 xor 1) xor 1 = 1
> (1 xor 0) xor 0 = 1
> (0 xor 1) xor 1 = 0
> (0 xor 0) xor 0 = 0

If P is a sequence of bits to be encrypted, called the plaintext, and K is any sequence of bits of the same length, called the key, then P xor K is called the cyphertext, C. The four equations displayed above imply that, in general, (P xor K) xor K = P. Consequently, an encryption and decryption method can be described by two simple instructions.

> To encrypt P: C ← P xor K
> To decrypt C: P ← C xor K

For example, suppose that the original plaintext is 11110000 and that the key is 10110001. To encrypt the plaintext we compute the exclusive or of the plaintext and the key, as shown below.

$$
\begin{array}{ll}
\phantom{\text{xor }}11110000 & \text{plaintext, P} \\
\underline{\text{xor }\ 10110001} & \text{key, K} \\
\phantom{\text{xor }}01000001 & \text{cyphertext, C}
\end{array}
$$

The cyphertext can be decrypted by simply computing the exclusive or of the cyphertext and the encryption key.

$$
\begin{array}{ll}
\phantom{\text{xor }}01000001 & \text{cyphertext, C} \\
\underline{\text{xor }\ 10110001} & \text{key, K} \\
\phantom{\text{xor }}1110000 & \text{plaintext, P}
\end{array}
$$

Exercise 10. Make your own example of a plaintext bit sequence and a key. Then encrypt it. Then decrypt your encryption. Check to be sure that you got the original message back.

Chapter 9
Truth for Statements with Multiple Connectives

This chapter shows how to do truth value calculations and make truth tables for statements with more than one connective. In the next chapter this material is applied to tracing program execution. After studying this chapter you should be able to:

1. Read and write correctly punctuated compound truth functions.
2. Translate complex statements between informal and logical English.
3. Make truth tables for compound truth functions.
4. Use those truth tables to find the truth value of a complex statement given the truth values of its elementary components.
5. Read truth tables from right to left in order to discover information about the elementary components of a statement, given information about the truth value of the whole statement.

Outline

9.1 Compound Statements

Recall that a compound statement is a statement which is constructed using one or more connectives. For example, the following statement is constructed using "and" and "or."

Today is Wednesday and it is hot or it is raining.

R. Lover, *Elementary Logic: For Software Development*,
DOI: 10.2007/978-1-84800-082-7, © Springer 2008

9.1.1   Computing Truth Values of Compound Statements

If the connectives used to make a compound statement are all truth functional then the truth value of that compound statement is determined by the truth values of its component statements and the truth functions associated with its connectives. Calculating the truth value of a compound statement is done by starting with the truth values of its most elementary components and applying the truth tables for the connectives, gradually building up to the whole compound statement. In order to do this it is necessary to know the order in which the truth values of intermediate component statements are to be evaluated.

Suppose, for example, that today is not Wednesday, that it is hot, and that it is raining. Is "Today is Wednesday and it is hot or it is raining." true or false? That depends upon which connective you evaluate first. If "and" is evaluated first then, obviously, "Today is Wednesday and it is hot" is false but "it is raining" is true, so the whole statement is true. But if "or" is evaluated first then "it is hot or it is raining" is true, but "Today is Wednesday" is false, so the whole statement is false. In spoken English we try to indicate which connective to evaluate first by speaking parts of the statement more rapidly than others, by pausing at certain points, and by saying one connective more loudly. For example, both statements below

Today is Wednesday and (pause) it is hot or it is raining.
Today is Wednesday AND (loudly) it is hot or it is raining.

would probably be understood to indicate that "or" is to be evaluated first, especially if the part after "AND" were spoken rapidly in an even tone of voice. On the other hand, both of these

Today is Wednesday and it is hot or (pause) it is raining.
Today is Wednesday and it is hot OR (loudly) it is raining.

would probably be understood to indicate that "and" is to be evaluated first, especially if the part before "OR" were spoken rapidly in an even tone of voice.

In written English we also have methods for indicating which connective to evaluate first. For example,

Today is Wednesday, and it is hot or it is raining.

indicates that "or" is to be evaluated first. On the other hand,

Today is Wednesday and it is hot, or it is raining.

indicates that "and" is to be evaluated first. Colons, semicolons, and commas are all used within compound written statements to indicate grouping.

While most English grammar teachers consider it barbaric, parentheses can be used to indicate which connective to evaluate first, as in the two statements below.

Today is Wednesday and (it is hot or it is raining).
(Today is Wednesday and it is hot) or it is raining.

Barbaric or not, when logical issues are important, parentheses are sometimes used to indicate the order in which logical operations are to be performed. Parentheses always come in matched pairs and are used to enclose a complete statement. In logical contexts, just as in mathematics and computer programming, parentheses are used with the rule that the most deeply nested operations are done first. For example, let P, Q, and R represent particular statements. In the statement displayed below, the number above a connective indicates the level of "nesting" of that connective, and the number below a connective indicates the order in which the connectives are to be evaluated. The level of nesting is the number of unmatched left parentheses to the left of the connective. The order of evaluation is to evaluate the most deeply nested first. Within a given level of nesting, connectives are evaluated from left to right.

$$
\begin{array}{ccccc}
0 & 2 & 1 & 2 & 3 \qquad \text{level of nesting}
\end{array}
$$

P and ((not Q) or (R and (not P)))

$$
\begin{array}{ccccc}
5 & 2 & 4 & 3 & 1 \qquad \text{order of evaluation}
\end{array}
$$

If P were true, Q were false, and R were false then the steps of the calculation of the truth value of the whole statement could be expressed as follows:

1. "not" in "not P" is the most deeply nested, "P" is true, so "not P" is false
2. "not" in "not Q" and "and" in "R and (not P)" are at the same level. The left to right evaluation order mentioned above requires "not" to be evaluated first. Since "Q" is false, "not Q" is true
3. Now the "and" in "R and (not P)" can be evaluated. Since "R" is false and "not P" is false, "(R and (not P))" is false
4. Since "not Q" is true, "(not Q) or (R and (not P))" is true
5. Finally, since "P" is true and "(not Q) or (R and (not P))" is true, it follows that "P and ((not Q) or (R and (not P)))" is true

Since what is important in such a calculation is the truth values of the statements, this reasoning could be expressed more briefly thusly.

1. "not P": is false because not true is false.
2. "not Q": is true because not false is true.
3. "R and (not P)": is false because false and false is false.
4. "(not Q) or (R and (not P))": is true because true or false is true.
5. "P and ((not Q) or (R and (not P)))": is true because true and true is true.

Exercise 1. Describe a similar calculation assuming that P, Q, and R are all true.

Expressing these calculations in English as described above works, but it is hard to do, hard to read, and time consuming. Fortunately, such time consuming descriptions are not necessary. In addition to parentheses, logicians have developed various other notations and ways of organizing calculations in order to make logic easier to use. For example, the calculation described above takes less space and is easier to understand as expressed below.

	0	2	1	2	3	level of nesting
P Q R	P and ((not Q) or (R and (not P)))					
T F F	T		F	F		T	initial values
	5	2	4	3	1	order of evaluation
					F	1
		T				2
				F		3
			T			4
	T					5

This can be abbreviated as:

P and ((not Q) or (R and (not P)))
T T   T F T F F   F T

Exercise 2. Express the result of Exercise 1 in summary form as shown above.

9.1.2   Reducing the Need for Parentheses

While parentheses are very useful, it is easy to get confused when you have several of them. Two ways of not needing so many of them, without introducing ambiguity, are described below.

9.1.2.1   Sequences of Conjunctions, Disjunctions, or Negations

If a statement is a sequence of conjunctions then the order in which the components are evaluated does not matter. For example,

"P and (Q and R)" always evaluates to the same value as "(P and Q) and R" no matter what values "P," "Q," and "R" have. Similarly, each of the following evaluates to the same value in every case.

    P and (Q and (R and S))
    P and ((Q and R) and S)
    (P and Q) and (R and S)
    ((P and Q) and R) and S

Similar identities are true no matter how long the series of conjunctions. Consequently, it is possible to omit parentheses in a series of conjunctions without creating ambiguity. So all four of the statements just displayed can be written "P and Q and R and S." In case some order needs to be specified, the conjunctions are assumed to be evaluated from left to right, i.e. as described by "((P and Q) and R) and S."

Sequences of disjunctions are treated similarly. Remember, however, that a mixture of conjunctions and disjunctions cannot be treated this way, e.g. under some circumstances, "P and (Q or R)" has a different truth value than "(P and Q) or R." However, the precedence rule described below will allow one of these to be written without parentheses.

Finally, a sequence of negations needs no parentheses because it can only be punctuated one way. "not (not P)" cannot be written as "(not not) P" because parentheses are only put around whole statements and "not not" is not a whole statement. So "not (not P)" can be written "not not P" and "not (not (not P))" can be written "not not not P" and so on.

9.1.2.2 Precedence Rules

The precedence rules of logic are like the precedence rules of arithmetic and algebra; they reduce the need for parentheses by indicating the order in which operations are to be evaluated when parentheses are absent. For example, in algebra multiplication and division are done before addition and subtraction, so that "a*b + c" is understood to abbreviate "(a*b) + c". If you want the addition done first then you must use parentheses, as in "a*(b + c)". Similarly, taking the additive inverse is done before multiplication, division, addition, and subtraction, so that "–a + b" is understood to abbreviate "(–a) + b". If you want the addition done first then you must use parentheses, as in "–(a + b)". Recall that precedence rules for truth functional connectives were introduced in Chap. 2 where they were called parenthesis dropping conventions. They were:

(a) ~ has the highest precedence of all.
(b) ∧, ∨, →, and ↔ have successively lower precedence.
(c) Matching pairs of parentheses can be removed if doing so does not cause ambiguity as to how to restore them. In particular, the outermost pair of parentheses can be dropped.

Here are two more introduced in this chapter.

(d) Operations at the same level of nesting are done from left to right.
(e) As discussed above, parentheses can be omitted within a series of conjunctions, disjunctions, or negations.

Recall that using symbols for connectives and using capital letters to stand for individual statements allows the logical structure of compound statements to be described and reasoned about in much more compact and easy to understand forms than when English is used. For example, consider the following sequence of expressions.

1. Today is Wednesday and it is hot or it is raining
2. (W and H) or R
3. (W ∧ H) ∨ R
4. W ∧ H ∨ R

Expression 1 is English, with ambiguity regarding which connective to evaluate first. Expression 2 uses letters to represent statements and resolves ambiguity by using parentheses. Expression 3 uses symbols for the connectives. Expression 4 uses the precedence rule to remove parentheses. Notice the extent to which 4 emphasizes logically important features of the original statement, while de-emphasizing logically unimportant features.

Exercise 3. Write expressions like Expressions 2, 3, and 4 above for each of the following statements. If the English is ambiguous about connectives, pick some reasonable order of evaluation and forge ahead. However, remember that in real life, if a statement is ambiguous, just picking some reasonable interpretation and forging ahead is likely to lead to misunderstandings. A good thing to do is to ask the author of the ambiguous statement what the intended meaning is. Here however you cannot do that.

(a) Today is Wednesday and it is raining and it is hot.
(b) Today is Wednesday or it is raining and it is not hot.
(c) Today is not Wednesday and it is not raining and it is not hot.
(d) Either today is Wednesday and it is not raining or it is not hot.
(e) Today is Wednesday and either it is not raining or it is not hot.
(f) It is not the case that today is Wednesday and it is raining and it is hot.
(g) Today is Wednesday and it is not the case that it is raining or it is hot.

Exercise 4. Finish the table below by inserting parentheses in "not P and Q or R" so that the connectives are evaluated in the order specified. Do not change the order of the connectives or the elementary statements.

| order | | | statement | |
not	and	or	using precedence rules	not using precedence rules
a. 1	2	3	not P and Q or R	((not P) and Q) or R
b. 1	3	2		
c. 2	1	3		
d. 2	3	1		
e. 3	1	2		
f. 3	2	1	not (P and (Q or R))	not (P and (Q or R))

9.2   How to Make Truth Tables for Compound Statements

Truth tables were used earlier to describe the truth functions associated with individual truth functional connectives. Here truth tables are extended to describe the truth functions associated more complex statements.

9.2.1   The Four Parts of a Truth Table

To make a truth table for a compound statement start by drawing crossed horizontal and vertical lines. It helps to use graph paper.

List of simple statements	Compound statement
List of all truth functionally possible combinations of truth values for the simple statements	Calculated truth values for compound statement

Then write the compound statement being analyzed in the upper right part of the table. In the upper left part list the elementary statements which make up the compound statement. If you use letters to represent the elementary statements it is customary to list them in alphabetic order. In the lower left part of the table put a column of Ts and Fs in such a way that every possible assignment of Ts and Fs for the elementary statements is represented by some row of Ts and Fs. If there are n elementary statements this will require 2 to the nth power rows of Ts and Fs. Finally, compute the truth value of the compound statement by using the truth tables for the basic connectives and the rules about the order in which connectives are to be evaluated. Record the results in the lower right part of the table. This whole process is easier to show by example that it is to describe in English. For example, the truth table for any statement of the form "P and (Q or R)" is

P	Q	R	P and (Q or R)	
T	T	T	**T**	T
T	T	F	**T**	T
T	F	T	**T**	T
T	F	F	**F**	F
F	T	T	**F**	T
F	T	F	**F**	T
F	F	T	**F**	T
F	F	F	**F**	F
			2	1 order of evaluation

Finally there is the issue of how to calculate the truth value of the compound statement for each row of the table. In this example column 1 (under "or") represents an intermediate step and is just included to make the table easier to make and read. Column 2 (under "and") is the only one that needs to be there. It is easier to fill in all of a column at once rather than to fill in the table row by row, because it is easier to remember the truth table for a single connective than to switch back and forth from one connective to another.

9.2.2 Organizing a Truth Table Calculation

In the lower left part of the table, each row is supposed to represent a different truth functionally possible combination of truth value assignments to the elementary statements. One way to be sure they are all listed is to follow the steps listed below.

Step 1: Under the rightmost elementary statement put alternating Ts and Fs until you have 2^N of them.

Step 2: After finishing a column, move left one statement and write another column of alternating groups of Ts and Fs. In each new column the groups should be twice as long as in the column to its right, but there will be half as many groups. So in the second column there are pairs of Ts followed by pairs of Fs, in the third column there are quadruples of Ts followed by quadruples of Fs and so on. Keep repeating this pattern until you run out of elementary statements.

It follows from Step 1 than that as the number of elementary statements increases by one, the number of rows in the truth table doubles, as shown in the table below.

Elementary statements	Rows in truth table
1	2
2	4
3	8
4	16
5	32
6	64
7	128
8	256
9	512
10	1,024

Here is another example, this time with four elementary statements.

Q	R	S	T	(S ∧ T)	∨	~	((Q ∧ R) ∨ S)	
T	T	T	T	T	**T**	F	T	T
T	T	T	F	F	**F**	F	T	T
T	T	F	T	F	**F**	F	T	T
T	T	F	F	F	**F**	F	T	T
T	F	T	T	T	**T**	F	F	T
T	F	T	F	F	**F**	F	F	T
T	F	F	T	F	**T**	T	F	F
T	F	F	F	F	**T**	T	F	F
F	T	T	T	T	**T**	F	F	T
F	T	T	F	F	**F**	F	F	T
F	T	F	T	F	**T**	T	F	F
F	T	F	F	F	**T**	T	F	F
F	F	T	T	T	**T**	F	F	T
F	F	T	F	F	**F**	F	F	T
F	F	F	T	F	**T**	T	F	F
F	F	F	F	T	**T**	T	F	F

Exercise 5. Make a truth table for each compound statement form below. Indicate which is the final column.

(a) ~(~P)

(b) ~(~(~P))

(c) $P \vee (P \wedge Q)$
(d) $P \wedge (P \vee Q)$
(e) $(P \vee Q) \wedge \sim P$
(f) $(P \wedge Q) \vee (Q \wedge P)$
(g) $(Q \vee (\sim Q))$
(h) $P \vee (\sim P)$
(i) $P \wedge (\sim P)$

9.3 Reading Truth Tables from Right to Left

Reading a truth table from left to right allows you to tell the truth value of a compound statement if you know the truth values of its component statements. Reading a truth table from right to left can give you some information about the truth values of the component statements if you know the truth value of the compound statement. For example, if you know that "P and (Q or R)" is true then, by investigating those rows in which its truth value is "T," you tell that P is true and that Q or R or both are true. Additionally, if the compound statement is false, then either P is false and Q and R can have any truth values or, P is true and both Q and R are false.

P	Q	R	P and (Q or R)	
T	T	T	**T**	T
T	T	F	**T**	T
T	F	T	**T**	T
T	F	F	**F**	F
F	T	T	**F**	T
F	T	F	**F**	T
F	F	T	**F**	T
F	F	F	**F**	F

The last example is so obvious that you may not even need to examine its truth table. However, if the compound statement is more complex you will probably need to examine its truth table. For example, without looking at the truth table below, if "(P or not Q) and ((Q or not R) or (R and not P))" were true, what could you determine about the truth values of P, Q, and R?

P	Q	R	(P or not Q) and ((Q or not R) or (R and not P))				
T	T	T	T	**T**	T	T	F
T	T	F	T	**T**	T	T	F
T	F	T	T	**F**	F	F	F
T	F	F	T	**T**	T	T	F
F	T	T	F	**F**	T	T	T
F	T	F	T	**T**	T	T	F
F	F	T	F	**F**	F	T	T
F	F	F	T	**T**	T	T	F

Exercise 6. For each of the following, try to determine what you can about the truth values of the component statements in case the compound statement is true. Then check your answers by finding or constructing a truth table for each one.

(a) ~(~P)
(b) ~(~(~P))
(c) P∨ (P ∧ Q)
(d) P ∧ (P ∨ Q)
(e) (P ∨ Q) ∧ ~P
(f) (P ∧ Q) ∨ (Q ∧ P)
(g) (Q ∨ (~Q))
(h) P ∧ (~P)
(i) (Q ∨ ~P) ∧ P
(j) (Q ∨ ~P) ∧ (P ∨ ~Q)
(k) (Q ∨ ~P) ∧ ~Q

Exercise 7. For each of the following, try to determine what you can about the truth values of the component statements in case the compound statement is false. Then check your answers by finding or constructing a truth table for each one.

(a) ~(~P)
(b) ~(~(~P))
(c) P ∨ (P ∧ Q)
(d) P ∧ (P ∨ Q)
(e) (P ∨ Q) ∧ ~P
(f) (P ∧ Q) ∨ (Q ∧ P)
(g) (Q ∨ (~Q))
(h) P ∧ (~P)
(i) (Q ∨ ~P) ∧ P
(j) (Q ∨ ~P) ∧ (P ∨ ~Q)
(k) (Q ∨ ~P) ∧ ~Q

Chapter 10
Tracing Program Execution

This chapter shows a few ways to apply the material in Chaps. 8 and 9 to tracing program execution. Pseudocode is used in place of a real programming language so that no background in any particular programming language is required. After studying this chapter you should be able to use truth functions to trace execution of programs forwards and backwards, no matter what programming language you use.

Outline

10.1   Tracing Program Execution Forwards

To trace the execution of an algorithm (or program) is to determine exactly what would happen if that algorithm were to be executed for specific input data. When tracing is done by hand it is normally recorded in a table, called a trace table. Most program development environments have automated trace facilities which take much of the drudgery out of tracing long and complex programs. Here we are concerned with simple algorithms and hand tracing, sometimes called *desk checking*.

The ability to trace the execution of a small algorithm, without running it on a computer, is fundamental to understanding what the algorithm does. If you can't trace it yourself by hand then you do not understand it. Often, doing a trace, while tedious, will help you understand the algorithm. Understanding it is of course a prerequisite for reasoning correctly about it.

R. Lover, *Elementary Logic: For Software Development*,
DOI: 10.2007/978-1-84800-082-7, © Springer 2008

10.1.1   Event Trace Tables

We begin with an example of a full event (or execution) trace using the algorithm MaxOf displayed below, using "#" to indicate comments and "←" for assignment of values to variables.

```
0       Algorithm MaxOf (LIST, N, MAX)
        # precondition: LIST is a nonempty list of numbers of length N
        # Postcondition: Returns the maximum element of LIST.

        # Initialize MAX to be first element of LIST
1       MAX ← LIST[1]
2       K ← 2
        # Examine the remainder of LIST, keeping track of the
        # largest element so far encountered in MAX.
3       While K <= N do            # '<=' means '<' or '='
4            If MAX < LIST[K] Then MAX ← LIST[K] End If
5            K ← K + 1
6       Repeat
7       Return MAX # MAX is now the maximum element of LIST.
        End Algorithm
```

Example 1. A full event (execution) trace table

A full event (or execution) trace of MaxOf applied to the input data set <3 4 6 2 > is recorded in the table below. The process of doing the trace consists of making this trace table.

Instruction executed	Resulting event	Remarks
MaxOf (LIST, N, MAX)	LIST ← 3 4 6 2 N ← 4	Initialize Variables
MAX ← LIST[1] K ← 2	MAX ← 3 K ← 2	

While K <= N do
    If MAX < LIST[K]
    Then MAX ← LIST[K]
    End If
    K ← K + 1
	K found to be <= N = 4
	MAX = 3 < LIST[2] = 4
	MAX ← 4
	
	K ← 3
		Start loop

While K <= N do
    If MAX < LIST[K]
    Then MAX ← LIST[K]
    End If
    K ← K + 1
	K found to be <= N = 4
	MAX = 4 < LIST[3] = 6
	MAX ← 6
	
	K ← 4
		Repeat loop

While K <= N do
    If MAX < LIST[K]
    Then MAX ← LIST[K]
	K found to be <= N = 4
	MAX = 4 not < LIST[4] = 2
	so no action
		Repeat loop

Instruction executed	Resulting event	Remarks
End If		
K ← K + 1	K ← 5	
While K < = N do	K found to be > N	End loop
Repeat	so skip loop body	
Return	exit algorithm with	Done!
	MAX = 6	

Although tedious, doing a step by step trace by hand of the execution of an algorithm forces whoever does it to pay attention to all the details. This way errors in the algorithm can sometimes be detected that would be missed by a less detailed examination of it.

Obviously, doing a full execution trace such as the one above would take a very long time with an algorithm of any complexity. Moreover, having to write so many things down is itself likely to lead to errors. As a result people generally take various shortcuts. One shortcut is to list only the line numbers of the instructions rather than the instructions themselves. Another shortcut is to be a bit less detailed about the values of variables. In this case the resulting table would look like this:

Example 2. An abbreviated event (execution) trace table

Stmt.	Resulting event	Remarks
0	LIST ← 3 4 6 2 and N ← 4	Initialize
1	MAX ← 3	
2	K ← 2	
3	K < = N	Start loop
4	MAX < LIST[2] so MAX ← 4	
5	K ← 3	
3	K < = N	Repeat loop
4	MAX < LIST[3] so MAX ← 6	
5	K ← 4	
3	K < = N	Repeat loop
4	MAX not < LIST[4] so no action	
5	K ← 5	
3	K > N so skip loop body	End loop
7	Exit algorithm with MAX = 6	Done!

10.1.2   Value Trace Tables

Another kind of shortcut is to record only certain kinds of events, such as transfer of control, output, or the assignment of values to variables. A trace that records only the assignment of values to variables is called a value trace or a variable trace. Done as a value trace the example above could be represented as follows.

Example 3. An abbreviated value trace table

Stmt.	LIST	N	MAX	K	Remarks
0	3 4 6 2	4	?	?	Initialize
1		4	3	?	
2		4	3	2	
4		4	4	2	
5		4	4	3	
4		4	6	3	
5		4	6	4	
5		4	6	5	Done!

Note that the value of N does not change. Variables whose values do not change are usually not given their own column in a value trace table.

Exercise 1. Do a value trace table of just P and MIN for the following algorithm, with LIST = < 7, 3, 5, 1 >.

```
0        Algorithm FindMin(LIST, N, MIN)
         # Preconditons: LIST is a list of N numbers with N > = 1.
         # Postcondition: MIN is the smallest element of LIST.

1                P ← 1                 # P points to the next element of LIST
2                MIN ← LIST[P]
3                While P < = N DO
4                        If LIST[P] < MIN Then MIN ← LIST[P] EndIf
5                        P ← P + 1
6                Repeat
7                Return MIN
         EndAlgorithm
```

Exercise 2. Do a value trace table for FindMin with LIST = < 3, 7, 1, 5 >.

10.1.3 *Tracing with Complex Conditions*

Your ability to trace the execution of many programs depends on your being able to do truth value calculations involving conjunction, disjunction, and negation. For example, suppose the following program fragment is executed, starting with $x = 3$, $y = 5$, and $z = 7$.

```
...
01    If not (2 * x > z) then y ← y + 1 Endif
02    x ← y + z
03    If ((z < x + y) and (x > y)) Print ('This is silly') EndIf
04    While ((x < 3 * y) or (y = x))
05              x ← x + 5
06              y← y + 1
07              Print (x, y, z)
08    EndWhile
...
```

What would be printed as a result of executing this program fragment? What would the final values of x, y, and z be? While these are not difficult questions, finding their answers certainly does depend upon knowing how to deal with the truth functions associated with "and," "or," and "not." Note the column reserved for "output" in this table. The beginning of a trace table for executing that program fragment is:

Line	x	Y	Z	Output	Comments
Initially	3	5	7		
1	3	6	7		~(2 * 3 > 7), so y ← y + 1
2	13	6	7		
3	13	6	7	This is silly	
4	13	6	7		13 < 3 * 6 and not x = y
5	18	6	7		
6	18	7	7		

Exercise 3. Finish the trace table above.

Exercise 4. Do a similar trace table but with x = 6, y = 4, and z = 8.

Exercise 5. Do a similar trace table but with x = 7, y = 5, z = 3

Exercise 6. Do a similar trace table but with x = 0, y = 0, z = 0

10.2   Tracing Program Execution Backwards

Occasionally it is useful (or fun) to try to execute a program in reverse. For example, if a program crashes or outputs an incorrect value as some point, executing backwards from that point can help diagnose the source of the error.

Example 4. Consider the instruction, I, below. What can you tell about the value of the variable a before I is executed from knowing the value of x after I is executed?

I If (a > 0) then x ← 3

1. After I is executed, either x = 3 or x not = 3.
2. Suppose x not = 3 after I.
    1. Then the condition (a > 0) was false before I, else x would = 3.
    2. So before I, a < = 0.
3. On the other hand, if x = 3 after I, nothing can be determined about the value of a before I. To see this consider the following
    1. If before I, a < = 0 and x = 3 then after I is executed x will still = 3.
    2. If before I, a > 0 then x ← 3, so after I, x = 3.
    3. Hence knowing x = 3 after I is consistent with any value of a before I.

Example 5. What can you tell about the values of a and b before instruction I, given what I prints?

I   If ((a > 0) or (b < 0)) then
                Print "yes"
        else
                Print "no"
        endif

1. If I prints "yes" then the condition ((a > 0) or (b < 0)) must have been true before I.
2. Hence a > 0 or b < 0 (or both) before I.
3. On the other hand if I prints "no" then ((a > 0) or (b < 0)) was false before I.
4. Hence both a > 0 and b < 0 were false before I.

Example 6. Consider the sequence of instructions I_1, I_2.

I_1:   If ((a = 0) and (b = 0)) then
                b ← 5
        else
                b ← 0
        endif

I_2:   if (not (a = 0 or b > 0) or (a = 3)) then
                c ← 7
        else
                c ← 4
        endif

Suppose just after executing I_2, c = 4. What can you tell about the value of a just before I_1 is executed?

    Working backwards, using the truth tables described earlier in the chapter, it can be seen that:

1. Since c = 4 after I_2, the else clause of I_2 was executed.
2. Hence (not(a = 0 or b > 0) or (a = 3)) is false before I_2 (and after I_1).

3. Since this is a false disjunction, both parts are false.
4. Hence not(a = 0 or b > 0) is false and a = 3 is false at end of I_1.
5. Hence a = 0 is true or b > 0 is true, and a = 3 is false after I_1.
6. Moreover, after I_1 either b = 0 or b = 5.
7. If b > 0 is true after I_1, the condition of I_1 was true before I_1.
8. So if b > 0 after I_1, b = 0 and a = 0 before I_1.
9. And if not b > 0 after I_1 then the condition of I_1 was false before I_1.

Notice that the conclusion of the argument above was not at all obvious at the beginning of the argument. Much of the power of logic comes from arguments of this sort that allow people to deduce new, hidden, implicit facts from known facts.

Exercise 7.

I: If((a = 0) and not(b = 0)) or (b = 0 and not(a = 0)) then
              Print "yes"
       else
              Print "no"
       endif

(a) If a and b are both = 0 before I, what will I print? Why?
(b) If a and b are both = 1 before I, what will I print? Why?
(c) If a = 0 and b = 7 before I, what will I print? Why?
(d) If a = 0 before I and I prints "no" then what can you tell about the value of b before I? Explain.

Exercise 8.

I: If not(a = 0 and b < > 0) and not(b = 0 and c < > 0) and c = 0 then
              Print "yes"
       else
              Print "no"
       endif

(a) If a = b = c = 0 before I what will I print? Why?
(b) If I prints "yes" what can you say about the values of a, b, and c? Why?
(c) If I prints "no" what can you say about the values of a, b, and c? Why?
(d) If a > b > c = 0 before I, what will I print? Why?

Exercise 9. Assume that the variables a and b have been assigned numeric values before I_1 followed by I_2 are executed. Let A represent the condition a = 0 and B represent the condition b = 0. For each of the four possible pairs of truth values for A and B, what can you say about the numeric values of c and d after the following two instructions are? Why?

I_1:   If not(a = 0 and b < > 0) then

        $c \leftarrow 0$

    else

        $c \leftarrow 3$

    endif

I_2:   If not(b = 0 and c < > 0) then

        $d \leftarrow 2$

    else

        $d \leftarrow 4$

    endif

(a) A and B both true.
(b) A true, B false
(c) A false, B true
(d) A and B both false.

Exercise 10. Given the following instructions from the middle of a program and assuming that a, b, and c have been assigned values before I_1.

I_1:   if a = 0 then b ← 1   else b ← 0 endif # So b = 0 or b = 1
I_2:   if b < > 0 then c ← 0 else c ← 1 endif # So c = 0 or c = 1

(a) If c = 0 after I_2 what can you say about a and b before I_1?
(b) If c = 1 after I_2 what can you say about a and b before I_1?

Part III
Logical Truth

Parts I and II were about specific statements expressed in informal English and how to express their logical form in aid of determining their material truth or falsity. In Part III there is an important shift in perspective. From now on, emphasis is on logical forms themselves, rather than specific statements which have those forms. The reason for this is that much of what we know about correct reasoning involves using forms of statements rather than using their material truth values.

Part III describes rules and criteria for determining logical properties of statements by analysis of the logical forms of those statements, without regard to their material truth or intended meaning. A notation similar to logical English is introduced to represent logical forms and to express rules and criteria for evaluating logical properties and relations such as consistency, redundancy, and equivalence of statement forms as well as correctness of arguments.

Chapter 11
Truth Functional Forms

In previous chapters the logical forms of specific statements expressed in English were discussed in aid of reasoning about their material truth values. Here, and in subsequent chapters there is an important shift in perspective. From now on, emphasis is on logical forms themselves, rather than specific statements which have those forms. The reason for this is that much of what we know about correct reasoning depends on forms of statements rather than material truth. After studying this chapter you should be able to:

1. Describe and use truth functional forms.
2. Describe and give examples of interpretations for truth functional forms.
3. Describe the conditions under which truth functional forms are said to be true or false for a given interpretation.
4. Distinguish among truth functionally true, false, and contingent forms.
5. Use properties of truth functional forms to help determine the logical status of statements expressed in English.
6. Use logical properties of forms to simplify statements and conditions.

Outline

11.1   Overview

Consider the following statements:

(a) It is raining or it is not raining.

R. Lover, *Elementary Logic: For Software Development*,
DOI: 10.2007/978-1-84800-082-7, © Springer 2008

(b) Today is Tuesday or today is not Tuesday.

(c) The Moon is green or the Moon is not green.

All of them are true. Moreover their truth does not depend upon ordinary facts. For example, you don't have to know anything about the weather to know that it is raining or it is not raining. Similarly you do not have to know the day of the week to know that today is Tuesday or today is not Tuesday. And you don't have to know anything about the Moon to know that the Moon is green or the Moon is not green. Statements like this are said to be necessarily true.

Another feature these examples share is that they all have the same form, i.e. they are all a disjunction of a statement and the denial of that statement. In fact, it is easy to see that all statements of that form are necessarily true.

Now consider the following arguments:

(d) It is raining. If it is raining then the picnic will be cancelled. Therefore the picnic will be cancelled.

(e) My car is old. If my car is old then my car probably needs repair. Hence my car probably needs repair.

Obviously, each of these arguments is correct. Moreover, they both have the same logical form. And it is easy to see that all arguments of that form are correct.

When statements and arguments are more complex it is no longer easy to see which statements are necessarily true and which arguments are correct. This is where the formal analysis described in this and subsequent chapters becomes useful. The diagram below may help clarify the overall strategy used here.

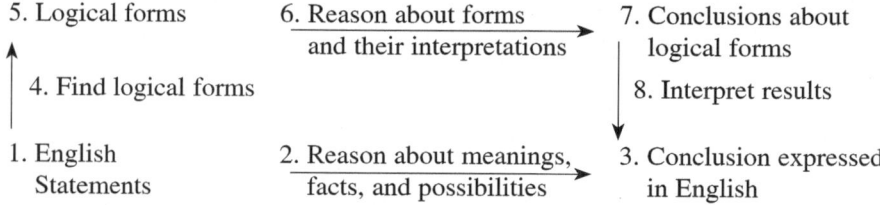

The path 1–2–3 represents the sort of reasoning most people do most of the time. Starting with statements expressed in ordinary English, they use informal reasoning to come to some conclusion about which statements are necessarily true or whether some argument is correct. One use of logical English is to help this process. For example, I might want to know whether the statement "76543 is prime or 76543 is not prime." is necessarily true. By noticing that "76543 is prime" and "76543 is not prime" are the only possibilities and understanding the meaning of "or" I might conclude that it is not possible for the disjunction to be false, hence that it is necessarily true.

The path 1–4–5–6–7–8–3 represents the alternative sort of reasoning described here in Part III. It is called formal reasoning. Starting as before with statements expressed in ordinary English the reasoner tries to find the logical forms of those statements. Reasoning about those forms results in conclusions about them. Those conclusions are then interpreted back to find conclusions about the original English statements. For example, I might want to know whether the statement "76543 is prime or 76543 is not prime." is true. This time I first find the form of the statement. Its form can be expressed as "S ∨ ~S." Then I remember that "S ∨ ~S" is a form which is true in all possible interpretations of it. Since the original statement is one possible interpretation of the form "S ∨ ~S" I conclude that the original statement is necessarily true.

On the face of it, ordinary informal reasoning seems much simpler, easier, and faster. And often it is. Unfortunately, while reasoning informally people often get confused, make mistakes, and come to incorrect conclusions.

Formal reasoning is one way to reduce the confusion and error associated with informal reasoning. After studying it people make fewer mistakes, even when they do informal reasoning. Carried to extreme, formal reasoning can be automated so that computers can be used to assist human reasoning. The simplest type of formal reasoning involves only truth functional statement forms, as discussed in this chapter.

11.2 Truth Functional Forms

Truth functional forms are terse notations similar to those of logical English. However, they do not abbreviate specific statements of English. Instead, they represent logical forms of statements completely abstracted from any particular English statements of which they are the forms. Most of what is known about rules and criteria of correct reasoning based only on truth functions involves only the forms of statements, not their meanings. Consequently, most of the rules and criteria of correct reasoning based only on truth functions are expressed in terms of truth functional forms. Following the next chapter, rules and criteria of correct reasoning based on quantifiers will be discussed.

Definition 1. An *atomic form* is an expression which is a single capital letter followed by zero or more lower case letters from near the beginning of the alphabet.

Example 1. P and Qaba are atomic forms. On the other hand, ∀xP(x) ∨ Q, R(c, x), and Rcx are not atomic forms. Notice that atomic forms do not have parentheses. Notice also that this definition is purely formal (syntactic) and atomic forms do not name, refer to, or abbreviate anything else.

Definition 2. F is a *truth functional form*, abbreviated *tff*, if and only if

1. F is an atomic form
2. F is of the form (~G) and G is a tff

3. F is of the form (G ∧ H) and both G and H are tffs
4. F is of the form (G ∨ H) and both G and H are tffs
5. F is of the form (G → H) and both G and H are tffs
6. F is of the form (G ↔ H) and both G and H are tffs

As in previous chapters, parentheses will be dropped where confusion is unlikely to result.

Example 2. P, Qab, ~P, ~Qab, P ∨ Qab, (P ∨ ~P), and (P ∨ ~P) → ~Qab are all truth functional forms by multiple applications of Definition 2.

11.3   Interpretations of Truth Functional Forms

Definition 3. An *interpretation* of a truth functional form is an assignment of a truth value (T or F) to each atomic form of that tff.

In the literature, interpretations are also called *models* and the approach to logic presented here is often called a model theoretic approach. Later the axiomatic approach to logic will be discussed briefly.

Example 3. P ∨ Qab is a tff. Its atomic forms are P and Qab. One interpretation of P ∨ Qab results from assigning T to P and T to Qab. Another interpretation results from assigning T to P and F to Qab. Another results from assigning F to P and T to Qab. Finally, one results from assigning F to P and F to Qab. These are the only possible interpretations for this tff. They are described more clearly and briefly in the following table, where each row below the components list represents a single possible interpretation.

P	Qab	
T	T	(first interpretation)
T	F	(second interpretation)
F	T	(third interpretation)
F	F	(fourth interpretation)

Note that an interpretation is just another way of describing a row of the lower left part of a truth table. If a tff is constructed from N atomic statement forms, then there are 2^N different interpretations of it, corresponding to the 2^N rows in the lower part of its truth table.

11.4   Truth Under an Interpretation

Recall that where truth functional connectives are used, the truth value of a compound statement depends only on the truth values of its component parts.

Definition 4. Let F be a truth functional form and I be an interpretation for F, then we define a *valuation function of I*, called *V*, whose domain is the atomic forms of F as well as all the truth functional forms that can be made from those atomic forms using truth functional connectives. Specifically, let G be any truth functional form built from the atomic forms of F, then $V(G) = T$ just in case

1. G is an atomic form and $V(G) = T$
2. G is of the form $(\sim H)$ and $V(H) = F$
3. G is of the form $(H \wedge J)$ and $V(H) = T$ and $V(J) = T$
4. G is of the form $(H \vee J)$ and $V(H) = T$ or $V(J) = T$
5. G is of the form $(H \rightarrow J)$ and $V(H) = F$ or $V(J) = T$
6. G is of the form $(H \leftrightarrow J)$ and $V(H) = V(J)$
7. Otherwise, $V(G) = F$

Example 4. If F is $P \vee Qab$ and I is the first interpretation described in Example 3 then $V_I(P) = T$ and $V_I(Qab) = T$, while if I is the second interpretation then $V_I(P) = T$ and $V_I(Qab) = F$, and so on for the other two interpretations.

Definition 5. Let F be a truth functional form and I be an interpretation for F, then if $V_I(F) = T$ then we say that *F is true under interpretation I*, and if $V_I(F) = F$ then we say that *F is false under interpretation I*.

Example 5.

(a) Since $V_I(P \vee Qab) = T$ if and only if $V_I(P) = T$ or $V_I(Qab) = T$ it follows that $P \vee Qab$ is true under I just in case P is true under I or Qab is true under I.
(b) Since $V_I(P \vee Qab) = F$ if and only if $V_I(P) = F$ and $V_I(Qab) = F$ it follows than $P \vee Qab$ is false under I just in case both P and Qab are false under I.

11.5   Truth Functional Truth, Falsity, and Contingency

Definition 6. A tff is said to be *truth functionally true*, abbreviated *TF-true*, just in case it is true under all of its interpretations, i.e. just in case its truth table has all Ts in its final column. TF-true tffs are also called *tautologies*.

Example 6. Consider the tff P ∨ ~P. Since it has only one atomic form, it has only two interpretations, call them I$_1$ and I$_2$, where I$_1$(P) = T and I$_2$(P) = F, as is shown in following truth table.

P	P ∨ ~P
T	T
F	T

Let V$_1$ be the valuation function of I$_1$. Then from Definition 4 it follows that V$_1$(P) = T, V$_1$(~P) = F, and V$_1$(P ∨ ~P) = T. Similarly, let V$_2$ be the valuation function of I$_2$. Then V$_2$(P) = F, V$_2$(~P) = T, and V$_2$(P ∨ ~P) = T. Hence, no matter what interpretation, I, is given to P, V$_1$(P ∨ ~P) = T. Correspondingly, the final column of the truth table for P ∨ ~P is all Ts. Hence P ∨ ~P is TF-true.

Definition 7. A tff is said to be *truth functionally false*, abbreviated *TF-false*, just in case it is false under all of its interpretations, i.e. just in case its truth table has all Fs in its final column. TF-false tffs are also called *contradictions*.

Example 7. Consider the tff P ∧ ~P. Since it has only one atomic form, it has only two interpretations, call them I$_1$ and I$_2$, where I$_1$(P) = T and I$_2$(P) = F, as is shown in following truth table.

P	P ∧ ~P
T	F
F	F

Let V$_1$ be the valuation function of I$_1$. Then from Definition 4 it follows that V$_1$(P) = T, V$_1$(~P) = F, and V$_1$(P ∧ ~P) = F. Similarly, let V$_2$ be the valuation function of I$_2$. Then V$_2$(P) = F, V$_2$(~P) = T, and V$_2$(P ∧ ~P) = F. Hence, no matter what interpretation, I. is given to P, V$_1$(P ∧ ~P) = F. Correspondingly, the final column of the truth table for P ∧ ~P is all Fs. Hence P ∧ ~P is TF-false.

Definition 8. A tff is said to be a *truth functionally contingent*, abbreviated *TF-contingent*, just in case it is neither logically true nor logically false, i.e. it is true in some of its interpretations and false in some of its interpretations.

Example 8. Consider the tff ~P. Since it has only one atomic form, it has only two interpretations, call them I$_1$ and I$_2$, where I$_1$(P) = T and I$_2$(P) = F, as is shown in following truth table.

P	~P
T	F
F	T

Let V_1 be the valuation function of I_1. Then from Definition 4 it follows that $V_1(P) = T$ and $V_1(\sim P) = F$. Similarly, let V_2 be the valuation function of I_2. Then $V_2(P) = F$ and $V_2(\sim P) = T$. Hence, $\sim P$ is true in some of its interpretations and false in others. Correspondingly, the final column of the truth table for $\sim P$ has some Ts and some Fs. Hence $\sim P$ is TF-contingent.

Strictly speaking, a form cannot have a truth value. Only statements have truth values. So what do Definitions 6–8 mean? When we say that a tff is TF-true that really means that all English statements of that logical form are true, no matter what truth values their atomic parts might have. Similarly, to say that a tff is TF-false really means that all English statements of that logical form are false no matter what truth values their atomic parts might have. Finally, to say that a tff is TF-contingent really means that some English statements of that form will be true and some will be false, depending on the truth values of their atomic parts.

Exercise 1. For each of the following tffs, determine whether it is TF-true, TF-false, or TF-contingent. Hint, find or make a truth table for each. Then examine its final column.

(a) $P \wedge \sim P$
(b) $P \vee \sim P$
(c) $P \leftrightarrow P$
(d) $P \leftrightarrow \sim P$
(e) $P \leftrightarrow \sim\sim P$
(f) $P \leftrightarrow \sim\sim\sim P$
(g) $P \rightarrow Q \vee P \rightarrow \sim Q$
(h) $P \rightarrow Q \vee \sim P \rightarrow Q$
(i) $P \rightarrow Q \vee Q \rightarrow P$
(j) $P \rightarrow Q \vee P \wedge \sim Q$
(k) $\sim(P \wedge Q) \leftrightarrow \sim P \wedge \sim Q$
(l) $\sim(P \wedge Q) \leftrightarrow \sim P \vee \sim Q$

The more general and more important concepts of *logical truth*, *logical falsity*, and *logical contingency* will be defined in Chap. 13. TF-true forms are among the forms that are logically true (logically necessary). TF-false forms are among the forms that are logically false (logically impossible). TF-contingent forms may be logically true, logically false, or logically contingent.

11.6 Using Forms to Find the Logical Status of English Statements

The first step in using the material above to help determine the logical status of an English statement is to express its logical structure by means of a truth functional form. For simple English statements, you may be able to go directly from

English to truth functional forms. But for complex statements, logical English may be a useful intermediate stage in this process. Below are some examples of logical English abbreviations for English statements and corresponding truth functional forms.

Example 9.

Logical English	Truth functional form
(a) Happy(Jill)	Hj
(b) TallerThan(Max, Joe)	Tmj
(c) LessThan(3, 85)	Lab
(d) LessThan(3, 5 + 33)	Lcd
(e) P(Alice) $\vee$ ~Q(Alice, Bill)	Pa $\vee$ ~Qab
(f) $4 + 2 = 99$	Eab
(g) $3*5 + 99*2 > 75$	Gab
(h) $\forall x P(x)$	P
(i) $\exists x P(x) \vee (\sim\exists x P(x) \rightarrow R(a, b))$	P $\vee$ (~P $\rightarrow$ Rab)
(j) $\exists x P(x) \vee \exists x \sim P(x)$	P $\vee$ Q
(k) $\forall x(P(x) \rightarrow \sim\exists y Q(x, y))$	P

Example 9a, b show the requirement that only single capital letters are used to represent predicates and that names are represented by single lower case letters. Example 9c shows that numbers are not just copied over into forms, they too are represented by a single lower case letter for each number. Example 9d, f, g show that definite descriptions such as 5 + 33 are also represented by single letters. Example 9e shows that truth functional structure carries over to tffs. Example 9h, k show that quantified statements are expressed by single capital letters followed by zero lower case letters. Finally, Example 9i, j show that truth functional structure which is not within the scope of a quantifier is represented even if some of the components are quantified. More will be said in the next chapter about quantifiers and logical forms for representing them.

Procedure TFL: Let S represent a statement expressed in ordinary English.

1. Express the logical structure of S as a tff, F.
2. Try to determine whether F is TF-true, TF-false, or TF-contingent by

   (a) Determining whether it is of a form known to be a TF-true, TF-false, or TF-contingent
   (b) Making a truth table for F and applying Definitions 6–8, thereby adding to your stock of known forms
   (c) Reasoning involving logical equivalence (see Chap. 14)
   (d) Reasoning using logical implication (see Chap. 15)

3. Draw the appropriate conclusion

   (a) If F is TF-true then S is necessarily true.
   (b) If F is TF-false then S is necessarily false (impossible).
   (c) If F is TF-contingent then this test does not establish the truth value of S. However, if S has no quantifiers then S is logically contingent in the sense defined in the Chap. 13. And if S does have quantifiers then Procedure QL in Chap. 13 may help establish the truth value of S.

Example 10. Suppose S is the statement "Everything is blue or something is not blue." Then logical English for S could be ∀xBlue(x) ∨ ∃x~Blue(x). But the tff for S will be a much less informative form such as P ∨ Q. This form is TF-contingent and S contains quantifiers, so this procedure fails even though it is obvious that S is necessarily true, a fact that can be established using Procedure QL in Chap. 13.

Example 11. Suppose S is the statement "Everything is blue and it is not the case that everything is blue." Then the logical English for S could be expressed by ∀xBlue(x) ∧~∀xBlue(x)), but the tff for S will be a form such as B ∧ ~B. Since the truth table for this form has all Fs in its final column, it is false in all of its interpretations, Hence S is false.

Example 12. Suppose S is the statement "Today is Monday and it is raining." Then logical English for S could be "Mon ∧ Rain." Hence the tff for S will be something like M ∧ R. Making a truth table for M ∧ R will show that it has one interpretation in which it is true and three in which it is false, hence it is TF-contingent, and therefore this Procedure TFL does not establish the truth value of S.

Example 13. Suppose S is the statement "Everything is blue or it is not blue." Then the logical English for S could be expressed by ∀x(Blue(x) ∨ ~Blue(x)). Hence the tff for S will be a much less informative atomic form such as B. Since the truth table for B has one T and one F in its final column B is TF-contingent, hence Procedure TFL does not establish the truth value of S.

Exercise 2. Use Procedure TFL to try to determine the truth value of each of the English statements below. First find logical English for each statement, then find an appropriate tff. Then do the truth table for that tff. Then apply Procedure TFL.

(a) Today is Monday and today is not Monday.
(b) Today is Monday or today is not Monday.
(c) If Today is Monday and today is not Monday then the Sun is cold.
(d) If a = 3 and not a = 3 then 5 = 0.
(e) If everything is blue then nothing is blue.
(f) If something is blue then something is blue.
(g) (If today is Monday then the Moon is blue) just in case (if the Moon is not blue then today is not Monday).

(h) (If today is Monday then the Moon is blue) just in case (if today is not Monday then the Moon is not blue).

(i) If it is not raining or it is not snowing and, moreover, it is raining then it is not snowing.

(j) If it is raining and either it is not snowing or it is not raining then is not snowing.

(k) It is not the case that today is Friday and that today is payday if and only if today is not Friday or today is not payday.

(l) It is not the case that today is Friday or that today is payday if and only if today is not Friday and today is not payday.

11.7 Application to Simplifying Statements and Conditions

Conditions in problem specifications and program instructions cannot be said to be true or false because they have no truth value. However, consider the condition "P(x) or not P(x)." It is obvious that no matter what value is given to x, the resulting statement would be true. It is common to say that such a condition is TF-true or to call it a tautology even though this is technically incorrect. Similarly conditions like "P(x) and not P(x)" are said to be TF-false or logically impossible. This way of speaking is followed in the discussion below. It is particularly appropriate for program instructions since when a program is written or compiled the program variables are placeholders, i.e. they are logical variables, but when a program is executed the program variables are assigned values and hence are names and not logical variables.

Knowing that a statement or condition is TF-true or TF-false can allow you to simplify it, e.g. in a problem specification or program instruction. You may even be able to eliminate the specification or instruction entirely. Below is a list of rules for simplifying conditions.

Procedure SC: Rules for Simplifying Statements and Conditions
When a condition can be simplified, the statements and instructions in which that condition appear may also be simplified.

Rule SC1. If a statement or condition is TF-true then it will be true under all circumstances.

For example, the condition part of the instruction

If ((x > 0) or not (x > 0)) then Print 'Hello' Endif

is TF-true, so it will print 'Hello' no matter what value x has. Consequently it can be simplified to just

Print 'Hello'.

Similarly, the loop

While ((x > 0) or not (x > 0))
# loop body
Endwhile

will repeat forever, no matter what the initial value of x is and no matter how the value of x is changed in the loop body.

Rule SC2. If a statement or condition is TF-false then is will be false under all circumstances.

For example, the condition part of the instruction

>   If ((x > 0) and not (x > 0)) then Print 'Goodbye' Endif

is TF-false, so it will not print "Goodbye" no matter what value x has. Consequently it can be simplified by being eliminated altogether.

A similar situation arises with conditions in statements. For example,

>   If ((x > 0) and not (x > 0)) then y > 5 else z = 7. Endif

can be simplified to just

>   z = 7.

Rule SC3. If a statement or condition is of the form "C ∨ S" where C is TF-true then that whole condition is itself TF-true so it can be eliminated.

For example, the condition part of the instruction

>   If (((x > 0) or not (x > 0)) or (y > 5)) then Print 'Hello' Endif

can be simplified to just

>   Print 'Hello'.

Similarly, the loop

>   While (((x > 0) or not (x > 0)) or (y > 5))
>   # loop body
>   Endwhile

can be simplified to just

>   Loop forever
>   # loop body
>   Endloop

Rule SC4. If a statement or condition is of the form "C ∧ S" where C is TF-true then that whole condition is true just in case S is true, so C can be eliminated.

For example, the condition part of the instruction

>   If (((x > 0) or not (x > 0)) and (y > 5)) then Print 'Hello' Endif

can be simplified to just

>   If (y > 5) then Print 'Hello' Endif

Rule SC5. If a statement or condition is of the form "C ∨ S" where C is TF-false then that whole condition is true just in case S is true, so C can be eliminated.

For example,

> If (((x > 0) and not (x > 0)) or (y > 5)) then z = 7 Endif.

can be simplified to

> If (y > 5) then z = 7 Endif.

Rule SC6. If a statement or condition is of the form "C ∧ S" where C is TF-false then that whole condition is itself TF-false, so S can be eliminated.

For example,

> If (((x > 0) and not (x > 0)) and (y > 5)) then Print Goodbye Endif

can be simplified by eliminating it entirely.

These examples are simple enough that they are easy to see and to avoid. In real life conditions and instructions can be much more complex. In addition the parts of TF-true and TF-false conditions can be spread out over more than one part of an instruction, as in the example below.

```
If (x = 0) then
        While (not (x = 0)
                Print 'Hello'
                x ← x + 1
        Endwhile
        Print 'Goodbye'
    Endif
```

Notice that "x = 0" in the first line contradicts "not (x = 0)" in the second line and that there is nothing between these lines which can change the value of x. The result is that the body of the while loop will never be executed. The whole instruction can be simplified to

> If (x = 0) then Print "Goodbye" Endif

Exercise 3. Use your knowledge of truth tables, TF-truth, and TF-falsity to simplify the following instructions. Note that in some cases there may be no way to simplify an instruction.

```
(a) If (x = 0) then
        If not (x = 0) then
                Print 'Hello'
        Endif
        Print 'Goodbye'
    Endif
```

```
(b) If (x = 0) then
        Print 'Goodbye'
        If not (x = 0) then
                Print ('Hello')
        Endif
```

Endif

(c) While (x = 0)
    While not (x = 0)
        $x \leftarrow x - 1$
    Endwhile
Endwhile

(d) If ((x = 0) or not (x = 0)) then
    $x \leftarrow x - 1$
Endif

(e) If (x > y and not y < 0 or not x > y and y < 0 or not y < 0 or x > y) then Print 'This is a mess' Endif

(f) If (not x > y or y < 0 or x > y and not y < 0 or not y < 0 or x > y) then Print 'This is a mess' Endif

Chapter 12
Truth Functional Properties of Program Designs

This chapter describes decision tables, also called decision-action tables. While they resemble truth tables in some respects, they are not truth tables. They can be used to plan and to document program designs. After studying this material you should be able to

1. Translate program designs expressed in English into equivalent program designs expressed as decision tables and vice versa.
2. Simplify decision tables.
3. Analyze program designs expressed as decision tables for consistency, completeness, and redundancy.

Outline

12.1 The General Form of Decision Tables

Decision tables (also know as decision logic tables, logic tables, and condition action tables) are often used to represent complex "If then else" or "case" control structure. They resemble truth tables in several respects. The general form of a decision table is:

Condition stub	Condition entries
Action stub	Action entries

R. Lover, *Elementary Logic: For Software Development*,
DOI: 10.2007/978-1-84800-082-7, © Springer 2008

12.2 Limited Entry Decision Tables

12.2.1 The Basic Form

Decision tables which have only Ts and Fs as condition entries and Ys or Ns as their action entries are called *limited entry decision tables*.

Example 1a. The specification If x is greater than 0 then assign y the value "positive" would be represented by the following decision table

x > o	T	F
y ← 'positive'	Y	N

Example 1b. The specification If x is greater than 0 then assign y the value "positive" otherwise assign y the value "negative" would be represented by the following decision table.

x > 0	T	F
y ← "positive"	Y	N
y ← "negative"	N	Y

The following example describes a more complex set of cases and introduces labels for rows and columns. The row labels C1, C2, and C3 refer to conditions. The row labels A1, A2, etc. refer to actions. The columns are labeled R1, R2, etc. because the information in each of those columns is intended to be interpreted as a rule for conditional action.

Example 2a. Everyone gets a printed sales flyer except those who are not rich, not paid up, and not high volume. Rich customers get a long catalog unless they are not paid up and not high volume. Poor customers get a long catalog just in case they are high volume. The only people who get nasty bills are those who are poor, not paid up, and not high volume. Others get a polite bill if and only if they are not paid up.

		R1	R2	R3	R4	R5	R6	R7	R8
C1	Customer rich	T	T	T	T	F	F	F	F
C2	Customer paid up	T	T	F	F	T	T	F	F
C3	High volume	T	F	T	F	T	F	T	F
A1	Print polite bill	N	N	Y	Y	N	N	Y	N
A2	Print nasty bill	N	N	N	N	N	N	N	Y
A3	Print long catalog	Y	Y	Y	N	Y	N	Y	N
A4	Print sales flyer	Y	Y	Y	Y	Y	Y	Y	N

If, as in Example 2a, a rule calls for more than one action then the convention is that the actions are to be executed one at a time from top to bottom, unless some other order is specified. Later more will be said about this and other control structure issues. For the present we will just follow the convention.

The process of constructing decision tables can be very helpful because it forces people to consider all possible cases and to be clear about what is supposed to happen in each different circumstance. After they are constructed, decision tables can help communicate important features of program design, even to people who know little or nothing about programming. A decision table can also be used to suggest test cases for programs that are supposed to implement the design expressed in the table. And after a program is written, a corresponding decision table can be used as part of its design documentation.

Steps for constructing a decision table.

Step 1. Find the simplest conditions in the program specifications.
Step 2. Find the simplest actions mentioned in the program specifications.
Step 3. Make a four part table with one row for column titles and one row for each simple condition in the upper half. The left half of the table should have a column for condition and action labels and a single wide column for the condition and action stubs (short descriptions). The right half of the table should have two to the nth power columns, where n is the number of simple conditions used.
Step 4. Fill in the condition and action entries using the program specifications.

Exercise 1. Make a decision table for the following specifications for calculating weekly pay for salespeople.

Everyone gets a base salary no matter what. Trainees get an additional $100 per week. Experienced salespeople in established territories are expected to sell at least $2,000 per week. If they do not then they get only their base salary. Anyone who sells more than $2,000 in a week gets a 10% commission on the amount over $2,000. Anyone selling in a new territory gets an additional 15% commission on the amount over $2,000.

12.2.2   Simplifying Tables with "Don't Care" Condition Entries

In the course of using decision tables people have invented a variety of ways to express them differently or make them easier to use. For example, when decision tables are implemented in programs, each rule can be represented by a separate conditional instruction. Rules 1 and 2 in Example 2a above would probably end up something like this:

```
If (Cust.is.rich and Cust.is.paidup and Cust.is.hivol) then
      print.long.cat
      print.sale.flyer
endif

If (Cust.is.rich and Cust.is.paidup and not Cust.is.hivol) then
      print.long.cat
      print.sale.flyer
endif
```

With eight rules we would get eight such instructions. The decision table may be very clear but the resulting program is unnecessarily complex and difficult to read. For example, note that Rules 1 and 2 both result in the same actions whether or not the customer is high volume. Consequently we could accomplish the same result with a single instruction:

If (Cust.is.rich and Cust.is.paidup) then
        print.long.cat
        print.sale.flyer
endif

The resulting program is significantly shorter and clearer. To represent this kind of simplification decision tables often use "-" to indicate "don't care" situations, as in Example 2b below.

Example 2b

		R12	R3	R4	R5	R6	R7	R8
C1	Customer rich	T	T	T	F	F	F	F
C2	Customer paid up	T	F	F	T	T	F	F
C3	High volume	–	T	F	T	F	T	F
A1	Print polite bill	N	Y	Y	N	N	Y	N
A2	Print nasty bill	N	N	N	N	N	N	Y
A3	Print long catalog	Y	Y	N	Y	N	Y	N
A4	Print sales flyer	Y	Y	Y	Y	Y	Y	N

Exercise 2. Try to simplify the Example 2b decision table further.

Another way of expressing decision tables is to replace "Y" and "N" in the action entries by "X" and " " (blank). People who use this notation often also use "Y" and "N" where "T" and "F" were used in Example 2. With these changes Example 2b becomes:

Example 2c

		R12	R3	R4	R5	R6	R7	R8
C1	Customer rich	Y	Y	Y	N	N	N	N
C2	Customer paid up	Y	N	N	Y	Y	N	N
C3	High volume	–	Y	N	Y	N	Y	N
A1	Print polite bill		X	X			X	
A2	Print nasty bill							X
A3	Print long catalog	X	X		X		X	
A4	Print sales flyer	X	X	X	X	X	X	

Exercise 3. Try to simplify the result of exercise 2.

Exercise 4. All the parts of this exercise refer to the following set of specifications. They all pertain to applicants for loans at a bank or loan company.

Specifications: An old applicant is one who has borrowed from us before. If an applicant does not qualify for a loan then write a polite rejection letter. Since we already have an applicant data record (name, address, etc.) for each qualifying old applicant we only need to update their record in the applicant file. For a qualifying new applicant we need to create a new applicant record in the applicant file. We do not create applicant records for non qualifying new applicants. For all applicants who qualify we also type new loan papers. Then we create a record describing that loan on the pending loan file.

(a) List the basic conditions used in the specifications.
(b) list the basic actions used in the specifications.
(c) Draw an appropriate complete limited entry decision table (like Example 2a). Fill in the condition stub, the condition entries, the action stub, and the action entries.
(d) Try to simplify your table. If it cannot be simplified then say why it cannot be simplified. If it can be simplified, use don't care (-) condition entries to represent simplifications.

12.3   Extended Entry Decision Tables

Another way in which decision tables can be made easier to use is to allow more than two condition alternatives (true or false). Sometimes we want to represent conditions that naturally divide things in more than two ways; e.g. $X < 0$, $X = 0$, or $X > 0$ or record status code = "FR," "SO," "JR," or "SR." When the condition entries are other than "T" or "F" they are called *extended condition entries*. The number of different possible cases associated with a condition is called its *modulus*. When the modulus of a condition is greater than two it is sometimes easier to indicate the condition status in the condition entry itself, as in the following condition stub.

                                                              Modulus

X value	>0	>0	=0	=0	<0	<0	3
X an integer	T	F	T	F	T	F	2

With n conditions, each true or false (modulus 2), the number of columns (rules) needed for a complete decision table is 2 to the nth power. More generally, the number of columns needed for a complete decision table is the product of the moduli of the conditions. In the example above the number of columns needed was 3 times 2, i.e. 6.

Exercise 5. Determine the number of Rules (columns) needed for a complete decision table for processing records where the transaction type can be "add," "change," or "delete," and the transaction code can be "FR," "SO," "JR," "SR," or "SP." Assume that each combination of transaction type and code requires different processing. What are the moduli of the two conditions?

Decision tables are also sometimes written with extended action entries which describe what to do rather than just using "X" and "" (or "Y" and "N"). For example, the last four columns of the bottom part of Example 2a could be rewritten:

	R1..R4	R5	R6	R7	R8
Condition stub	...	Condition	Entries	Condition	Entries
Print bill type	...	None	None	Polite	Nasty
Print ad type	...	Both	Flyer	Both	None

Exercise 6. Take your result from Exercise 2 and rewrite it with extended action entries as above.

Exercise 7a. Construct a pair of decision tables for calculating insurance origination fees according to the following specifications. Make your tables compact by using "don't care" condition entries, extended condition entries, and extended action entries as appropriate. Have one table for each kind of insurance.

At one time the consumer loan laws of one state allowed lenders to charge insurance origination fees for the life insurance and for the accident and health insurance they could offer borrowers. Borrowers are not required to buy either kind of insurance. For each of the two kinds of insurance the origination fee is: $0 if the amount of indebtedness is less than $250, $1 if the amount is between $250 and $500, and $2 if the amount is greater than $500. Borrowers occasionally renew their loans, i.e. borrow more before the original loan is completely repaid. In that case they can again choose none, one, or both kinds of insurance and another loan origination fee can be charged for each kind of insurance except that no more than two origination fees for each type of insurance can be charged in any one year period. Your decision tables should assign the appropriate fee for each of the two kinds of insurance, i.e. your action entries should specify what insurance origination fee to assign under various circumstances for each of the two kinds of insurance.

Exercise 7b. What is the advantage of doing two separate tables over one combined table? Hint: How big would a combined table be?

Exercise 8. Construct a decision table to express the following specifications. Make your tables compact by using "don't care" condition entries, extended condition entries, and extended action entries as appropriate. The subroutine is to update a single master inventory file record using a single transaction record from a transaction file. The subroutine is inside a loop which goes through both files, but this part only deals with a single record from each file. Transactions are of type "Add," "Change," or "Delete." If the transaction type is "Add" and master.key is not equal transaction. key then a new master record is added to the master file. If the transaction type is "Add" and master.key = transaction.key then an error message is printed and no other action is taken. If the transaction type is "Change" or "Delete" and master.key = transaction.key then the master record is changed or deleted, but if the two keys are not equal then an error message is printed and no other action is taken.

12.4 Decision Tables and Other Control Structures

As was mentioned earlier, if a rule in a decision table calls for more than one action then by convention the actions are to be executed in order from top to bottom. If some other order is intended this can be indicated by numbering the entries in the action entry part of the table.

Various exit actions can be included among the action entries of a decision table. Among them are "call," "return," "go to," "repeat," and "stop." "Call" is used to cause a temporary exit to another decision table (or other kind of program specification) with the assumption that the called decision table will end with a "return." "Return" is implicitly the last action of every rule, unless some other exit action is explicitly given. "Goto" (followed by a table name) is sometimes used, but is not consistent with fashionably structured programming. It should be avoided unless you have a very good reason to use it. "Repeat" indicates that the whole table is to be executed again, from the top. It allows decision tables to represent loops. Finally, "stop" indicates execution is to cease at that point.

Example 3. This example shows a decision table representing a loop. The specifications it is supposed to represent are to be implemented in a subroutine that begins by opening a file and assigning the variable "Answer" the value "none". Then it repeats the following actions until Answer = "Y" or there are no more records to read.

	R1	R2	R3	R4
File closed	T	F	F	F
More records	–	F	T	T
Answer = "Y"	–	–	T	F
Open file	Y	N	N	N
Answer ← "none"	Y	N	N	N
Read next record	N	N	N	Y
Get value for answer	N	N	N	Y
Repeat	Y	N	N	Y
Return	N	Y	Y	N

Rule 1 represents the fact that at the beginning of the subroutine the file is supposed to be closed and the first thing to be done is to open the file and initialize "Answer" to "none". Notice that if the file is closed then we don't care about the other conditions. Rule 2 is used in case the file is open and there are no more records to read. In this case we do not care what the value of Answer is, we just want to return to the calling program. If the file is open and there are more records to read and Answer is not already assigned "Y" then R4 describes the repeating loop body actions, i.e. a record is read, a new value of Answer is obtained, and the table is repeated. Note that it is the table that is repeated, not just the loop body. When Answer = "Y" Rule 3 is executed to cause return to the calling program. Below is some pseudocode which might represent this table.

```
If (file is closed) then
        open file
        Answer ← "none"
else
        while (there are more records and not Answer = "Y") do
                read next record
                get value for Answer
        endwhile
endif
return
```

Exercise 9. Make a decision table for the following specifications. The subroutine is to delete a record from a sequential access file. It is to do this by opening the master file, creating a new master file, and copying records from the master file to the new master file until it has read the record to be deleted. It does not copy that record to the new master file. Then it copies the remaining records from the master file to the new master file, closes both files, and returns to the calling program. It is assumed that each record has a KEY field and that the subroutine is given the key value of the record to be deleted.

12.5 Consistency, Completeness, and Redundancy of Decision Tables

When decision tables are used to express program specifications they can help detect defects such as functional incompleteness, inconsistency, and redundancy in those specifications. This is especially true if the original specifications are verbal or are written in English. Unfortunately, if decision tables are used incorrectly they can introduce those same defects. In any case decision tables should always be checked for completeness, consistency, and redundancy as described below.

A decision table is complete just in case it has a rule for each possible combination of condition values for its conditions. A complete decision table tells what to do in every possible circumstance. It should be noted, however, that "Do nothing" is a perfectly acceptable action, since in many cases a given part of a program is not supposed to do anything. Of course, doing nothing must be distinguished from forgetting to specify an action for a particular set of conditions. In practice you may have to ask the specifier about particular situations where an explicit specification is missing.

Two rules in a decision table are inconsistent iff they have the same condition values and different actions. Inconsistent rules tell you to do different things under the same circumstances. If any pair of rules in a decision table is inconsistent then the whole table is also said to be inconsistent. Note that carefully constructed decision tables would not be inconsistent because by definition they have only one rule for each combination of conditions. In practice, however, inconsistencies can creep in when specifications get complicated or people get confused.

A rule in a decision table is said to be redundant iff it has the same condition values and specifies the same actions as some other rule in the table. It is especially easy to introduce redundancy or even inconsistency by using "don't care" condition values too freely while simplifying decision tables.

Exercise 10. Imagine that you have been given the following English description of a subroutine that is to implement the RECCHECK problem specifications given below. Each execution of the routine is to check data from one student record. Input for RECCHECK is a single student record with many fields. Among those fields are the TIME field, the CODE field, and the AGE field. The initial output specifications described below.

If the TIME field is "day" and the AGE field has a value less than 24 then if the CODE field is "trad" then the subroutine should return "OK." Under these same conditions if the CODE field is not "trad" then the subroutine should return "NG." If the time field is not "day" then the subroutine should return "NG" unless the AGE field has a value greater than or equal to 24, in which case it should return "OK."

(a) Make a limited entry decision table from the specifications above. "Limited entry" means you use Ts and Fs as the only condition entries and Ys and Ns as the only action entries. The fact that this is a subroutine means that the last action for each rule should be to return to the calling program. For this exercise, explicitly express the return action, e.g. RETURN ("OK").

(b) Use your decision table to determine what action is specified for a record with TIME = "night," AGE = 17, and CODE = "trad."

(c) For what combinations of conditions does your decision table specify no action, i.e. for what conditions are these specifications incomplete?

(d) In attempting to improve the specifications for RECCHECK you ask the specifier for additional information. The specifier gives you the following additional specifications.

Additional specifications for RECCHECK:

1. If AGE is less than 24 and TIME is not "day" and CODE is not "trad" then the subroutine should return "OK."

2. If CODE is "trad" and AGE is less than 24 and TIME is "day" then return "OK."
3. If TIME is not "day" and CODE is "trad" and AGE is not less than 24 then return "OK."

For each of the three new specifications determine whether it is redundant, inconsistent with the original specifications, or is a nonredundant addition to those specifications. In each case explain your answer.

Chapter 13
Quantified Forms

This chapter extends the concepts of Chap. 11 to include quantifiers and variables. After studying this material you should be able to:

1. Describe how truth functional logic differs from quantificational logic.
2. Describe and use well formed forms (wffs).
3. Describe and give examples of interpretations for wffs.
4. Describe the conditions under which wffs are true or false for a given interpretation.
5. Describe the conditions under which wffs are said to be logically true, logically contingent, or logically false.
6. Use knowledge of the logical status of wffs to determine the logical status of statements expressed in ordinary English.

Outline

13.1 How Truth Functional Logic Differs from Quantificational Logic

The part of logic described in this chapter is called quantificational logic or predicate logic. It is the core of modern logic. When the term "logic" is used, without qualification, quantificational logic is usually what is meant. Consequently, properties

R. Lover, *Elementary Logic: For Software Development*,
DOI: 10.2007/978-1-84800-082-7, © Springer 2008

and relations you might expect to be called "quantificational" are usually just called "logical." For example, quantificational truth, quantificational consistency, etc. are called logical truth, logical consistency and so on.

Truth tables can be used to determine whether a tff is TF-true, TF-false, or TF-contingent. The procedure of making a truth table, if properly done, is guaranteed to come to an end after a finite number of steps and is guaranteed to determine which category a statement belongs to. Unfortunately there is no such step by step "decision procedure" for classification of forms involving quantifiers.

13.2   Well Formed Forms

Definition 1. A *predicate letter* is any uppercase letter, with or without subscripts, used as part of a form as defined below, e.g. P, P_0, P_1,... An *identifier letter* is any lower case letter near the beginning of the alphabet, with or without subscripts, used as part of a form as defined below, e.g. a, a_0, a_1, ... A *logical variable* is any lower case letter near the end of the alphabet, with or without subscripts, used as part of a form as defined below, e.g. w, w_0, w_1,...

Predicate letters are the formal counterparts of predicates in English. Identifier letters are the formal counterparts of names and definite descriptions. Logical variables are formal place holders.

Definition 2. A predicate letter followed by zero identifier letters is called a *statement letter*. A predicate letter followed by one or more identifier letters, e.g. Pa, Pab, Q_7cac, ...is called an *atomic predicate form*. If an atomic predicate form has N identifier letters then in that context the predicate letter is said to be an *N-place predicate letter*.

Atomic predicate forms are just like the atomic forms of Chapter 11 except that capital letters followed by zero identifier letters are now called statement letters.

Definition 3. A *universal quantifier* is the symbol ∀ followed by a logical variable. An *existential quantifier* is the symbol ∃ followed by a logical variable, e.g. ∀x, ∀y, $∀z_3$,... ∃x, ∃y, $∃z_3$, ...

Well formed forms, defined below, are intended to represent the logical forms of statements which may involve quantifiers. The expressions called "well formed forms" here are traditionally called "well formed formulas."

Definition 4. F is a well formed form (wff) if and only if

1. F is a statement letter,
2. F is an atomic predicate form,
3. F is of the form (~G) and G is a wff,
4. F is of the form (G ∧ H) and both G and H are wffs,
5. F is of the form (G ∨ H) and both G and H are wffs,

6. F is of the form (G → H) and both G and H are wffs,
7. F if of the form (G ↔ H) and both G and H are wffs, or
8. F is the result of modifying a wff, H, by

    (a) replacing all instances of an identifier letter in H, by a variable, v, not already in H,

    (b) prefixing the resulting expression by ∀v or ∃v, and

    (c) except when H is an atomic predicate form, enclosing the expression to the right of the quantifier in parentheses.

9. Finally, in case clause 8 is used to construct F, the part of F to the right of the quantifier is called the *scope of the quantifier* and each instance of v in it is said to be *quantified* and to be *bound by* that quantifier.

Wffs are not logical English. They are not abbreviations for statements, rather, they are placeholders for statements. They represent logical forms of statements stripped of all meaning. For example, "∀xPxa" represents the logical form of statements such as "All things are taller than John." and "∀xPxx" represents the logical form of statements such as "Everything is equal to itself."

Example 1. Every statement letter and every atomic predicate form is a wff. Below are some more wffs.

(a) ∀xPxa   Pxa is the scope of ∀x and the x in Pxa is bound by ∀x.

(b) ∀xPxx   Pxx is the scope of ∀x and both instances of x are bound by ∀x.

(c) ∃zQzza   Qzza is the scope of ∃z and both instances of z are bound by ∃z.

(d) ∀xPx ∨ ∃xPx   The scope of ∀x is the first Px and its x is bound by ∀x. The scope of ∃x is the second Px and its x is bound by ∃x.

(e) ∀x(Px ∧ ∃yPy)   The scope of ∀x is (Px ∧ ∃yPy). The scope of ∃y is Py. The x in Px is bound by ∀x and the y in Py is bound by ∃y.

(f) S → ∀x(∃yRxy)   The scope of ∀x is (∃yRxy). The scope of ∃y is Rxy. In Rxy, x is bound by ∀x and y is bound by ∃y.

(g) ∀z(Pz → Rzb ∨ Q)   The scope of ∀z is (Pz → Rzb ∨ Q). Both instances of z are bound by ∀z.

(h) ∀x(Px ↔ ∃yQxy)   The scope of ∀x is (Px ↔ ∃yQxy) and both instances of x are bound by ∀x. The scope of ∃y is Qxy and the instance of y is bound by ∃y.

Example 2. On the other hand, the following are not wffs.

(a) Pa→   because → requires a wff on each side.

(b) ∀x(Px → ∃xPx)   because x is quantified in (P(x) → ∃xP(x)), so ∀x cannot be prefixed to it.

(c) ∀x(∃xPx)   because x is already quantified in ∃xPx.

(d) ∃yPx   because y could not have been the result of substituting y for an identifier letter in P....

Exercise 1. Identify the scope of each quantifier and tell which instances of which variables are bound by what quantifiers.

(a) $\forall xPx \land \exists yPy$
(b) $S \rightarrow \forall x \exists yRxy$
(c) $\forall z(Pz \rightarrow Rzb)$
(d) $\forall x(Px \leftrightarrow \exists yQxy)$
(e) $\forall x(Pxy \leftrightarrow \exists y(Qxy \lor Rx))$
(f) $Pb \rightarrow \exists x \forall y(Qxyx \lor \forall zQzyx)$

13.3   Interpretations of Wffs

Here the concept of an interpretation is extended from interpretations for truth functional forms to interpretations for wffs. This is done by defining an interpretation of F to consist of a set, D, called the domain of the interpretation and a valuation function, V. V associates an element of D with each identifier letter of F and V associates an N-place relation on D for each N-place predicate letter of F. Different interpretations of a wff provide a basis for finding examples of meaningful statements that have the logical form represented by the wff.

Definition 5. If F is a wff then the set of statement letters, identifier letters and predicate letters in F is called the *vocabulary of F.*

Definition 6. An interpretation, I, of a wff, F, is a pair <D, V> where D is a non-empty set and V is a function whose domain is the vocabulary of F and where:

1. If L is a statement letter in F then V(L) = T or V(L) = F,
2. If b is an identifier letter of F then V(b) ∈ D, and
3. If P is an N-place predicate letter of F then V(P) is a set of N-tuples of elements of D, i.e. an N-place relation on D.

   Notice that V is not defined for the variables of a wff. In extensions of interpretations, as defined later, V is extended so it is defined for variables also.
   If b is an identifier letter in the vocabulary of F then equations such as "V(b) = 22" will often be written "b is interpreted as 22" or "b is assigned to 22." And if P is a predicate letter in the vocabulary of F then equations such as "V(P) = {x | x a prime number}" will often be written "P is interpreted as the property of being a prime number" or "P is assigned to the property of being a prime number."

Example 3. Suppose F is the wff "$\forall x(Gxb \rightarrow \sim Gbx)$." Then b is the only identifier letter of F, G is its only predicate letter, and {b, G} is the vocabulary of F. A few interpretations of F are described below.

(a) One interpretation of F is <D, V> where
    D = {1, 2, 3}, V(b) = 2, and V(G) = {<1, 2>, <2, 3>}.

(b) Another interpretation of F is <D, V> where
D = {Mercury, Venus, Earth}, V(b) = Mercury, and D(G) = {<Earth, Mercury>, <Mercury, Venus>, <Venus, Earth>}.

(c) Another interpretation of F is <D, V> where
D = the set of all rational numbers, V(b) = 3/5, and V(G) = the less than relation on rational numbers.

(d) Another interpretation of F is <D, V> where
D = the set of all programming languages, V(b) = Ruby, and V(G) = the IsOlderThan relation on programming languages.

In general, the domain of an interpretation can be any nonempty set, the values associated with the identifier letters can be any elements of that set, and the relations associated with N-place predicates can be any set of N-tuples of elements of the domain.

Example 4. Suppose F is the wff "P ∧ ∃yBay ∨ Rabc." Then P is a statement letter of F, a, b, and c are the identifier letters, B is a two-place predicate letter, R is a three-place predicate letter, and {P, a, b, c, B, R} is the vocabulary of F.

(a) One interpretation of F is
D = the set of all positive integers, V(a) = 2, V(b) = 3, V(c) = 5, V(P) = T, V(B) = the LessThan relation on D, and V(R) = the IsTheSumOf relation on D, i.e. Rabc if an only if a is the sum of b and c.

(b) Another interpretation of F is
D = The set of cities in the United States, V(a) = Chicago, V(b) = Kalamazoo, V(c) = Detroit, V(P) = F, V(B) = the WestOf relation on D, and V(R) = the IsBetween relation on D, i.e. Rabc if and only if a is between b and c.

Recall that the number of interpretations of a truth functional form composed of N atomic forms is 2^N. With well formed forms, however, because the number of sets is infinite, the number of interpretations of any wff is infinite. This is one of the reasons that quantificational logic is harder than truth functional logic.

13.4 Truth of Wffs in an Interpretation

Definition 7. Let I = <D, V> be an interpretation of a wff F and v be a variable in F. Then *an extension of I to v*, denoted I_v = <D, V_v>, is an interpretation identical to I except that $V_v = V \cup \{<v, d>\}$ for some element d of D.

Note that extending I to I_v amounts to treating the variable v as if it were an identifier letter with interpretation d. Consequently we can write "In I_v v is interpreted as d."

Example 5. Let F be (Pa ∨ Qa) ∧ ∀xRx ∧ ∃yBcy. Then a and c are the identifier letters of F and B, P, Q, and R are the predicate letters of F. One interpretation, I, of F is described below.

D = {Jack, Jill, Dick, Jane}
V(a) = Jane
V(c) = Jill
V(B) = {<Jack, Jill>, <Jill, Dick>}
V(P) = {Jill, Dick}
V(Q) = {Jack, Jill, Jane}
V(R) = {Jack, Jill}

Since there are four elements of D there are four ways to extend I to x. One extension of I to x would result from extending V to V_x so that $V_x(x)$ = Jack. Another extension of I to x would result from extending V so that $V_x(x)$ = Jill. A third extension would make $V_x(x)$ = Dick, and the fourth would make $V_x(x)$ = Jane.

Each of these extensions could be extended to y. One extension of I_x to y would result from extending V_x to V_{xy} so that $V_{xy}(x)$ = Jack and $V_{xy}(y)$ = Jack. Another extension of I_x to y would result from extending V_x to V_{xy} so that $V_{xy}(x)$ = Jack and $V_{xy}(y)$ = Jill.

All together there are four different ways to extend I to x and for each of these there are four different ways to extend I_x to y. Hence there are 16 different ways to extend I to x and y, one for each different way of assigning an element of D to x and a (not necessarily different) element of D to y.

An interpretation of a wff represents one way to give meaning to it. A wff is said to be true in an interpretation if it is true when its vocabulary is understood to have the meanings given them by I.

Definition 8. A wff, F, is true in an interpretation, I = <D, V>, of F if and only if

1. F is a statement letter and V(F) = T,
2. F is an atomic predicate form, $Pi_1i_2.i_N$, and $<V(i_1), V(i_2), ... V(i_N)>$ is an element of the N place relation on D that I associates with P,
3. F is of the form (~G) and G is false in I,
4. F is of the form (G ∧ H) and both G and H are true in I,
5. F is of the form (G ∨ H) and G is true in I or H is true in I,
6. F is of the form (G → H) and G is false in I or H is true in I,
7. F is of the form (G ↔ H) and G and H have the same truth value in I,
8. F is of the form ∃vH(v) and H(v) is true in some extension of I to v, or
9. F is of the form ∀vH(v) where H(v) is true in every extension of I to v.
10. Finally, *F is false in I* if and only if it is not true in I.

When clause 8 or clause 9 if this definition is applied, the variable v is said to be *instantiated* in the corresponding extended interpretation. The instantiated variable, v, functions like an identifier letter in H(v). The extended interpretation, I_v, functions exactly like an ordinary interpretation of H(v).

Each time a clause of Definition 8 is applied, the forms that result are simpler, either by involving one less truth functional connective or by involving one less quantifier. However, repeated application of Definition 8 will require considering more and more forms and more and more extended interpretations.

Example 6. Using the interpretation, I, described in Example 5 above and applying Definition 8 we have that (with parentheses restored)

$$F = ((Pa \lor Qa) \land \forall xRx) \land \exists yBcy.$$

(a) In order for F to be true in I both $((Pa \lor Qa) \land \forall xRx)$ and $\exists yBcy$ must be true in I.
(b) In order for $(Pa \lor Qa) \land \forall xRx$ to be true in I, both $(Pa \lor Qa)$ and $\forall xRx$ must be true in I.
(c) In order for $Pa \lor Qa$ to be true in I, either Pa or Qa must be true in I.
(d) But Pa is false in I because V(a) = Jane, V(P) = {Jack, Jill}, and hence Jane is not an element of V(P).
(e) On the other hand, Qa is true in I since V(a) = Jane, V(Q) = {Jack, Jill Jane}, and therefore Jane is an element of V(Q).
(f) So $Pa \lor Qa$ is true in I.
(g) On the other hand, $\forall xRx$ is false in I because if V is extended so $V_x(x) = $ Dick we have an extension I_x of I to x in which $V_x(x) \sim\in V_x(R)$.
(h) Hence the original wff, F, is false in I
(i) For the sake of completeness, note that $\exists yBcy$ is true in I. This is because V(c) = Jack and <Jack, Jill> $\in$ V(B). So if I is extended so that y is interpreted as Jill, then we have an extension of I to I_y in which <Jack, $V_y(y)> \in$ V(B), i.e. in which Bcy is true.

Notice that once you have an interpretation for a set, F, of wffs, you also have an interpretation for any other wffs whose vocabulary is included in the vocabulary of F. For example, $\exists xRx$ is true in I because there is an extension of I to x in which Rx is true, e.g. any extension in which V(x) = Jack or V(x) = Jill.

Exercise 2. Using the interpretation described in Example 5, determine the truth value of each of the following wffs in I. Explain your reasoning.

(a) $Pc \rightarrow Qc$
(b) $\forall xBcx$
(c) $\exists x\forall yBxy$
(d) $\exists x\exists yBxy$

13.5 Logical Truth of Wffs

Definition 9. A *wff is logically true*, abbreviated *L-true*, just in case it is true in all of its interpretations. A *wff is logically false*, abbreviated *L-false*, just in case it is false in all of its interpretations. A *wff is logically contingent*, abbreviated *L-contingent*, just in case it is not logically true and not logically false, i.e. it is true in some of its interpretations and false in others.

The idea behind this definition is that a wff is logically true just in case it is true no matter how it is interpreted. A wff is logically false just in case it is false no matter how it is interpreted.

Example 7. L-true wffs

(a) All TF-true tffs
(b) $\forall x(Px \vee \sim Px)$
(c) $\forall xPx \leftrightarrow \forall yPy$
(d) $\forall x(Px \leftrightarrow Qx) \leftrightarrow \forall x(Qx \leftrightarrow Px)$
(e) $\forall x(Px \wedge Qx) \rightarrow \forall xPx$
(f) $\forall x(Px \leftrightarrow \sim\sim Px)$
(g) $\forall x\forall y((Pxy \vee Qxy) \leftrightarrow (Qxy \vee Pxy))$
(h) $Pa \rightarrow \exists xPx$
(i) $\exists x(Px \wedge Qx) \rightarrow \exists yPy$
(j) $\forall x((Px \rightarrow Qx) \wedge Pa) \rightarrow Qa$

Example 8. L-false wffs

(a) All TF-false tffs
(b) $\exists x(Px \wedge \sim Px)$
(c) $\exists x(Px \leftrightarrow \sim Px)$
(d) $\forall x(Px \rightarrow Qx) \wedge \exists x(Px \wedge \sim Qx)$
(e) $\exists xPx \wedge \forall y \sim Py$
(f) $\exists x\exists yPxy \wedge \forall x\forall y \sim Pxy$

Example 9. L-contingent wffs

(a) All statement letters
(b) All atomic predicate forms
(c) $\forall xPx$
(d) $\exists xPx$
(e) $\forall xEy(Pxy \wedge Pyx)$
(f) $\forall x(Px \rightarrow Qx)$

To show that a wff is not L-true it is sufficient to find a single interpretation in which it is false. This is called finding a *counterexample* to the claim that the wff is L-true. To show that a wff is not L-false it is sufficient to find a single interpretation in which it is true. This is called finding a counterexample to the claim that the wff is L-false. To show that a wff is L-contingent it is sufficient to show that it is not L-true and not L-false, i.e. it is sufficient to find an interpretation in which it is false and another interpretation in which it is true.

Example 10. In Example 7b it is claimed that $\forall x(Px \vee \sim Px)$ is L-true, i.e. that it is true in all its interpretations. To see why this is so let $I = <D, V>$ be any interpretation of F and let I_x be any extension of I to x. Suppose x is interpreted as d in I_x. Then either d $\in V_x(P)$ or d $\sim\in V_x(P)$. Hence Px is true or Px is false in I_x. If Px is true then so is Px $\vee \sim Px$. While if Px is false then $\sim Px$ is true, so again Px $\vee \sim Px$ is true. Since the choice of I and I_x were completely general, $\forall x(Px \vee \sim Px)$ is true in all of its interpretations.

Example 11. In Example 8b it is claimed that ∃x(Px ∧ ~Px) is L-false, i.e. that ∃x(Px ∧ ~Px) is false in all of its interpretations. Suppose, to the contrary, that there were some interpretation, I, in which ∃x(Px ∧ ~Px) were true. Then there would have to be an extension I_x of I and an element d of D in which Px ∧ ~Px was true with x interpreted as d. Since if Px ∧ ~Px were true in I_x, both Px and ~Px would have to be true in I_x. If ~Px were true in I_x, Px would be false in I_x. But then Px would be both true and false in I_x. This is not possible. Hence the supposition that there is an interpretation in which ∃x(Px ∧ ~Px) is true must itself be false. Hence there is no interpretation in which ∃x(Px ∧ ~Px) is true. Hence ∃x(Px ∧ ~Px) is false in every one of its interpretations.

Example 12. In Example 9c it is claimed that ∀xPx is L-contingent, i.e. that it has interpretations in which it is true and other interpretations in which it is false. To do this we must show that there is at least one interpretation of ∀xPx in which it is true and there is at least one interpretation in which it is false. To show ∀xPx is true in some of its interpretations, let I be an interpretation of ∀xPx where D = the set of all integers and P is interpreted as the property of being an integer. Clearly ∀xPx is true in I. To show ∀xPx is false in some of its interpretations let I be an interpretation in which P is interpreted as the property of being an elephant and let D include something which is not an elephant, e.g. Leo the lion. Then ∀xPx is false in I. Hence ∀xPx is L-contingent.

Exercise 3. Show that each of the following wffs are L-true

(a) ~∀xPx → ∃x~Px, i.e. if it is not the case that everything has property P then there is something which does not have property P.
(b) ~∃xPx → ∀x~Px, i.e. if it is not the case that something has property P then everything lacks the property P.
(c) Pa → ∃xPx, i.e if a has property P then something has property P.
(d) ∀xPx → Pa, i.e. if everything has property P then a (whatever it is) has property P.

Exercise 4. Show that each of the following wffs are L-false.

(a) ∀x(Px ↔ ~Px), i.e. everything has property P if and only if it does not have property P.
(b) ∀x(Px → Qx) ∧ ∃x(Px ∧ ~Qx), i.e. if anything has property P then it has property Q and also there is something that has property P but does not have property Q.
(c) ∃xPx ∧ ∀y~Py, i.e. there is something with property P and everything is such that it does not have property P.
(d) ∃x∃yRxy ∧ ∀x∀y~Rxy, i.e. there is an ordered pair of things such that they bear the relation R to each other, in that order, and also for any ordered pairs of things, those things do not bear the relation R to each other in that order.

Exercise 5. For each of the following L-contingent wffs, try to find an interpretation in which it is true and an interpretation in which it is false.

(a) ∀xPx, i.e. everything has property P.
(b) ∃xPx, I.e. something has property P.
(c) ∀xEy(Pxy ∧ Pyx), i.e. for everything there is a second thing such that they bear the relation P to each other in that order and also in the reverse order.
(d) ∃x∀y(Pxy → Qyx), i.e. there is some one thing such that it bears the relation P to it and everything bears the relation Q to it.

13.6 Using Wffs to Determine the Logical Status of English Statements

In this chapter the terms used to describe the logical status of statements have been distinct from the terms used to describe wffs, as is shown in the table below:

Statements	Wffs
True	True in I
False	False in I
Necessarily true	Logically true, L-true
Necessarily false, impossible	Logically false, L-false
Contingent	Logically contingent, L-contingent

However, in many discussions of logic these distinctions are ignored or made using slightly different terms. For example, statements are often said to be logically true, logically false, logically contingent, and so on. Moreover, wffs are often said to be necessarily true, necessarily false, and so on.

The following is a generalization of the procedure TFL described earlier for trying to determine whether an English language statement, S, is necessarily true, necessarily false, or contingent.

Procedure QL. Let S represent a statement in English.

1. Express the logical form of S as a wff, F, of quantificational logic
2. Try to determine whether F is L-true, L-false, or L-contingent by
   1. Determining whether it is of a form known to be L-true, L-false, or L-contingent.
   2. Doing a truth table to see whether it is TF-true, TF-false, or TF-contingent (thereby adding to your stock of known forms),
   3. Reasoning involving interpretations for quantificational wffs as discussed in this chapter,
   4. Reasoning involving logical equivalence (see Chapter 14), or
   5. Reasoning using logical implication (see Chapter 15).
3. If step 2 succeeds then apply the following rules:

1. If F is L-true then S is necessarily true.
2. If F is L-false then S is necessarily false (impossible).
3. If F is L-contingent S is contingent.
4. If step 2 fails then the procedure fails.

Example 13. If S is "Everything is purple or not purple" then S is necessarily true. In case this was not obvious the procedure could be applied thus.

1. One way to express the logical form of S is $\forall x(Px \lor \sim Px)$.
2. $\forall x(Px \lor \sim Px)$ is in the list of L-true wffs.
3. Hence S is necessarily true by step 3.1 of the procedure.

Example 14. If S is "All people are mortal and some are not mortal" then S is necessarily false.

1. One way to express the logical form of S is $\forall x(Px \to Qx) \land \exists x(Px \land \sim Qx)$
2. $\forall x(Px \to Qx) \land \exists x(Px \land \sim Qx)$ is in the list of L-false wffs
3. Hence S is necessarily false by step 3.2 of the procedure

Exercise 6. Apply Procedure QL to each of the following statements. Hint: you can use the lists of L-true, L-false, and L-contingent wffs given in Examples 6–8. Explain your reasoning.

(a) All programs have bugs.
(b) There is something which is green and not green.
(c) If all men are mortal and Socrates in a man then Socrates is mortal.
(d) File7 is open and File7 is not open.

13.7   Conditions Revisited

Definition 10. An *open well formed form (open wff)* is the expression that results from replacing one or more instances of an identifier letter in a wff or open wff with a variable not already in the wff or open wff. In contexts where both open and ordinary wffs are discussed, an ordinary wff is often said to be a *closed wff*.

Despite its wording, Definition 10 is not circular. To get an open wff you start with an ordinary (closed) wff and replace one or more instances of an identifier letter with a variable not already in it. Then you get another open wff by replacing one or more instances of an identifier letter in the newly constructed open wff with a variable not already in the previously opened wff. This process can be repeated until you run out of identifier letters in the increasingly more open wffs.
Notice that open wffs are not built up from simpler forms the way ordinary wffs are, so, for example, just because F is an open wff and G is an open wff it does not follow that $F \lor G$ is an open wff. Open wffs are obtained only by modifying wffs in the way described in the definition above.

Definition 11. Variables not bound by any quantifier in an open wff are said to be *free variables* in that open wff.

Open well formed forms are intended to represent the logical forms of conditions which may involve quantifiers.

Example 16. Some open wffs

(a) ∀xPxy   Pxy is the scope of ∀x and the x in Pxy is bound by ∀x, but y is free.

(b) ∀xPxy ∨ ExPxa The scope of ∀x is the first Px and its x is bound by ∀x, but y is free. The scope of ∃x is the second Px and its x is bound by ∃x.

(c) ∀x(Pxz ∧ EyPzy) The scope of ∀x is (Pxz ∧ EyPzy). The scope of ∃y is Pyz. The x in Px is bound by ∀x and the y in Py is bound by ∃y, but both instances of z are Free.

(d) Sz → Rxyz   All three variables are free.

On the other hand, ∀x(Px ∧ Qx) is not an open wff because x is bound by ∀x so it cannot also be free.

There are two different ways of describing how truth and falsehood in an interpretation apply to open wffs. One is to say that open wffs have no truth value with respect to an interpretation. Consider the open formula Rxg in an interpretation where R is interpreted as the taller than relation, g is interpreted as a name for a particular person, George, and x is an uninterpreted (or uninstantiated) variable. It seems reasonable to say that Rxg is neither true nor false in this situation.

But what about Rxg ∨ ~Rxg and Rxg ∧ ~Rxg? There is some temptation to declare that Rxg ∨ ~Rxg is true and that Rxg ∧ ~Rxg is false no matter how x might be interpreted. This attitude leads to an alternative way of treating truth for open wffs. This treatment defines an open wff to be true in an interpretation just in case its universal closure is true in that interpretation, where the universal closure of an open wff is the result of prefixing it with a universal quantifier for each its free variables. e.g. the universal closure of Rxy is ∀x∀yRxy. Moreover, an open wff is said to be false in an interpretation just in case its existential closure is false in that interpretation, where the existential closure of an open wff is the result of prefixing it with an existential quantifier for each of its free variables, e.g. the existential closure of Rxy is ∃x∃yRxy. Finally, an open wff has no truth value in an interpretation just in case it is neither true nor false in that interpretation. Such an open wff could be said to be contingent in that interpretation. For example, Rxg would have no truth value (or be contingent) in any interpretation in which George was not the tallest nor the shortest thing in the domain of the interpretation. But Rxg ∨ ~Rxg would be true and Rxg ∧ ~Rxg would be false in any interpretation of R and g. Fortunately, it turns out that the difference between these two ways of treating truth for open statements is not important for what follows, so it will be left as an open issue here.

13.8 Summary of Classifications

The large number of definitions in this chapter may have left the reader a bit confused. The diagrams below may help clarify things a bit. They summarize the relations among the terms defined earlier.

closed wffs classifications		
truth functional	Examples	quantificational
TF-true	P ∨ ~ P	L-true
	⋯⋯⋯⋯⋯⋯⋯⋯⋯⋯⋯⋯	
	∀xQx ∨ ∃x~Qx	
	⋯⋯⋯⋯⋯⋯⋯⋯⋯⋯⋯⋯	L-contingent
TF-contingent	P	
	⋯⋯⋯⋯⋯⋯⋯⋯⋯⋯⋯⋯	
	∀xQx ∧ ∃x~Qx	L-false
	⋯⋯⋯⋯⋯⋯⋯⋯⋯⋯⋯⋯	
TF-false	P ∧ ~ P	

open wffs (conditions) classifications

In a specific interpretation, I = <D, V>, an open wff may be:

True of all things in I
True of some things in I and false of some things in I
False of all things in I

Whether open formulas should be said to have a truth value in I was left as an open question.

In general open wffs may be:	Examples
True of all things in all interpretations	Px ∨ ~Px
True of some things in some interpretations and false of some things in some interpretations	Px
False of all things in all interpretations	Px ∧ ~Px

Chapter 14
Logical Equivalence

Logical equivalence is important because logically equivalent statements, conditions, or instructions generally accomplish the same thing. As a result, it is often possible to substitute a simpler, faster running, or more easily understood expression for an equivalent but more complex, slower running, or harder to understand expression. On the other hand, knowing that two things are not logically equivalent strongly suggests that one cannot be substituted for the other. After studying this chapter you should be able to:

1. Use previously established logically equivalent forms to determine that two statements are logically equivalent.
2. Use truth tables to determine that two statements are logically equivalent.
3. Use arguments involving interpretations of wffs to determine that two statements are logically equivalent.
4. Recognize various logically inequivalent statement forms.
5. Use logical equivalence to simplify statements and conditions.
6. Use logical equivalence to determine whether a set of statements is redundant and whether one statement is redundant with respect to a set of statements.

Outline

R. Lover, *Elementary Logic: For Software Development*,
DOI: 10.2007/978-1-84800-082-7, © Springer 2008

14.1   Truth Functional Equivalence

Recall that two statements are materially equivalent just in case they have the same truth value. For example, it might be that today is Tuesday and that it is raining. In that case the statement "Today is Tuesday" and the statement "It is raining" are materially equivalent. But this equivalence is contingent. For example, if it is still raining tomorrow then the first statement will be false while the second is true, so tomorrow the two will not be materially equivalent.

On the other hand, logical equivalence of two statements requires that it be necessary that the two statements have the same truth value. For example, the statement "Today is Tuesday or it is raining" and the statement "It is raining or today is Tuesday" must necessarily have the same truth value in all circumstances, i.e. they are logically equivalent. More generally any two statements, one of the form "$P \vee Q$" and the other of the form "$Q \vee P$" are logically equivalent. As with logical truth, an analysis of logical forms and their interpretations will often help to determine logical equivalence in complex cases. Truth functional equivalence, defined below, is the easy case of logical equivalence.

Definition 1. Two tffs, F_1 and F_2, are *truth functionally equivalent*, abbreviated *TF-equivalent*, just in case $F_1 \leftrightarrow F_2$ is TF-true, i.e. $F_1 \leftrightarrow F_2$ has all Ts in its main column, i.e. $F_1 \leftrightarrow F_2$ is a tautology. The symbol $\equiv$ will be used here to represent truth functional equivalence. For example, $P \equiv Q$ will represent the claim that P is TF-equivalent to Q.

Example 1. Let P, Q, and R be any tffs and let T represent any TF-true tff and F represent any TF-false tff, then the following TF-equivalence claims are true.

(a) $P \wedge Q \equiv Q \wedge P$
(b) $P \vee Q \equiv Q \vee P$
(c) $(P \wedge Q) \wedge R \equiv P \wedge (Q \wedge R)$
(d) $(P \vee Q) \vee R \equiv P \vee (Q \vee R)$
(e) $P \wedge (Q \vee R) \equiv (P \wedge Q) \vee (P \wedge R)$
(f) $P \vee (Q \wedge R) \equiv (P \vee Q) \wedge (P \vee R)$
(g) $P \vee F \equiv P$
(h) $P \wedge T \equiv P$
(i) $P \vee {\sim}P \equiv T$
(j) $P \wedge {\sim}P \equiv F$

To show that F_1 and F_2 are not TF-equivalent it is only necessary to find a single row of the truth table for $F_1 \leftrightarrow F_2$ it which it is false.

Example 2. The pair of tffs in each row are not logically equivalent.

(a) P	~P
(b) P ∧ Q	P ∨ Q
(c) P → Q	Q → P
(d) ~(P ∨ Q)	~P ∨ ~Q

Exercise 1. Determine whether each pair of tffs below are TF-equivalent by using truth tables.

(a)	P	~~P
(b)	~P	~~~P
(c)	P ∧ Q	Q ∧ P
(d)	~(P ∨ Q)	~P ∧ ~Q
(e)	P ∨ Q	Q ∨ P
(f)	P ∨ (Q ∧ R)	(P ∨ Q) ∧ R
(g)	P ∧ (Q ∨ R)	(P ∧ Q) ∨ (P ∧ R)
(h)	P ∨ (Q ∧ R)	(P ∨ Q) ∧ (P ∨ R)
(i)	P ∨ Q	~(~P ∧ ~Q)
(j)	~(P ∧ Q)	~P ∧ ~Q
(k)	P ∨ ~Q	~(~P ∧ Q)
(l)	P ∧ Q ∨ ~P ∧ ~Q	P ↔ Q
(m)	~(P ↔ Q)	(P ∧ ~Q) ∨ (~P ∧ Q)

14.2 Applications of Truth Functional Equivalence

Recall that in algebra, one expression can be replaced by another provided the two expressions are algebraically equivalent, e.g. $a^2 + 2ab + b^2$ can be replaced by $(a + b)^2$ and if $a = 2x$ then $(a + b)^2 = (2x + b)^2$. Similarly, one statement can be replaced by another provided the two are logically equivalent. In particular, a simpler statement can replace a more complex statement provided the two are logically equivalent.

14.2.1 Equivalence and Simplification of Program Instructions

In programming language instructions a condition can be substituted for another which is TF-equivalent without changing the behavior of the program. For example, the following two instructions will result in the same program behavior, assuming that short cut evaluation is not used.

If not(X > 0 or Y < 0) then
      Print 'Hello'
Else
      Print 'Goodbye'
Endif

If not(X > 0) and not(Y < 0) then
      Print 'Hello'
Else
      Print 'Goodbye'
Endif

To see why this is so, let "P" represent "X > 0" and "Q" represent "Y < 0" Then examine the truth table for the equivalence $\sim(P \vee Q) \leftrightarrow \sim P \wedge \sim Q$ displayed below.

P	Q	$\sim(P \vee Q)$	$\leftrightarrow$	$\sim P \wedge \sim Q$
T	T	F	T	**T** F F F
T	F	F	T	**T** F F T
F	T	F	T	**T** T F F
F	F	T	F	**T** T T T

Here the fact that the equivalence is a tautology guarantees that there are no circumstances under which the two instructions could result in different behavior, no matter what values X and Y might have. Even short cut evaluation would not be a problem in this example, unless Y were undefined.

On the other hand, the following two instructions will not always result in the same behavior.

1. If X > 0 and (Y < X or Y < 0) then
      Print 'Hello'
  Else
      Print 'Goodbye'
  Endif

2. If (X > 0 and Y < X) or Y < 0 then
      Print 'Hello'
  Else
      Print 'Goodbye'
  Endif

To see why these instructions could result in different behaviors, examine the truth tables for the two conditions. In them "P" stands for "X > 0", "Q" stands for "Y < X", and "R" stands for "Y < 0."

P	Q	R	P and (Q or R)		(P and Q) or R	
T	T	T	**T**	**T**	**T**	**T**
T	T	F	**T**	**T**	**T**	**T**
T	F	T	**T**	**T**	**F**	**T**
T	F	F	**F**	**F**	**F**	**F**
F	T	T	**F**	**T**	**F**	**T**
F	T	F	**F**	**T**	**F**	**F**
F	F	T	**F**	**T**	**F**	**T**
F	F	F	**F**	**F**	**F**	**F**

In most cases the two statements are materially equivalent, i.e. they have the same truth value. In the two underlined cases they are not materially equivalent. The truth value assignments in those two cases describe the circumstances under which the two instructions would result in different behaviors. For example, if X and Y were both −7. In general, if X is not >0 and Y is <0 the two instructions will behave differently. Also notice that the truth value of "Y < X" makes no difference in these two cases. While this is a simple example, this kind of information can be invaluable when you are trying to read or debug a program.

Exercise 2. Use truth tables to determine which of the following pairs of programming language instructions are TF-equivalent. In case they are not, specify the conditions under which they will give rise to different behaviors. Assume that shortcut evaluation is not used.

(a) If x > 0 and (y < x or z < y) then Print 'Hello' Endif
    If (x > 0 and y < x) or z < y then Print 'Hello' Endif

(b) If not (x > 0 and not z < y) then Print 'Hello' Endif
    If z < y or not x > 0 then Print 'Hello' Endif

(c) If not (x > 0 and z < y) then Print 'Hello' Endif
    If not z < y or not x > 0 then Print 'Hello' Endif

(d) If (x > 0 or not y < x) and z < y then Print 'Hello' Endif
    If not z < y and (not y < x or x > 0) then Print 'Hello' Endif

(e) While (not(x > 0 and y < z))
        print (x, y)
        x ← x - y
    endwhile

    While (not y < z and x > 0)
        print (x, y)
        x ← x − y
    endwhile

(f) While (not(x > 0 and not y < z))

```
        print (x, y)
        x ← x − y
endwhile
```

```
While (x > 0 or not y < z))
        print (x, y)
        x ← x − y
endwhile
```

14.2.2   *Equivalence and Simplification of SQL Select Instructions*

If P and Q are TF-equivalent, then Q can be substituted for P in SQL SELECT instructions, assuming there are no null fields in the data table involved. For example, the following two SQL instructions give the same results because their WHERE conditions are TF-equivalent.

```
SELECT description, color, sell_price
FROM items
WHERE not (color = blue or on_hand < 100)
```

```
SELECT description, color, sell_price
FROM items
WHERE not (color = blue) and not (on_hand < 100)
```

To see that this is so, let P represent "color = blue" and Q represent "on_hand < 100", then the truth table for the equivalence is:

P	Q	$(\sim(P \vee Q)) \leftrightarrow (\sim P \wedge \sim Q)$					
T	T	F	T	**T**	F	F	F
T	F	F	T	**T**	F	F	T
F	T	F	T	**T**	T	F	F
F	F	T	F	**T**	T	T	T

The fact that the equivalence is a tautology shows that there are no circumstances under which the two SQL statements could generate different reports, no matter what data was in the table, as long as there were no null data values.

Exercise 3. Use truth tables to determine which of the following pairs of SQL instructions are TF-equivalent. In case they are not, specify the conditions under which they could give rise to different reports. Do not assume anything about what data is in the tables, but do assume that there are no nulls in the data tables.

(a) SELECT supplier, item_number
    FROM suppliers
    WHERE not (unit_price = 3.00 and qty100_price > 500.00)

    SELECT supplier, item_number

FROM suppliers
WHERE not (unit_price = 3.00) and not (qty100_price > 500.00)

(b) SELECT supplier, item_number
FROM suppliers
WHERE not (item_number = 11111 and not (qty100_price > 300.00))

SELECT supplier, item_number
FROM suppliers
WHERE qty100_price > 300.00 or not (item_number = 11111)

(c) SELECT item_number, sell_price
FROM items
WHERE color = 'blue' and on_hand < 100 or on_order = 0

SELECT item_number, sell_price
FROM items
WHERE (color = 'blue' or on_hand < 100) and (color = 'blue' or on_order = 0)

(d) SELECT description, color
FROM items
WHERE (on_hand < on_order or on_hand < 100) and sell_price < 9.00

SELECT description, color
FROM items
WHERE on_hand < on_order or (on_hand < 100 and sell_price < 9.00)

14.3 Logical Equivalence

14.3.1 Logical Equivalence of Wffs

Definition 2. Two wffs, F1 and F2, are logically equivalent, abbreviated *L-equivalent*, if and only if $F_1 \leftrightarrow F_2$ is logically true. This is equivalent to saying that two wffs are logically equivalent if and only if they have the same truth value in every interpretation of them. The symbol $\equiv$ will be extended here to represent logical equivalence as well as truth functional equivalence, so $F_1 \equiv F_2$ will represent the claim that F_1 is logically equivalent to F_2.

If two statements are TF-equivalent, then they are L-equivalent, so if $F_1 \leftrightarrow F_2$ is a tautology then $F_1 \equiv F_2$ in this extended sense of $\equiv$.

Example 3. Let P and Q be one-place predicate letters, R be a two-place predicate letter, and b be an identifier letter, then the following L-equivalences hold.

(a) $\forall xPx \equiv \forall yPy$
(b) $\forall xPx \equiv \sim\exists x{\sim}Px$
(c) $\exists xPx \equiv \sim\forall x{\sim}Px$
(d) $\forall x\forall yRxy \equiv \forall y\forall xRxy$

(e) $\exists x \forall y Rxy \equiv \exists y \forall x Ryx$
(f) $\forall x Px \rightarrow Q \equiv Q \lor \exists x{\sim}Px$
(g) $\forall x(Px \land Qx) \equiv \forall x Px \land \forall x Qx$
(h) $\exists x(Px \lor Qx) \equiv \exists x Px \lor \exists x Qx$
(i) ${\sim}(Px \land Qx) \equiv {\sim}Px \lor {\sim}Qx$
(j) $Px \rightarrow Qx \equiv {\sim}Qx \rightarrow {\sim}Px$
(j) ${\sim}\forall x(Px \rightarrow Qx) \equiv \exists x(Px \land {\sim}Qx)$
(k) $\forall x Px \rightarrow P \equiv P \lor {\sim}\forall x Px$
(l) $P \lor {\sim}\forall x Px \equiv P \lor \exists x{\sim}Px$
(m) $\forall x(Px \land Qx) \equiv \forall x Px \land \forall x Qx$
(n) $\exists x(Px \lor Qx) \equiv \exists x Px \lor \exists x Qx$

Example 4. The pair of wffs in each row are not logically equivalent.

(a) $\forall x(Px \lor Qx)$ $\forall x Px \lor \forall x Qx$
(b) $\forall x \exists y Qxy$ $\exists y \forall x Qxy$
(c) $\exists x(Px \land Qx)$ $\exists x Px \land \exists x Qx$
(d) $\forall x(Px \rightarrow Qx)$ $\forall x Px \rightarrow \forall x Qx$

14.3.2 Logical Equivalence of Conditions

Two conditions can be accidentally (contingently) equivalent in the sense of being true of exactly the same things, e.g. the condition "x is a student in my class who is taller than 7 feet" and the condition "x is a student in my class who is on our basketball team" might accidentally be true, but there is no necessary connection between them

On the other hand, the condition "x is tall and x is green" is necessarily true of exactly the same things as is the condition "x is green and x is tall."

Definition 3. Two open wffs (conditions), $C_1 v_1 v_2 \ldots v_n$ *and* $C_2 v_1 v_2 \ldots v_n$ *with free variables* $v_1 v_2 \ldots v_n$, *are logically equivalent if and only if they are true and false of the same n-tuples of things in all their interpretations. They are logically inequivalent if and only if there is some interpretation in which there is at least one n-tuple of things for which they have different truth values.*

Definition 4. If $C_1 v_1 v_2 \ldots v_n$ *is any condition with free variables* $v_1 v_2 \ldots v_n$ *then* $\forall v \forall v2 \ldots \forall v_n C_1 v_1 v_2 \ldots v_n$ *is called the* universal closure *of* $C_1 v_1 v_2 \ldots v_n$.

Definition 2 above is equivalent to saying that two conditions with the same free variables are logically equivalent just in case their universal closures are logically equivalent in the sense of Definition 1 above.

Example 5. The following pairs of conditions are logically equivalent.

(a) Px ∨ Qx   Qx ∨ Px
(b) ∀xRxy   ~∃x~Rxy
(c) ~∀zQxyz   ∃z~Qxyz
(d) ∀x(Rxy → Qxy)   ∀x(~Qxy ∨ Rxy)
(e) ~(Px ∧ Qx)   ~Px ∨ ~Qx
(f) Px → Qx   ~Qx → ~Px

Exercise 4. Explain why the following logical equivalence claims are true.

(a) ∀xPx ≡ ∀yPy
(b) ∀xPx ≡ ~∃x~Px
(c) ∃xPx ≡ ~∀x~Px
(d) ∀x∀yPxy ≡ ∀y∀xPxy

Exercise 5. For each of the pairs of wffs below, find an interpretation in which one of them is true and the other is false. Hint for item c the fact that every pen in my desk has either red ink or black ink is not the same as every pen in my desk having red ink or every pen in my desk having black ink.

(a) P   ~P
(b) P ∧ Q   P ∨ Q
(c) ∀x(Px ∨ Qx)   ∀xPx ∨ ∀xQx
(d) ∃x(Px ∧ Qx)   ∃xPx ∧ ∃xQx
(e) ∀x∃yQxy   ∃y∀xQxy
(f) ∀x∃yQxy   ∀x∃yQyx

The following procedure, while not guaranteed to determine logical equivalence in every case, will work in most simple cases.

Procedure LEQ. Let S_1 and S_2 be two statements.

1. Represent the logical form of S_1 by the wff F_1 and the logical form of S_2 by the wff F_2.
2. Try to determine whether F_1 and F_2 are logically equivalent by:
   1. Showing that F_1 and F_2 are instances of known equivalent forms,
   2. Using truth tables to show that they are truth functionally equivalent, or
   3. Reasoning about quantifiers, variables, and interpretations.
3. Interpret the results of your effort.
   1. If F_1 and F_2 are logically equivalent then S_1 and S_2 are logically (necessarily) equivalent.
   2. Otherwise, the test fails and no definite conclusion can be drawn.

Obviously if the wffs representing the logical forms of S_1 and S_2 are instances of forms already known to be logically equivalent then S_1 and S_2 are logically equiva-lent. For example, suppose S_1 is "If every record in this file was processed yesterday then today is Friday" and S_2 is "Today is Friday or there is a record in this file that was not processed yesterday." The logical forms of S_1 and S_2 can be expressed as $\forall xPx \rightarrow Q$ and $Q \vee \exists x\sim Px$ respectively. Since this is (an instance of) logical equivalence f in Example 3 above, S_1 and S_2 are logically equivalent by clause 2.1 of Procedure LEQ.

Even when quantifiers are present, it is often possible to show that two statements are logically equivalent by using truth tables, without having to deal with quantifiers. For example, suppose S_1 is "If every record in the payroll file was processed yesterday and today is Friday then we will be paid today." and S_2 is "Either not every record in the payroll file was processed or today is not Friday or we will be paid today." One way to express the logical forms of S_1 is to represent it by the wff, $P \wedge Q \rightarrow R$, not bothering to represent the quantificational structure of S_1. In the same spirit, the logical structure of S_2 can be represented by $\sim P \vee \sim Q \vee R$. The truth table for these two wffs is given below.

P	Q	R	$P \wedge Q \rightarrow R$		$(\sim P \vee \sim Q) \vee R$	
T	T	T	T	**T**	F	**T**
T	T	F	T	**F**	F	**F**
T	F	T	F	**T**	T	**T**
T	F	F	F	**T**	T	**T**
F	T	T	F	**T**	T	**T**
F	T	F	F	**T**	T	**T**
F	F	T	F	**T**	T	**T**
F	F	F	F	**T**	T	**T**

Since the final column of each truth table is the same, the two wffs are truth functionally equivalent. Hence S_1 and S_2 are logically equivalent by clause LEQ 2.2.

When recognizing instances of previously established logically equivalent forms and doing truth tables both fail, it may be useful to reason about quantificational structure. Consider, Example 2b, the pair of wffs $\forall xPx$ and $\sim \exists x\sim Px$. To show that they are logically equivalent it is sufficient to show that in all their interpretations if one of them is true then the other is true and if one of them is false then the other is false. Let I be any interpretation and suppose that $\forall xPx$ is true in I. By definition this means that Px is true of everything in the domain of I, i.e. that Px is true in every extension I_x of I to x. Therefore, it is not the case that there is something in the domain of I of which Px is false. And this implies that $\exists x\sim Px$ is false in I, hence $\sim \exists x\sim Px$ is true in I. On the other hand, suppose $\forall xPx$ is false in I. This means that it is not the case that Px is true of everything in the domain of I. Hence, there is something in the domain of I of which Px is false. Hence $\exists x\sim Px$ is true in I. Hence $\sim \exists x\sim Px$ is false in I. Hence the two wffs are logically equivalent.

14.4 Applications of Logical Equivalence

14.4.1 Simplification of Problem Specifications

Definition 5. If S is a finite set of statements or wffs, the notation ($\wedge$S) will be use to denote the conjunction of the elements of S.

Example 5. If S = {P $\vee$ Q, ~Q, R $\rightarrow$ $\forall$xHx) then ($\wedge$S) = (P $\vee$ Q) $\wedge$ (~Q) $\wedge$ (R $\rightarrow$ $\forall$xHx).

Using this notation makes it easy to describe extensions of various logical terms originally defined on individual statements or wffs to finite sets of statements or wffs. Here are some examples.

Definition 6. A finite set, S, of wffs is L-true, L-false, or L-contingent just in case ($\wedge$S) is L-true, L-false, or L-contingent. Two sets of wffs, S_1 and S_2, are L-equivalent just in case ($\wedge S_1$) and ($\wedge S_2$) are L-equivalent.

Since problem specifications are sets of statements or conditions, to show that two problem specifications, S_1 and S_2, are L-equivalent, it is sufficient to show that ($\wedge S_1$) $\equiv$ ($\wedge S_2$).

14.4.2 Detecting Redundancy

Definition 7. A wff R is logically redundant relative to a collection of wffs S just in case ($\wedge$S) is logically equivalent to ($\wedge$(S $\cup$ {R})). This amounts to saying that adding R to S would not change the conditions under which ($\wedge$S) would be true.

For example, let S = {(P $\vee$ Q), (~(P $\wedge$ Q))} and let R be P$\rightarrow$Q. Then R is not logically redundant relative to S, as is shown by the middle part of the truth tables below.

				not redundant	redundant
P Q	(P $\vee$ Q)$\wedge$~(P $\wedge$ Q) = ($\wedge$S)	($\wedge$S)$\wedge$(P $\rightarrow$ Q)	($\wedge$S)$\wedge$~(P $\leftrightarrow$ Q)
T T	T FF T	F F T	F FF T
T F	T TT F	T F F	T TT F
F T	T TT F	T T T	T TT F
F F	F FT F	F F T	F FF T

On the other hand, "~(P$\leftrightarrow$Q)" is redundant relative to S, as is shown by the right-most part of the truth tables above.

Exercise 6. Determine whether the statement on the right is logically redundant relative to the set of statements on the left.

	Set of statements	Statement
(a)	{P}	$Q \vee (\sim Q)$
(b)	{P $\wedge$ ($\sim$P)}	Q
(c)	{P $\vee$ Q, Q $\vee$ R, $\sim$Q}	R $\wedge$ P
(d)	{P $\rightarrow$ Q, Q $\vee$ R, $\sim$P}	$\sim$Q

Sometimes a set all by itself is said to be redundant, rather than saying that a statement is redundant relative to a set. Specifically, a finite set of statements, S, is said to be logically redundant if and only if there is a proper subset, B, of S such that ($\wedge$S) is logically equivalent to ($\wedge$B). Another way to say this is to say that S is L-redundant if and only if one or more of its statements could be removed without changing the truth table of its conjunction, i.e. if and only if one of its statements is L-redundant relative to the rest of it.

For example, the truth tables above show that S itself is not logically redundant, because if either component of S is removed, S becomes the set consisting of just the other component, and neither component has a truth table equivalent to ($\wedge$S). On the other hand, the fact that $\sim$(P$\leftrightarrow$Q) is TF-redundant relative {(P $\vee$ Q), ($\sim$(P $\wedge$ Q))} implies that {(P $\vee$ Q), ($\sim$(P $\wedge$ Q)),$\sim$(P$\leftrightarrow$Q)} is redundant.

Exercise 7. Determine which of the following sets of statements are L-redundant and which are not. Note that showing that a set of statements is not L-redundant requires separately investigating what happens when each element of S is removed, e.g. by removing each component of the original set S in turn and, for each of them, comparing the truth table for ($\wedge$S) with the truth table for ($\wedge$S) with that element of S removed. You might also find some shortcut in particular cases.

(a) {P, $\sim$P, $\sim\sim$P}
(b) {P$\wedge$Q, (P$\wedge$Q}
(c) {P$\wedge$Q, P, Q}
(d) {P$\vee$Q, Q$\vee$R, P$\vee$R}

Chapter 15
Logical Implication and Validity

Recall that logic is about general criteria and methods of correct reasoning expressed in arguments. When used to analyze arguments that have already been constructed, logic is being used critically. When used to create new arguments logic is being used constructively. The next chapter describes some methods for using logic constructively. This chapter describes some methods for using logic critically. After studying it you should be able to:

1. Explain what it means for an argument to be valid.
2. Describe the relations among true premises, true conclusions, validity, and soundness. Give examples of arguments having various logical characteristics and explain why certain combinations of those characteristics are impossible.
3. Explain the difference between formal and informal methods of showing validity.
4. Use informal methods to determine whether simple arguments are valid or invalid and explain your conclusions.
5. Use the truth table test to investigate the validity of arguments.
6. Use reasoning based on quantifiers and interpretations of wffs to investigate the validity of arguments.

Outline

R. Lover, *Elementary Logic: For Software Development*,
DOI: 10.2007/978-1-84800-082-7, © Springer 2008

15.1   Logical Implication and Validity

15.1.1   Logical Implication

Definition 1. A finite set of statements, P, logically implies a statement C just in case it is not possible for all the elements of P to be true and C false.

Another way to put this definition is that P logically implies C means that if all the statements in P were true then C would have to be true. It follows from this definition that to show that P does not logically imply C it is sufficient to find a single possible situation in which ($\land$P) would be true and C would be false. This definition also implies that if two statements are logically equivalent then each logically implies the other.

15.1.2   Logical Validity

When statements such as are mentioned in Definition 1 are presented as an argument then Definition 2 applies.

Definition 2. An argument with premises P and conclusion C is *valid* just in case ($\land$P) logically implies C.

An equivalent way to express Definition 2 is to say than an argument is valid just in case it is logically impossible for all of its premises to be true and its conclusion false. The general problem of determining whether an argument is valid is very hard. Fortunately, there are many useful easy cases.

Example 1. Compare the following arguments.

Premise	The program crashed.
Conclusion	There is a syntax error in the program.

Premise	The error was a syntax error or a run time error.
Premise	The error was not a syntax error.
Conclusion	The error was a run time error.

The first argument is not valid, because the premise could be true and the conclusion false. For example the program could be syntax error free and could have crashed because a file was missing from a storage device.

The second argument is valid, because the conclusion could not possibly be false if the premises were both true. Another way to say this is to say that the premises of the second argument logically imply its conclusion.

15.1.3   Soundness

Definition 3. An argument is *sound* just in case it is valid and all of its premises are true.

Sound arguments are the gold standard of reasoning because *the conclusion of a sound argument must be true!* Used critically, showing that an argument is sound (valid and that its premises are all true) allows us to conclude that its conclusion is true. Used constructively, sound reasoning helps people discover new truths by reasoning validly from true premises to new true conclusions.

Exercise 1. Suppose you could establish that an argument was valid but that its conclusion was false. What would that imply about its premises?

The terms "valid" and "sound" are often incorrectly applied to statements. Strictly speaking only arguments can be valid or invalid, sound or unsound. Similarly, "true" and "false" are sometimes incorrectly applied to arguments. Strictly speaking only statements (such as premises and conclusions) can be true or false.

Understanding the relations among validity and soundness of arguments as well as truth and falsity of their premises and conclusions is fundamental to being able to use logic. It is also difficult. The examples and exercises below are designed to make these relations a bit clearer.

Each row of the table below lists one combination of truth or falsity of premises and conclusions and validity and soundness of arguments. Some of these combinations are possible and some are not. The following examples discuss some rows of the table. Similar discussions of the other rows are left as exercises. For each row the problem is to determine whether there could be an argument with the combination of properties listed in that row. If there could be such an argument then give an example of one. If no such argument is possible then explain why.

Row	Premises	Conclusion	Validity	Soundness
1	All T	T	V	S
2	All T	T	V	U
3	All T	T	I	S
4	All T	T	I	U
5	All T	F	V	S
6	All T	F	V	U
7	All T	F	I	S
8	All T	F	I	U
9	Some T Some F	T	V	S
10	Some T Some F	T	V	U
11	Some T Some F	T'	I	S
12	Some T Some F	T	I	U
13	Some T Some F	F	V	S
14	Some T Some F	F	V	U
15	Some T Some F	F	I	S
16	Some T Some F	F	I	U
17	All F	T	V	S
18	All F	T	V	U
19	All F	T	I	S
20	All F	T	I	U

Row	Premises	Conclusion	Validity	Soundness
21	All F	F	V	S
22	All F	F	V	U
23	All F	F	I	S
24	All F	F	I	U

Example 2. Row 1: Could there be an argument with all true premises and a true conclusion which is valid and sound? Yes. These are the ideal kinds of arguments. The classic example is

> All men are mortal.
> Socrates is a man.
> Socrates is mortal.

All the premises are true and the conclusion is true. The argument is valid because, even without knowing that the premises are true, it is clear that if they were true then the conclusion would also have to be true, i.e. it is not possible for the premises to all be true while the conclusion is false. The argument is sound because it is valid and all its premises are true.

Example 3. Row 2: Could there be an argument with all true premises and a true conclusion which is valid but not sound? No. By definition if an argument is valid and all its premises are true then it is sound.

Example 4. Row 8: Could there be an argument with all true premises and a false conclusion which is invalid and unsound? Absolutely. Almost any argument in which the conclusion has nothing to do with the premises is an example. Here is one.

> All men are mortal.
> Socrates is a man.
> 5 < 3.

All the premises are true, the conclusion is false. The truth of the premises has nothing to do with the conclusion, so the argument is invalid. Since it is invalid it must also be unsound.

Example 5. Row 9: Could there be an argument with some true and some false premises and a false conclusion which is valid and sound? No. To be sound all its premises must be true.

Example 6. Row 10: Could there be an argument with some true and some false premises and a true conclusion which is valid and unsound? Yes. Here is an example.

> All horses are animals.
> All animals are mammals.
> All horses are mammals.

The first premise is true and the second is false. So it is not sound. The conclusion is true. Moreover, if both premises were true then the conclusion would have to be true.

Example 7. Row 22: Could there be an argument with all false premises and a false conclusion which is valid and unsound? Yes. Here is an example.

> All horses have wings.
> All things with wings can write computer programs.
> All horses can write computer programs.

Both premises and the conclusion are false and, hence, the argument is unsound. But it is valid. If the premises were true then the conclusion would also have to be true. The point is that validity cannot be determined by just knowing the truth or falsity of premises and conclusion. Validity depends upon the relation between the premises and the conclusion. Here is another example, where the truth values of the premises and conclusion are unknown.

> All galaxies more than one billion light years from Earth have black holes in their centers.
> The next galaxy we discover which is more than one billion light years from earth has a black hole in its center.

This argument is obviously valid, but its validity has nothing to do with the truth or falsity of its premise or conclusion, since we know it is valid but we do not know the truth values of its premise and conclusion.

Exercise 2. For each of the remaining rows of the table, do an analysis as was done in the examples above. This is not as laborious a task as it may seem. You can eliminate several rows at a time, for example an argument cannot be sound and invalid, so rows 3, 7, 11, 15, 19, and 23 can all be treated at once. The hard part will be coming up with example arguments for some of the rows that are possible.

15.2 Determining Validity

15.2.1 Degrees of Formality

The various ways of trying to determine whether an argument is valid differ in degree of formality.

Trying to establish by informal methods that a specific argument or argument form is valid consist of (1) including the definitions of the terms used in the argument as implicit premises, (2) ignoring the actual truth or falsity of the premises and conclusion, and (3) trying to establish that in all logically possible cases in which the premises would all be true, the conclusion would also have to be true. Hence the ability to think hypothetically about all logical possibilities is critical to determining validity. Establishing validity by informal means can range from being easy to being extremely difficult.

To establish that an argument or argument form is invalid by informal methods it is only necessary to find a logically possible example in which all the premises of the argument would be true while the conclusion was false. This usually involves using the definitions of terms and may involve appeal to the actual truth or falsity of premises and conclusions, since any actual situation is also a logically possible situation.

Analyzing individual arguments for validity by using informal methods is often much easier than using formal methods, and sometimes it is just the right thing to do. However, it can also be very time consuming and unreliable. Fortunately there are methods for determining the validity or invalidity of arguments by using the argument forms while de-emphasizing or ignoring the meanings of the terms used in the arguments. These formal methods are very powerful. They embody the parts of logic which are best understood.

However, there are important tradeoffs between informal and formal methods. While informal methods can be very powerful they tend to focus attention on the details of a specific problem while formal methods tend to lead to general conclusions about all arguments of a certain form. Formal methods are often more trouble to use than informal methods. However, properly applied, formal methods can reduce confusion and lead to correct results that are difficult to get informally. Moreover, the study of formal methods helps people use informal methods with fewer errors. Finally, purely formal methods can be automated while informal methods cannot, at least not now, be automated. The formal methods discussed here might be called partially formal since they involve informal reasoning used to discuss statement forms and argument forms. Formal reasoning will be discussed briefly in the next chapter.

15.2.2 Arguments and Corresponding Conditionals

Corresponding to every argument with premises $P_1 \ldots P_n$ and conclusion C there is a conditional statement of the form "If P_1 and $P_2 \ldots$ and P_n, then C." While closely related to each other, an argument and its corresponding conditional are not the same thing. An argument is a collection of two or more statements while the corresponding conditional is a single statement. An argument may be valid or invalid, sound or unsound, but it may not be true or false. The corresponding conditional may be true or false, but it may not be valid, invalid, sound, or unsound. The truth table test below exploits the close relation between an argument and its corresponding conditional.

Example 8. The statement

> If today is Friday then today is payday.

is a conditional statement. It is either true or false. It is not an argument. The corresponding argument is

> Since today is Friday, it must be that today is payday.

Because it is an argument it is either valid or invalid but it is neither true nor false. In the conditional statement "Today is Friday" is called the antecedent and in the argument it is called a premise. The statement "Today is payday." is called the consequent of the conditional statement and it is called the conclusion of the argument.

Example 9. If an argument has several premises then forming the corresponding conditional requires conjoining the premises with "and." For example, the following argument:

> It is raining or it is snowing.
> If it is raining then the sidewalk is wet.
> If it is snowing then the sidewalk is frozen.
> The sidewalk is wet or it is frozen.

has the following corresponding conditional:

> If ((It is raining or it is snowing) and (If it is raining then the sidewalk is wet) and (If it is snowing then the sidewalk is frozen)) then (The sidewalk is wet or it is frozen.)

Example 10. The logically relevant aspects of Example 9 can be more clearly expressed using wffs. Let R represent "It is raining," S represent "It is snowing," W represent "The sidewalk is wet," and F represent "The sidewalk is frozen." Then, using logical notation for connectives, the argument of Example 9 is represented by

$$R \vee S$$
$$R \rightarrow W$$
$$S \rightarrow F$$
$$\overline{W \vee F}$$

The corresponding conditional is

$$((R \vee S) \wedge (R \rightarrow W) \wedge (S \rightarrow F)) \rightarrow (W \vee F)$$

Exercise 3. Write the conditional corresponding to the following argument, as was done in the Example 9.

> For every number there is a number such that their sum = 0.
> 3 is a number.
> There is a number such that it plus 3 = 0.

Exercise 4. Use predicate letters, variables, quantifiers, symbols for connectives to represent the argument of Exercise 3 and the corresponding conditional, as was done in Example 10.

15.2.3 *Truth Functional Validity*

Definition 4. If an argument can be shown to be valid using truth functional considerations alone, then it is said to be *truth functionally valid*.

15.2.3.1 Informal Methods

Example 11. Recall some of the examples discussed in Chap. 4.

(a) Today is Monday
   Tomorrow must be Friday.

Clearly invalid. Any Monday not followed by a Friday is a counterexample. Since all Mondays are like that, there are lots of counterexamples.

(b) The sky is dark and it is raining just west of here.
   It will probably rain here soon,

This is an inductive argument, as indicated by the word "probably" in the conclusion. So its validity is not relevant. As an inductive argument, if rainy weather around "here" generally travels from West to East and this is all the information available about this specific situation then this is a fairly good inductive argument.

(c) $A = 3, B = 5$
   Therefore $A + B = 8$.

If the definition of integer addition is allowed as an implicit premise then this is a valid argument.

(d) This is a compound argument.

   Since the file is sorted.
   It must be in ascending or descending order.

Valid, given the definition of "sorted" as an implicit premise.

   It must be in ascending or descending order.
   It is not in ascending order.
   Hence it is in descending order.

Also valid since it is not possible for there to be only two possibilities and have one eliminated, without the other possibility being the case.

(e) I have tested this program with hundreds of test cases.
   It worked correctly in each case.
   This program is correct.

Not valid. Anyone who has done much program testing will tell you that it is possible to test a program thousands of times and still have undetected errors. Even the weaker conclusion "Hence this program is probably correct" would not make this a good inductive argument.

(f) The program used to work perfectly.
   Then you modified it.
   Now it doesn't work perfectly.
   You ought to work on it some more.

Clearly invalid. Perhaps you ought not to be allowed near it ever again or perhaps someone else also worked on it and they introduced the problem.

(g) FCOUNT must be = 0 or > 0 at line 20.
   If FCOUNT > 0 at line 20 then FILE5 will be opened or else a file-not-found message will be sent just in case the trace flag is set.
   The trace flag cannot be set if FCOUNT = 0 at line 20.
   If FCOUNT = 0 at line 20 and FILE5 is not opened and a file-not-found message is not sent then the trace flag is not set.

Valid. Note that the third premise guarantees that if FCOUNT = 0 at line 20 then the trace flag cannot be set. The conclusion includes the condition that FCOUNT = 0 at line 20. That alone implies that the trace flag is not set.

While most of these examples are easy, Example 2g is difficult enough that it takes some careful reasoning to see that it is valid. When arguments are sufficiently complex, informal methods often fail. In those cases, formal methods can help.

Exercise 5. Use informal methods. If the argument is valid, explain why. If it is invalid, give a counterexample.

(a) Today is Monday
   Tomorrow must be Tuesday.

(b) The error is in subroutine X or subroutine Y.
   If the error were in subroutine Y then someone would probably have reported a problem with subroutine Y.
   No one has reported a problem with subroutine Y.
   The problem must be in subroutine X.

(c) The rest of the program works perfectly.
   If there is a problem with the program it must be in the new procedure.

(d) If today is Friday then today is payday. Moreover, today is Friday.
   Hence, today is pay day.

(e) If x were 5 at line 2,020 then the program would have crashed.
   It did crash.
   So probably x was 5 at line 2,020.

(f) If he is telling the truth then I am a monkey's uncle.

(g) If the program was run yesterday then a run log entry for it would have been made.
   No run log entry for it was made.
   Moreover, if the program was not run yesterday then the records in it are not current.
   Hence the records in it are not current.

(h) If a run log entry for it was made then the program ran yesterday.
   No run log entry for it was made.
   Moreover, if the program was not run yesterday then the records in it are not current.
   Hence the records in it are not current.

15.2.3.2   More Formal Methods

The Truth Table Test Applied to an Individual Argument

To perform this test you first find the conditional statement that corresponds to the argument. Then you do a truth table for that conditional statement and then apply the following rules. Unless the argument is very short, it usually helps to abbreviate the argument using logical English. Here are the details.

The Truth Table Test for Validity of an Individual Argument:

1. Determine the logical structure of the corresponding conditional, perhaps expressing it in logical English.
2. Do the truth table for the corresponding conditional.
3. Draw the appropriate conclusion:
   (a) f the conditional is a truth functional tautology then the argument is valid.
   (b) If the conditional is a truth functional contradiction then the argument is invalid.
   (c) If the conditional is truth functionally contingent then the truth table test fails and the argument might be valid or it might be invalid, depending on details that are not adequately dealt with by the truth table test.

For example, to test the argument 'Since it is raining, it follows that it is raining or it is snowing.' you would construct the conditional statement "If it is raining then it is raining or it is snowing" and then do the following truth table, using R to abbreviate "It is raining." and S to abbreviate 'It is snowing'.

R	S	If R then (R or S)	
T	T	T	T
T	F	T	T
F	T	T	T
F	F	T	F

Since the truth table for the conditional has all Ts in its final column the conditional is a tautology and the corresponding argument is truth functionally valid by clause 3.1 of the test.

Exercise 6. This exercise is about the following argument.

If subroutine A had been executed then X would have been zero at line 500. If X had been zero at line 500 then subroutine B would not have been executed. But subroutine B was executed. Hence, subroutine A was not executed.

(a) List the premises and conclusion of this argument.
(b) Using A to represent the claim that subroutine A was executed, X to represent the claim that X is zero at line 500, B to represent the claim that subroutine B was executed, and using symbols for connectives, express the form of the argument.
(c) Do the truth table test for validity of the argument. What can you conclude about it from the test?

The Truth Table Test Applied to an Argument Form

Two statements have the same (sentential) form iff the part of their structures that can be represented with truth functional connectives and punctuation is the same. For example, statements that do not have any truth functional connectives, such as "Today is Monday.," "This program has bugs in it.", and "All the records in this file have been processed." all have the same sentential form. Such statements are often called truth functionally atomic statements because they cannot be broken into simpler statements. Similarly, "Today is Tuesday and tomorrow is Friday" has the same sentential form as "This program has bugs in it and tomorrow is Monday." Their common form is that of two statements separated by "and." This is often represented by saying they have the form "S ∧ T." Individual statements that share the same form are said to be instances of that form.

Two arguments are said to have the same (sentential) form just in case their premises and conclusions can be matched one to one so that corresponding premises and conclusions have the same sentential form. Individual arguments that share the same argument form are said to be instances of that argument form.

The Truth Table Test for Validity of Argument Forms:

1. Express the form of the corresponding conditional as a wff.
2. Do the truth table for the conditional wff.
3. Draw the appropriate conclusion
   (a) If the conditional form corresponding to an argument form is a truth functional tautology than every argument of that form is valid.
   (b) If the conditional form corresponding to an argument form is a truth functional contradiction then every argument of that form is invalid.
   (c) If the conditional form corresponding to an argument form is truth functionally contingent then the test fails and some of the arguments of that form are valid while others are invalid.

For example, all arguments of the following form are valid.

P, If P then Q
$\overline{\qquad Q \qquad}$

The truth table of the corresponding conditional is

P	Q	$(P \land (P \to Q)) \to Q$		
T	T	T	T	T
T	F	F	F	T
F	T	F	T	T
F	F	F	T	T

Applying the truth table test shows that all arguments of the corresponding form are valid. For example

Today is Friday.
If today is Friday then today is payday.
Today is payday.

Another valid argument form is:

If P then Q, If Q then R
    If P then R

The truth table of the corresponding conditional is

P	Q	R	$((P \rightarrow Q) \land (Q \rightarrow R)) \rightarrow (P \rightarrow R)$				
T	T	T	T	T	T	T	T
T	T	F	T	F	F	T	F
T	F	T	F	F	T	T	T
T	F	F	F	F	T	T	F
F	T	T	T	T	T	T	T
F	T	F	T	F	F	T	T
F	F	T	T	T	T	T	T
F	F	F	T	T	T	T	T

Here again the truth table test shows that all arguments of the corresponding form are valid. For example

If today is Friday then today is payday.
If today is payday then I can pay bills tomorrow.
If today is Friday then I can pay bills tomorrow.

On the other hand, every argument of the form:

P or not P (which is always true)
P and not P (which is always false)

is invalid, although this is so bizarre a form of argument that this fact is not very useful. Just for the record, here is the truth table of the corresponding conditional.

P	$((P \lor \sim P) \rightarrow (P \land \sim P)$		
T	T	F	F
F	T	F	F

Applying the truth table test gives the result that all arguments of the corresponding form are invalid. For example,

$(3 \le 5) \lor \sim(3 \le 5)$
$(3 < 5) \land \sim(3 < 5)$

Finally, the truth table test fails on arguments of the form:

P, Q
 R

P	Q	R	$(P \land Q) \rightarrow R$	
T	T	T	T	T
T	T	F	T	F
T	F	T	F	T
T	F	F	F	T
F	T	T	F	T
F	T	F	F	T
F	F	T	F	T
F	F	F	F	T

The truth table test indicates that some arguments of this form are valid and some are not. For example the argument

> All records in this file have been processed.
> The Jones record is a record in this file.
> The Jones record has been processed.

is a valid argument of this form, while the argument

> All records in this file have been processed.
> The Jones record is a record in this file.
> The moon is made of green cheese.

is an invalid argument of this form.

Exercise 7. Apply the truth table test to each of the following argument forms.

(a) $\dfrac{\sim(P \wedge Q), R \leftrightarrow \sim P, P \rightarrow \sim R, Q}{P}$

(b) $\dfrac{\sim(\sim P \vee \sim Q), \sim P}{P \rightarrow Q}$

(c) $\dfrac{P \rightarrow \sim(Q \wedge R), \sim P \vee Q}{\sim R}$

(d) $\dfrac{\sim P \vee Q, \sim Q \vee R}{\sim R \rightarrow \sim P}$

(e) $\dfrac{\sim(P \vee Q), \sim(P \wedge \sim Q)}{P \leftrightarrow Q}$

(f) $\dfrac{P \vee \sim Q, Q \vee \sim R, \sim P \vee Q}{\sim Q}$

15.2.4 *Logical Validity*

The truth table test fails when applied to many valid arguments.

For example, consider the following argument:

> All men are mortal. Socrates is a man.
> Socrates is mortal.

The truth table test applied to this argument works as follows. The truth functional form of the argument is

$$\frac{P, Q}{R}$$

and the corresponding conditional has the form $P \wedge Q \rightarrow R$. The truth table for this conditional has some Ts and some Fs in its final column, so the conditional is truth functionally contingent. Yet the original argument is clearly valid, as can be seen by reasoning about the quantificational structure of the argument.

Unfortunately, there is no decision procedure like the truth table test for arguments whose validity or invalidity depends upon predicates and quantifiers, although there are decision procedures for special cases such as arguments whose predicate symbols are all 1-place predicate symbols. As a result, luck, experience, and cleverness must be relied upon to determine logical validity in general.

Here is an example of an informal approach to showing validity or invalidity of an argument. Here is a specific, but invalid, argument.

> All martians can fly. Tweety can fly.
> Tweety is a martian.

To see that this is so, consider the following counterexample. Suppose it is true that all martians can fly. But Tweety, my pet parakeet, can fly even though it is not a martian. Hence we have an example in which the premises are all true but the conclusion is false. Hence the argument is not valid.

Exercise 8. Use an informal approach to showing the validity or invalidity of each of the following arguments.

(a) All birds are bipeds., Chalky is not a biped.
    Chalky is not a bird.

(b) All birds are bipeds., The current President is not a bird.
    The current President is not a biped.

(c) All birds are bipeds., Everything is a biped.
    Everything is a bird.

(d) All birds are bipeds., Everything is a bird.
    Everything is a biped.

(e) Tweety is a bird.
    Everything is a bird.

(f) Tweety is a bird.
    Something is a bird.

(g) Everything is a bird.
    My cat is a bird.

(h) Something is a bird.
    My cat is a bird.

Here is an example of a more formal approach to showing validity or invalidity. Here is a valid argument form.

> $\forall x(Hx \rightarrow Mx)$, Hs
> Ms

To see why this argument is valid, consider any interpretation, I, in which both premises are true. Then Hs is true in I. Moreover, $\forall$x(Hx $\rightarrow$ Mx) is true in I. Hence Hx $\rightarrow$ Mx is true of every element, d, of the domain of I. Since V(s) is an element of the domain of I, Hs $\rightarrow$ Ms is true in I. Hence it is not the case that Hs is true in I and Ms is false in I. Hence, if Hs is true in I then Ms is true in I. This same reasoning applies to any other interpretation of the conditional. Hence the corresponding argument is valid.

Notice that the same reasoning applies to any argument whose form can be represented by

$\forall$x(Hx $\rightarrow$ Mx), Hs
Ms

For example, let Hx be interpreted as "x is human," Mx as "x is mortal," and s be interpreted as a name for Socrates. Then the argument below is valid.

All humans are mortal. Socrates is a man.
Socrates is mortal.

Here is another example of the same form

All martians can fly. Xabfeeg is a martian.
Xabfeeg can fly.

Exercise 9. Determine which of the following argument forms are valid and which are not valid. If an argument form is valid explain why it is valid, i.e. explain why the corresponding conditional must be true in all of its interpretations. If it is invalid, give a counterexample, i.e. give an interpretation in which all the premises are true and the conclusion is false.

(a) $\forall$x(Px $\rightarrow$ Qx), ~Qa
~Pa

(b) $\forall$x(Px $\rightarrow$ Qx), ~Pa
~Qa

(c) $\forall$x(Px $\rightarrow$ Qx), $\forall$xQx
$\forall$xPx

(d) $\forall$x(Px $\rightarrow$ Qx), $\forall$xPx
$\forall$xQx

(e) Pa
$\forall$xPx

(f) Pa
$\exists$xPx

(g) $\forall$xPx
Pa

(h) $\exists$xPx
Pa

Chapter 16
Rules of Inference

The purpose of this Chapter is to describe rules of inference for truth functional reasoning. There are rules of inference for quantificational reasoning, but they are more complex and will not be discussed here. After studying this material you should be able to:

1. Describe two important limitations of truth table tests.
2. Explain what a rule of inference is and give examples.
3. Recognize important rules of inference by name.
4. Explain why rules of inference are useful.

Outline

16.1   Limitations of Truth Table Tests

Truth tables are extremely useful tools for some kinds of critical reasoning, e.g. for checking the validity of arguments, the consistency of sets of statements, and so on. But truth tables also have serious limitations. For example, as the number of statements being analyzed increases the resulting tables become very large very quickly. For example, to show that the argument

$$P \rightarrow Q, Q \rightarrow R, R \rightarrow S, S \rightarrow T, T \rightarrow U, \sim U$$
$$\overline{\sim P}$$

R. Lover, *Elementary Logic: For Software Development*,
DOI: 10.2007/978-1-84800-082-7, © Springer 2008

is valid by use of a truth table would require a table with sixty four rows. Using the rules of inference described below, five easy applications of the rule called *modus tollens* would do the job.

Another serious limitation of truth tables is that they are not of much use in constructive reasoning, i.e. if you want to create a new valid argument. On the other hand, rules of inference are designed for exactly that task. Consequently, they can be used to discover new (hidden) knowledge, as while solving puzzles, testing programs for correctness, or debugging programs.

16.2   Rules of Inference

16.2.1   Formal Rules of Inference

Definition 1. A *formal rule of inference* is a rule that describes the claim that a conclusion of a certain form may validly be inferred from a finite list of premises of certain forms. Such rules are often displayed in the following way:

$$\frac{P_1, P_2, ..., P_n}{C}$$ (list of premise forms separated by commas)

(conclusion form)

For example, the claim that from premises of the form P and $P \rightarrow Q$, the conclusion Q may validly be inferred would be displayed thusly.

$$\frac{P, P \rightarrow Q}{Q}$$

A specific instance of this rule of inference would be that from the premises "Today is Tuesday." and "If today is Tuesday then the payroll file should be backed up today. the conclusion "The payroll file should be backed up today." may be validly inferred.

16.2.2   Correct and Incorrect Rules of Inference

Definition 2. If the claim made by a rule of inference is true then the rule is said to be a *correct rule of inference*, otherwise it is said to be an *incorrect rule of inference*.

Any valid argument form can be redescribed as a rule of inference. Such rules are sometimes said to be valid rules of inference, although it is better to call them correct rules of inference. Correct rules of inference never lead you from true premises to false conclusions. That is why they are so useful. If you restrict your reasoning to such rules, then your reasoning will be correct, your arguments valid, and, if your premises are true, then your arguments will be sound and your conclusions will be true.

16.3   Some Truth Functional Rules of Inference

Truth functional rules of inference are rules of inference whose correctness can be established solely by analysis of the truth functional structure of the sentence forms involved. There are also rules of inference involving program instructions. Some of these rules will be discussed in Chap. 19

16.3.1   Examples of Correct Rules of Inference

There are many correct rules of inference and many ways to organize them. In the examples below, the rules on the left are called *introduction rules* because in each case a connective that was not in the premises is present (introduced) in the conclusion. Each rule has a name, for example, the rule on the left of the first row below is called ∧-introduction, the rules on the left of the second row are called ∨-introduction, and so on. The rules on the right are called *elimination rules* because in each case one or more connectives that were in the premises is not in the conclusion. The rules on the right of the first row are called ∧-elimination, the rule on the right of the second row is called ∨-elimination, and so on.

Introduction rules		*Elimination rules*	
$\dfrac{P,\ Q}{P \wedge Q}$	$\wedge$-intro.	$\dfrac{P \wedge Q}{P} \quad \dfrac{P \wedge Q}{Q}$	$\wedge$-elim.
$\dfrac{P}{P \vee Q} \quad \dfrac{P}{Q \vee P}$	$\vee$-intro.	$\dfrac{P \vee Q,\ P \rightarrow R,\ Q \rightarrow R}{R}$	$\vee$-elim.
$\dfrac{\dfrac{P}{Q \wedge \sim Q}}{\sim P}$	$\sim$-intro.	$\dfrac{\sim P}{Q \wedge \sim Q}$ $\dfrac{}{P}$	$\sim$-elim.
$\dfrac{\dfrac{P}{Q}}{P \rightarrow Q}$	$\rightarrow$-intro.	$\dfrac{P \rightarrow Q,\ P}{Q}$	$\rightarrow$-elim.
$\dfrac{P \rightarrow Q,\ Q \rightarrow P}{P \leftrightarrow Q}$	$\leftrightarrow$-intro.	$\dfrac{P \leftrightarrow Q}{P \rightarrow Q} \quad \dfrac{P \leftrightarrow Q}{Q \rightarrow P}$	$\leftrightarrow$-elim

Some other correct rules of inference along with commonly used names for them are described below.

$$\frac{P, P \to Q}{Q}$$ (*modus ponens* or affirming the antecedent)

$$\frac{P \to Q, \sim Q}{\sim P}$$ (*modus tollens* or denying the consequent)

$$\frac{P \to Q, Q \to R}{P \to R}$$ (hypothetical syllogism or chain argument)

$$\frac{P \lor Q, \sim P}{\sim Q}$$ (disjunctive syllogism)

$$\frac{P \to Q, R \to S, P \lor R}{Q \lor S}$$ (constructive dilemma)

$$\frac{P \to Q}{P \to (P \land Q)}$$ (absorption)

$$\frac{P \land Q}{P}$$ (simplification)

$$\frac{P \land Q}{Q \land P}$$ ($\land$ is commutative)

$$\frac{P \lor Q}{Q \lor P}$$ ($\lor$ is commutative)

$$\frac{P \leftrightarrow Q}{Q \leftrightarrow P}$$ ($\leftrightarrow$ is commutative)

$$\frac{P}{\sim\sim P} \qquad \frac{\sim\sim P}{P}$$ (double negation intro and elim.)

$$\frac{P \land (Q \lor R)}{(P \land Q) \lor (P \land R)}$$ ($\land$ distributes over $\lor$)

$$\frac{P \lor (Q \land R)}{(P \land Q) \lor (P \land R)}$$ ($\lor$ distributes over $\land$)

$$\frac{\sim (P \lor Q)}{P \land \sim Q} \qquad \frac{\sim P \land \sim Q}{\sim (P \lor Q)}$$

(DeMorgan's laws)

$$\frac{\sim (P \land Q)}{P \lor \sim Q} \qquad \frac{\sim P \lor \sim Q}{\sim (P \land Q)}$$

Example 1. Correct uses of rules of inference

valid inference   rule used

a. From $\underline{A \wedge (B \vee C)}$ $\wedge$-elimination
   infer $B \vee C$

b. From $\underline{(A \vee B) \rightarrow C, \sim C}$ modus tollens
   infer $\sim(A \vee B)$

c. From $\underline{\sim(A \vee B)}$ $\vee$-introduction
   infer $(\sim(A \vee B)) \vee E$

Note that Example 1b and 1c form a chain of valid argument forms. Taken together they show that the argument form

$$\frac{(A \vee B) \rightarrow C, \sim C}{(\sim (A \vee B)) \vee E}$$

is valid.

16.3.2 *Some Properties of Rules of Inference*

The general rule used above to obtain correct rules of inference is that an argument form is valid if and only if the corresponding rule of inference is correct. Some additional general principles about rules of inference are:

1. *The Order of Premises Rule*: The premises of a rule of inference can be written in any order without affecting the correctness of the rule. For example, the denying the consequent rule can be written either as

$$\frac{P \rightarrow Q, \sim Q}{\sim P} \quad \text{\textit{or as}} \quad \frac{\sim Q, P \rightarrow Q}{\sim P} \quad \text{(premises in either order)}$$

2. *The Repetition Rule*: Premises and previously derived conclusions can be repeated at any later stage of an argument. For example, recall the first argument of this chapter.

$$\frac{P \rightarrow Q, Q \rightarrow R, R \rightarrow S, S \rightarrow T, T \rightarrow U, \sim U}{\sim P}$$

A sequence of five uses of *modus tollens* and repetition will show that this argument is valid, without doing a 64 row truth table.

$\underline{P \rightarrow Q,\ Q \rightarrow R,\ R \rightarrow S,\ S \rightarrow T,\ T \rightarrow U,\ \sim U}$	
$\underline{P \rightarrow Q,\ Q \rightarrow R,\ R \rightarrow S,\ S \rightarrow T,\ \sim T}$	*modus tollens*, repetition
$\underline{P \rightarrow Q,\ Q \rightarrow R,\ R \rightarrow S,\ \sim S}$	*modus tollens*, repetition
$\underline{P \rightarrow Q,\ Q \rightarrow R,\ \sim R}$	*modus tollens*, repetition
$\underline{P \rightarrow Q,\ \sim Q}$	*modus tollens*, repetition
$\underline{\sim P}$	*modus tollens*, repetition

3. *The Premise Strengthening Rule*: If you have a correct rule of inference then you can add any additional premises (above the line) and the result will also be a correct rule. Another way to look at this is to say that if conclusion C follows validly from a set of premises, S, then C also follows from premises $S \cup \{P\}$ where P is any statement, i.e. the set of premises of a valid argument can be strengthened by adding more premises without affecting the validity of the argument.

4. *The Conclusion Weakening Rule*: If you have a correct rule of inference then you can add the disjunction of the conclusion with any statement P and the result will also be a correct rule. Another way to look at this is to say that if conclusion C follows validly from a set of premises, S, then $C \vee P$ also follows from premises S where P is any statement, i.e. the conclusion of a valid argument can be weakened by disjoining any statement to the conclusion without affecting the validity of the argument.

5. *The Tautology Rule*: Every tautology follows validly from the null (empty) set of premises. In diagram form this can be expressed by

$$\frac{}{\text{any tautology}} \text{ (tautology rule)}$$

6. *The equivalence substitution rules*: If two statements are truth functionally equivalent then (any instances of) one may be substituted for (any instances of) the other in any statement and the result will be truth functionally equivalent to the first. In diagrammatic form this could be expresses by

$$\frac{P \leftrightarrow Q}{S(P) \leftrightarrow S(Q)} \text{ (substitution rule 1, or just sub1)}$$

where S(P) is any statement and S(Q) is the result of substituting Q for one or more instances of P in S.

For example, recall that $(\sim(P \wedge Q)) \leftrightarrow ((\sim P) \vee (\sim Q))$. Consequently, by substitution of $(\sim(P \vee Q))$ for $((\sim P) \wedge (\sim Q))$ in $(R \wedge ((\sim P) \vee (\sim Q)))$ we know that $(R \wedge ((\sim P) \vee (\sim Q))) \leftrightarrow (R \wedge (\sim(P \wedge Q)))$.
This rule is often combined with the rule

$$\frac{P \leftrightarrow Q, Q}{P}$$

to get another substitution rule

$$\frac{P \leftrightarrow Q, S(P)}{S(Q)} \text{ (substitution rule 2, or just sub2)}$$

Continuing the example above, if we somehow knew that a statement $(R \wedge ((\sim P) \vee (\sim Q)))$ was true then since we also know that $(\sim(P \wedge Q)) \leftrightarrow ((\sim P) \vee (\sim Q))$ we could apply rule 2 to conclude that $(R \wedge (\sim(P \wedge Q)))$ was also true.

Whichever form of the substitution rule is used, it is important to be clear about what is being substituted for what in what statement. Note also that if S(P) has more than one instance of P in it, Q may be substituted for just some or all of them. For example both

$$\frac{R \leftrightarrow (\sim (\sim R), R \to (P \vee R)}{\sim (\sim R) \to (P \vee R)} \text{ (substituting } \sim(\sim R) \text{ for just one instance of R in}$$
$$R \to (P \vee R) \text{ using sub1)}$$

and

$$\frac{R \leftrightarrow (\sim (\sim R)), R \to (P \vee R)}{(\sim (\sim R) \to (P \vee \sim (\sim R))} \text{ (substituting } \sim(\sim R) \text{ for both instances of R in}$$
$$R \to (P \vee R) \text{ using sub2)}$$

Exercise 1. Identify one correct rule of inference that could be used to justify each of the following inferences. If no single correct rule can justify the inference, say so.

(a) If the file were sorted in ascending order the Adams record would be first. Moreover, the file is sorted in ascending order. Hence the Adams record is first.

(b) If the file were sorted in ascending order the Adams record would be first. Moreover, the Adams record is not first. Hence the file is not sorted in ascending order.

(c) Today is Tuesday and it is raining here now. Hence today is Tuesday.

(d) Today is Tuesday or it is raining here now. Today is not Tuesday. Therefore it is raining here now.

(e) If x = 5 then y = 7. Also, if a > 0 then b < 0. Moreover, x = 5 or a > 0. Consequently, y = 7 or b < 0.

(f) If x = 5 then y = 7. However, ~(y = 7). Hence, ~(x = 5).

(g) $\dfrac{(x = 3) \leftrightarrow (y < 0)}{(y < 0) \leftrightarrow (x = 3)}$

(h) ~(~(S ∧ T)). Hence S ∧ T.

(i) $\dfrac{S \to (T \vee Q)}{S \to (S \wedge (T \vee Q))}$

(j) $\dfrac{}{\sim (S \wedge (T \vee Q)) \vee \sim (\sim (S \wedge (T \vee Q))}$

(k) $\dfrac{S \leftrightarrow (R \wedge (\sim Q)), (R \wedge S) \leftrightarrow (T \vee S)}{(R \wedge S) \leftrightarrow (T \vee (R \wedge (\sim Q)))}$

Exercise 2. First translate the following chain argument into symbolic form. Then identify the rules of inference used in the argument. Clearly identify which premises and conclusions are used for each use of a rule of inference.

Argument: If the file is sorted then it is in ascending order or descending order. Moreover the file is sorted. Hence it is in ascending order or descending order. However, it is not in ascending order. Hence it must be in descending order.

Exercise 3. Given the following three premises, apply valid rules of inference to them to arrive at four conclusions that differ from the premises and from the example given below. For each of the four inferences you may use any of the three given premises or any of the conclusions you have from previous inferences. For each inference, tell what inference you are making and give a name of rule you are applying.

$$\text{Premises: } A \wedge (B \vee C), B \rightarrow\, \sim D, \sim\sim D$$

16.3.3 Examples of Incorrect Rules of Inference (Formal Fallacies)

Finally, a rule of inference could be incorrect. To say that a rule of inference is incorrect is to say that it could lead from true premises to a false conclusion. Incorrect rules of inference correspond to invalid patterns of reasoning. Some of them are so common that they have Latin names. They are often called formal fallacies. A few of them are listed below.

$$\frac{P \rightarrow Q, Q}{P} \qquad \text{(affirming the consequent)}$$

$$\frac{P \rightarrow Q, \sim P}{\sim Q} \qquad \text{(denying the antecedent)}$$

$$\frac{P \rightarrow Q}{Q \rightarrow P} \qquad \text{(converting a consequent)}$$

$$\frac{P \vee Q, P}{\sim Q} \qquad \text{(improper disjunctive syllogism)}$$

Exercise 4. For each of the incorrect rules above, give a counterexample that shows that the rule is incorrect.

Chapter 17
Proof

The last chapter described some truth functional rules of inference. The purpose of this Chapter is to show how to use such rules to construct proofs. After studying this material you should be able to:

1. Construct valid arguments using rules of inference.
2. Explain several different senses of the term 'proof'.
3. Explain the difference between and tradeoffs between formal and informal proof methods.
4. Apply the proof methods explained here to proving the truth functional validity of argument forms and proving that statement forms are tautologies
5. Describe and use direct, conditional, and indirect proof strategies.
6. Be able to construct simple arguments using rules of inference and facts from specific subjects such as mathematics.

Outline

R. Lover, *Elementary Logic: For Software Development*,
DOI: 10.2007/978-1-84800-082-7, © Springer 2008

17.1   Kinds of Proof

17.1.1   Different Senses of Proof

The word "proof" is used in many different ways. In the broadest sense, a proof is just an argument intended to explain why some statement is true. The idea is that if you already believe the premises of the argument and you see that the conclusion follows logically from the premises, and if you are rational, then you should be persuaded that the conclusion is also true.

Many years ago a friend of mine was assigned to teach a differential equations course to a class of engineering students. The students had heard horror stories about the difficulty of differential equations courses, especially those that included 'proofs' of the theorems. On the first day of the course my friend announced to the class that they were not going to have to do proofs of the theorems but that they were going to have to explain why the theorems were true. The students breathed a sigh of relief, the course proceeded smoothly, and my friend only explained his "noble lie" to them at the end of the course. The moral of the story is that a rose by any other name would not smell as sweet.

The principle concern of logic is not the truth or falsity of premises and conclusions but the validity of arguments. From a logical point of view a proof is an argument or chain of arguments intended to demonstrate that the final conclusion of the sequence follows necessarily from the original premises. In this sense a proof may be correct or incorrect, depending upon whether its component arguments are valid or invalid.

In a stricter sense, a sequence of arguments is not really a proof unless all its component arguments are valid. Unless the context indicates otherwise this is the sense of the word which will be used in this book.

In some contexts an even stricter sense of proof is used in which all the component arguments have to be valid and the premises also have to be true, i.e. all the component arguments have to be sound. In this sense what a proof proves is that its conclusion is true.

Finally, for something to be a proof it is often required that each statement of the proof be associated with an explicit justification or reason. This is the sort of proof you may recall from logic or mathematics courses.

17.1.2   Formal vs Informal Proofs

At one extreme, a purely formal proof is a proof whose validity can be determined by examining the forms of the component statements, without regard to their meanings. At the other extreme, a purely informal proof is a proof whose validity can be determined by considering facts the author of the argument believes are not in question, e.g. "obvious" facts and the meanings of the component statements, without regard to their form. Most proofs found outside of logic books are informal or semiformal, i.e. partly formal and partly informal.

Formal proofs tend to be long, very detailed, and boring. On the good side, they make everything very explicit and errors in them are usually easy to check. Computer programs can be written to check the correctness of formal proofs. Informal proofs tend to be shorter, much less detailed, and more interesting. They can also be difficult to understand. It is far easier to be fooled by an informal argument than by a formal one, and it is difficult or impossible to write computer programs to check their correctness.

Here is a joke that illustrates the point about informal proofs sometimes being hard to understand. A mathematics professor was doing an informal proof on the blackboard. He started on one side of the room and filled several panels of blackboard before he wrote "Obviously $Y < 0$" on the board. Whereupon he stepped back, stared at the board for a while then paced back and forth for several minutes, all the time staring at the various steps of the proof. Then he left the room without saying a word. The students waited for a very long time. Finally the Professor rushed back into the room and proudly exclaimed "Yes, it is obvious!"

Context determines the level of formality that is appropriate for a proof. Considerable formality is appropriate in the context of learning to reason correctly. Formal reasoning often seems like walking using baby steps. However, formality makes reasoning clearer and less subject to misunderstanding. Formality can play the same role in learning to use logic that training wheels can play in learning to ride a bicycle. Formality helps you learn the formal rules of correct reasoning. Once you know the rules then you are in a better position to take informal shortcuts.

17.2 Two Ways of Organizing Proofs

Recall that for every argument there is a corresponding conditional statement. Moreover, an argument is truth functionally valid just in case the corresponding conditional is a tautology. The two ways of organizing proofs described below correspond to analyzing the validity of arguments expressed as arguments versus analyzing the corresponding conditional to determine that it is a tautology. The general form of a proof organized the first way is

Line	Assumes	Statement	Justification
1.	1	P_1	Premise
2.	2	P_2	Premise
.		.	
.		.	
n.	n	P_n / C	Premise / conclusion
n + 1	?,...,?	Statement	Justification
n + 2	?,...,?	Statement	Justification
.		.	
.		.	
N	?,...,?	C	Justification (for the conclusion, C)

Each line, often called a step, of such a proof has four columns. Column 1 is simply a line number. Column 2 is a list of the assumptions the statement in that row depends upon. Column 3 is a statement of the proof. Column 4 is a justification for asserting that statement. In formal proofs of this kind, justifications are premises of the argument or they refer to formal rules of inference or formalized expressions of the definitions of terms or facts assumed about a specific area of application. Justifications in informal proofs do the same job but are expressed informally. This general form may be supplemented in various ways to make its purpose clearer. Here is an example of such a proof.

Example 1. A proof of validity of an argument form

The argument form below is written horizontally with "/" between the premises and the conclusion in order to save space on the page.

$$P \rightarrow Q, (\sim R) \rightarrow (\sim Q), P / R$$

One (formal) proof of R from these three premises is the following. The numbers in the right hand column are the line numbers of the specific previous lines to which the rule of inference referred to in that line is applied in order to deduce the statement to its left.

Line	Assumes	Statement	Justification
1.	1	$P \rightarrow Q$	Premise
2.	2	$(\sim R) \rightarrow (\sim Q)$	Premise
3.	3	P / R	Premise / conclusion
4.	1,3	Q	$\rightarrow$ elim. 1,3
5.	1,3	$\sim (\sim Q)$	$\sim\sim$ intro. 4
6.	1,2,3	$\sim (\sim R)$	Modus tollens 2,5
7.	1,2,3	R	$\sim\sim$ elim. 6

A second way to organize a proof starts with the corresponding conditional. The general form is

Theorem: The statement to be proved, e.g. $(P_1 \wedge P_2 \wedge ...P_n) \rightarrow C$
Proof

Line	Assumes	Statement	Justification
1.	?,...?	Statement 1	Justification
2.	?,...?	Statement 2	Justification
.		.	
.		.	
N.	(blank)	Statement to be proved e.g. $(P_1 \wedge P_2 \wedge ... P_n) \rightarrow C$	Justification

Since the statement to be proved is not an argument it has no premises. Consequently premises are not available as justifications. However, all the truths of logic (e.g. tautologies), the rules of inference, definitions, and previously proved statements in the subject are available. Note that the last line under "assumes" is blank because at this point all assumptions have been discharged. Also the last statement in the proof is the theorem itself. Typically the antecedent is assumed in preparation for a conditional proof. Here is the proof of Example 1. reorganized this way.

Example 2. Proof from Example 1 reorganized

Theorem: $(((P \to Q) \land (\sim R \to \sim Q)) \land P) \to R$
Proof:

Line	Assumes	Statement	Justification
1.	1	$((P \to Q) \land (\sim R \to \sim Q)) \land P$	Assume for CP
2.	1	P	$\land$ elim. 1
3.	1	$(P \to Q) \land (\sim R \to \sim Q)$	$\land$ elim. 1
4.	1	$\sim R \to \sim Q$	$\land$ elim. 3
5.	1	$P \to Q$	$\land$ elim. 3
6.	1	Q	$\to$ elim. 2, 5
7.	1	$\sim\sim Q$	$\sim\sim$ intro. 6
8.	1	$\sim\sim R$	modus tollens 4, 7
9.	1	R	$\sim\sim$ elim. 8
10.		$(((P \to Q) \land (\sim R \to \sim Q)) \land P) \to R$	$\to$ intro. 1, 9

While the second form is somewhat longer, it is widely used, so it is a good idea to be familiar with it.

17.3   Three Proof Strategies

There are many strategies for organizing the arguments that constitute a proof. Three of the most common are described below. The examples in this section will be about proving the validity of argument forms. In the next chapter, proofs about nonlogical issues will be discussed.

17.3.1   Direct Proof

A direct proof starts with premises and forges ahead applying one rule of inference after another until the conclusion is reached. It does not involve making any temporary "assumptions" as do conditional and indirect proofs. Example 1 above uses a direct proof strategy.

Example 1 Repeated (direct proof of validity of an argument form)

1.	1	$P \to Q$	Premise
2.	2	$(\sim R) \to (\sim Q)$	Premise
3.	3	P / R	Premise / conclusion
4.	1,3	Q	$\to$ elim. 1,3
5.	1,3	$\sim (\sim Q)$	$\sim\sim$ intro. 4
6.	1,2,3	$\sim (\sim R)$	modus tollens 2,5
7.	1,2,3	R	$\sim\sim$ elim. 6

In general there are infinitely many other proofs that would prove the same thing, although most of them would be longer than this one.

The proof given shows that all arguments of its form are valid. For example, if P is replaced by "Today is Tuesday", Q is replaced by "We have a class today", and R is replaced by "It is raining" then the fact that the argument form is valid tells us that the following argument is valid.

> If today is Tuesday then we have a class today.
> If it is not raining then we do not have a class today.
> Today is Tuesday.
> Therefore it is raining.

The proof above shows equally that the following argument is valid, where P is replaced by "$x > 0$", Q is replaced by "$y = 1$", and R is replaced by "$z = 5$".

> $(x > 0) \to (y = 1)$
> $(\sim(z = 5)) \to \sim(y = 1)$
> $x \geq 0$
> $z = 5$

Exercise 1. Fill in columns 2 and 4 for the following (formal) proof of the correctness of the argument form

$$A \to (B \wedge C), \sim C / \sim A$$

Proof:

1.	$A \to (B \wedge C)$		
2.	$\sim C / \sim A$		
3.	$(\sim B) \vee (\sim C)$		
4.	$\sim(B \wedge C)$		
5.	$\sim A$		

Exercise 2. If A is replaced by "Today is Tuesday", B is replaced by "We have a class today", and C is replaced by "It is raining" then what specific argument does the proof of Exercise 1 show to be valid?

Exercise 3. If A is replaced by "x > 0", B is replaced by "y = 1", and C is replaced by "z = 5" then what specific argument does the proof of Exercise 1 show to be valid?

17.3.2 Conditional Proof

The rule for → introduction is also called the rule of conditional proof. The idea behind the rule is that if, by assuming P, you can validly infer Q then, without assuming P, you may validly infer P → Q. This form of proof is very useful if the conclusion of the argument is a statement of conditional form.

Example 3. A conditional proof

1.	1	(A ∨ B) → C	premise
2.	2	(A ∨ B) → D	premise
		/ (A ∨ B) → (C ∧ D)	/ conclusion
3.	3	A ∨ B	assume (for conditional proof, CP)
4.	1,3	C	→ elim. 1,3
5.	2,3	D	→ elim. 2,3
6.	1,2,3	C ∧ D	∧ intro. 4,5
7.	1,2	(A ∨ B) → (C ∧ D)	→ intro. 3,6
			(discharges assumption 3)

The conditional proof strategy is especially useful for proving conclusions which are themselves of conditional form. The idea is that you get to introduce the antecedent of the conclusion as an additional temporary assumption, derive the consequent of the conditional based on that assumption, then conclude the conditional itself. Note the use of a temporary assumption starting at line 3. At line 7 the assumption in 3 is said to be discharged.

Here is a proof that the corresponding conditional is a tautology.

Theorem: (((A ∨ B) → C) ∧ ((A ∨ B) → D)) → ((A ∨ B) → (C ∧ D))

Proof:

1.	1	((A ∨ B) → C) ∧ ((A ∨ B) → D)	assume for CP
2.	1	(A ∨ B) → C	∧ elim. 1
3.	1	(A ∨ B) → D	∧ elim. 1
4.	4	A ∨ B	assume (for CP)
5.	1,4	C	→ elim. 2,4
6.	1,4	D	→ elim. 3, 4
7.	1,4	C ∧ D	∧ intro. 5, 6
8.	1	(A ∨ B) → (C ∧ D)	→ intro. 4, 7
9.		(((A ∨ B) → C) ∧ ((A ∨ B) → D)) → ((A ∨ B) → (C ∧ D))	→ intro. 1, 8

Exercise 4. Use conditional proof to prove the following argument forms are valid. Then rewrite to prove that the corresponding conditional is a tautology. Hint, in some cases you may have to use the rule of conditional proof more than once in a single proof.

a. A → C, B → D/(A ∧ B) → (C ∧D)
b. A → B, ~C → ~A/A → (B ∧ C)
c. A → (B → C)/(A ∧ B) → C

17.3.3   *Indirect Proof*

The rules for ~ introduction and ~ elimination are the basis for what are called indirect proofs (or proofs by contradiction or proofs by reduction to absurdity). The contradiction or absurdity involved is "Q and not Q". The strategy for using ~ elimination to prove that P is true is to consider what would be the case if P were false, i.e. if ~P were true, and then derive a contradiction from this hypothesis, blame the contradiction on the hypothesis, and conclude that P must after all be true. Similarly the strategy for using ~ introduction to prove that ~P is true is to consider what would be the case if ~P were false, i.e. if P were true, derive a contradiction from that hypothesis, blame the contradiction on the hypothesis, and conclude that ~P is true after all.

Example 4. An indirect proof of validity

1.	1	~P → Q ∧ R	Premise
2.	2	~R / P	Premise / conclusion
3.	3	~P	assume (for IP)
4.	1,3	Q ∧ R	→ elim. 1,3 (or MP 1,3)
5.	1,3	R	∧ elim. 4
6.	1,2,3	R ∧ ~R	∧ intro. 5,2 (a contradiction. Blame on 3)
7.	1,2	P	~ elim. 3,6 (assumption in 3 discharged)

Here again note the use of a temporary assumption. At line 7 the assumption at line 3 is denied, and it is said to be discharged, in this case by use of ~ elimination.

Here is a proof that the corresponding conditional is a tautology.

Theorem: ((~P → Q ∧ R) ∧ ~R) → P

Proof:

1.	1	(~P → Q ∧ R) ∧ ~R	assume for CP
2.	1	~R	∧ elim. 1
3.	3	~P	assume (for IP)

4.	1,3	$Q \wedge R$	$\rightarrow$ elim. 1,3 (or MP 1,3)
5.	1,3	R	$\wedge$ elim. 4
6.	1,3	$R \wedge {\sim}R$	$\wedge$ intro. 5,2 (a contradiction)
7.	1	P	$\sim$ elim. 3,6 (assumption discharged)
8.		$(({\sim}P \rightarrow Q \wedge R) \wedge {\sim}R) \rightarrow P$	$\rightarrow$ intro. 1, 7

Any theorem can be proved in a variety of ways. Here, for example, is a direct proof of validity of the argument form of Example 4.

Example 5. Shows that indirect proof is not the only way the theorem of Example 4 can be proved

1.	1	${\sim}P \rightarrow Q \wedge R$	Premise
2.	2	${\sim}R$ / P	premise / conclusion
3.	2	${\sim}Q \vee {\sim}R$	$\vee$ intro. 2
4.	2	${\sim}(Q \wedge R)$	de Morgan 2
5.	1,2	${\sim}({\sim}P)$	modus tollens 1,4
6.	1,2	P	$\sim\sim$ elimination 5

Example 6. Another example of indirect proof

1.	1	$(R \vee Q) \rightarrow P$	Premise
2.	2	$P \rightarrow (S \wedge T)$	Premise
3.	3	$({\sim}S) \vee ({\sim}T)$ / ${\sim}(R \vee Q)$	premise / conclusion
4.	4	$(R \vee Q)$	assume (for IP)
5.	1,4	P	$\rightarrow$ elim. 1,4
6.	1,2,4	$S \wedge T$	$\rightarrow$ elim. 2,5
7.	3	${\sim}(S \wedge T)$	de Morgan 3
8.	1,2,3,4	$(S \wedge T) \wedge {\sim}(S \wedge T)$	$\wedge$ intro. 6, 7
11.	1,2,3	${\sim}(R \vee Q)$	$\sim$ intro. 4, 8

Exercise 5. Use the indirect proof strategy to prove the validity of each of the following argument forms. Do not also prove the corresponding conditional is a tautology.

a. $P \vee Q, P \vee {\sim}Q$ / P
b. $P \rightarrow (Q \wedge R), R \rightarrow (S \wedge T), ({\sim}Q) \vee ({\sim}T)$ / ${\sim}P$
c. $(S \wedge T) \vee Q, (S \wedge T) \vee R, R \rightarrow {\sim}Q$ / $(S \wedge T)$
d. $P \rightarrow Q, {\sim}R \rightarrow {\sim}Q, P$ / R

Exercise 6. For each of the following arguments, either construct a formal proof of it or show a counterexample to it. Note: a counterexample to an allegedly valid argument form could be given by specifying an assignment of truth values of the elementary statements involved which made all the premises true and the conclusion false. A counterexample to an allegedly valid argument form could also be given by showing an instance of that form with obviously true premises and a false conclusion. In your proofs you can use any mixture of direct, conditional, and indirect strategies. Some may require more than one. Do not use "tautology" as a justification for any line in a proof.

a. $P \to Q, Q \to R, R \to S, S \to T, T \to U, \sim U / \sim P$
b. $((P \to Q) \to R) / (P \to (Q \to R))$
c. $(P \to (Q \to R)) / ((P \to Q) \to R)$
d. $(P \to (Q \to R)) / ((P \wedge Q) \to R)$
e. $((P \wedge Q) \to R) / (P \to (Q \to R))$
f. $((P \to R) / (P \vee Q) \to R$
g. $((P \to R) / (P \wedge Q) \to R$

Exercise 7. For each of the following alleged theorems of logic (tautologies), either construct a formal proof of it or show a counterexample to it. Note: a counterexample to an alleged tautology could either be an assignment of truth values which was not all ts in its final column or an instance of the statement form which is false. In your proofs you can use any mixture of direct, conditional, and indirect strategies. Some may require more than one. Do not use "tautology" as a justification for any line in a proof.

a. $((P \vee Q) \to R) \to ((P \to R) \vee (Q \to R))$
b. $((P \wedge Q) \to R) \to ((P \to R) \wedge (Q \to R))$
c. $((P \to R) \wedge (Q \to R) \to ((P \wedge Q) \to R)$
d. $\sim(P \wedge Q) \leftrightarrow (\sim P \wedge \sim Q)$
e. $\sim(P \vee Q) \leftrightarrow (\sim P \wedge \sim Q)$
f. $((P \to R) \wedge (Q \to \sim R)) \to \sim(P \wedge Q)$
g. $((P \wedge Q) \vee (P \wedge \sim Q))$

17.4   Applying Logic to Specific Subjects

Rules of inference can be used in aid of reasoning about specific subjects in two ways, with and without allowing nonlogical information about the specific subjects as justifications in the proofs.

17.4.1   *Using Instances Of General Forms*

Recall that truth tables can be done for individual statements and arguments as well as for statement and argument forms. Similarly, when the sentence letters in abstract proofs of the validity of argument forms are replaced by specific statements then the result is a proof of the validity of an argument about a specific subject. Consider the following examples.

Example 7. Recall Example 1.

1.	1	P → Q	Premise
2.	2	(~ R) → (~ Q)	Premise
3.	3	P / R	premise / conclusion
4.	1,3	Q	→ elim. 1,3
5.	1,3	~ (~ Q)	~~ intro. 4
6.	1,2,3	~ (~R)	modus tollens 2,5
7.	1,2,3	R	~~ elim. 6

Consider what happens to this proof if x > 0, y = 1, and z = 5 are used in place of P, Q, and R. The result is

1.	1	x > 0 → y = 1	Premise
2.	2	(~ z = 5) → > (~ y = 1)	Premise
3.	3	x ≥ 0 / z = 5	premise / conclusion
4.	1,3	y = 1	→ elim. 1,3
5.	1,3	~ (~ y = 1)	~~ introduction 4
6.	1,2,3	~ (~z = 5)	→ elim. 2,5
7.	1,2,3	z = 5	~~ elimination 6

This particular argument is about numbers, but the justifications used do not refer to any facts about numbers, they refer entirely to facts about logic. The specific proof above is called an instance of the more general proof. Any general proof of the validity of an argument form can be instantiated in infinitely many specific ways, giving rise to infinitely many specific applications.

Exercise 8. In each of the following, write the instance of the general proof that results if P is replaced by "Today is Tuesday", Q is replaced by "We have a meeting today", R is replaced by "It is raining", S is replaced by "It is snowing", and T is replaced by "Today is Thursday".

a. The proof in Example 5.
b. The proof in Example 6.
c. The proof in Example 7.
d. The proof in Example 8.

17.4.2 *Adding Nonlogical Justifications*

When constructing proofs about a particular subject the previously established facts peculiar to that subject can be used as justifications for lines of the proof. Of course if a proof uses justifications that are peculiar to a particular subject then what is proved is not completely general, rather it is true of that particular subject.

Example 8. Proof of a theorem of arithmetic

1.	1	$(x = 0) \to (y = 1)$	Premise
2.	2	$\sim(y = 1) / (x < 0) \vee (x > 0)$	Premise / conclusion
3.	1,2	$\sim(x = 0)$	m.t. 1,2
4.		$(x = 0) \vee ((x < 0) \vee (x > 0))$	Arithmetic
5.	1,2	$((x < 0) \vee (x > 0))$	d. syll 3,4

What is new here is the use of "arithmetic" to justify line 4. It is not a fact about logic that any number x is less than zero, equal to zero, or greater than zero. This is a fact of arithmetic. The proof shows something about arithmetic as well as something about logic. Since logic is assumed in all other subjects, this proof would be said to be about arithmetic.

Recall that logic is completely gen eral. Logic alone will not tell you anything specific about a subject. For example, logic alone guarantees that either it is raining or it is not raining, but it does not determine which. However, if some facts about a subject are already known then logic can help discover other (previously unknown) facts about that subject. For example, if it is known that it is raining and that if it is raining then the picnic is cancelled then logic will guarantee that the picnic is cancelled.

Moreover, most interesting subjects are not just collections of isolated facts. Usually some of the facts of a subject are more general and more fundamental than others. In the sciences the most general facts are called laws of nature, e.g. laws of physics, chemistry, biology, etc. In our legal system we have constitutional laws with which other lesser laws are not supposed to conflict. In mathematics we have axioms of geometry, arithmetic, algebra, topology, etc.

When logic is applied to a particular subject, such as arithmetic or computing, less emphasis is placed on determining which arguments are valid and more emphasis is placed on determining which statements about the subject are true. Another way to put this is to say that there is a shift from concern about validity to concern about soundness. Corresponding to this shift there is a slight change in the way proofs are usually presented.

When a proof of a statement within a particular subject is attempted, all the previously established statements of that subject are available as justifications for the lines of the proof. In addition, definitions are allowed as justifications. In some contexts reports of observations or even appeals to authority are allowed. After a proof is successfully completed, the proven statement joins the ranks of previously established statements and it is available the next time a proof of some other statement is attempted.

Statements that are proved to be consequences of the basic statements (laws, axioms, principles, and definitions) of a highly organized subject are often called theorems of that subject, e.g. theorems of arithmetic, geometry, or computer science. In other cases statements for which proofs are offered are not called theorems. For example, while proofs are often used in investigating crimes, there are no theorems of criminology. Although there is some variation in how proofs are presented, they are often organized as in Example 9 below.

Recall that for every argument there is a corresponding conditional statement. Consequently all of the proofs previously given that show that some argument is valid can be turned into theorems about their subject matter. For example the theorem of arithmetic and the proof of it that correspond to the argument of Example 9 is given below.

Example 9. Conditional corresponding to Example 9

Theorem: $(((x = 0) \rightarrow (y = 1)) \wedge \sim(y = 1)) \rightarrow (x < 0) \vee (x > 0)$
Proof:

1.	1	$(((x = 0) \rightarrow (y = 1)) \wedge \sim(y = 1))$	Assume (for CP)
2.	1	$((x = 0) \rightarrow (y = 1))$	$\wedge$ elim. 1
3.	1	$\sim(y = 1)$	$\wedge$ elim. 1
4.	1	$\sim(x = 0)$	$\rightarrow$ elim. 2,3
5.	1	$(x = 0) \vee ((x < 0) \vee (x > 0))$	arithmetic
6.	1	$((x < 0) \cdot (x > 0))$	d syll 5,4
7.		$(((x = 0) \rightarrow (y = 1)) \wedge \sim(y = 1)) \rightarrow (x < 0) \vee (x > 0)$	$\rightarrow$ intro. 1,6

Exercise 9. Using the style of Example 10, construct proofs of the following theorems. Suggestion: Use the fact that $(x = 0) \vee ((x < 0) \vee (x > 0))$ and $(y = 0) \vee ((y < 0) \vee (y > 0))$ and $(z = 5) \vee ((z < 5) \vee (z > 5))$.

a. $(x = 0 \rightarrow z = 5) \wedge \sim(z < 5 \vee z > 5) \rightarrow \sim x = 0.$
b. $(((x = 0 \vee y = 1) \rightarrow z = 5) \wedge \sim (x < 0 \vee x > 0)) \rightarrow z = 5$
c. $(((y = 1 \rightarrow (z = 5 \wedge x = 0)) \wedge \sim z = 5) \rightarrow \sim y = 1$
d. $((y = 1 \rightarrow (z = 5 \vee x = 0)) \wedge y = 1 \wedge \sim z = 5) \rightarrow x = 0$

Chapter 18
Algorithmic Unsolvability Proofs

This short chapter describes what it means for a problem to be algorithmically unsolvable and gives a proof that the halting problem is algorithmically unsolvable. After studying this material you should be able to:

1. Explain what it means for a problem to be algorithmically unsolvable.
2. Describe the halting problem and explain the proof of its unsolvability.
3. Describe the program equivalence problem and the verification problem and explain what their algorithmic unsolvability means.

Outline

18.1   Algorithmic Solvability and Unsolvability

Recall that the term "program" and "algorithm" are often used as synonyms and that where a distinction between them is made, an algorithm is a plan for a program. Programs are written to solve certain kinds of problems. The problems which can be solved by means of computer programs, involve transforming information that can be represented in digital form. More precisely, a functional problem specification is an ordered pair, <D, S>, where D represents the set of data to be transformed, called the domain of the problem, and S represents the condition that anything must satisfy in order to solve the problem. S must represent a function, i.e. for each x there must be at most one y such that S(x, y) is true.

Example 1. Some algorithmic problem specifications

R. Lover, *Elementary Logic: For Software Development*,
DOI: 10.2007/978-1-84800-082-7, © Springer 2008

(a) The problem of finding the absolute value of any real number.

      D = the set of real numbers.

      S(x, y) is true iff x is a real number and y is the absolute value of x.

(b) The problem of finding the smaller of any pair of real numbers.

      D = the set of pairs of real numbers.

      S(x, y) is true iff x is a pair of real numbers and y is the smaller of the elements of x.

(c) The problem of finding the sum of any nonempty finite sequence of numbers.

      D = the set of all finite sequences of numbers.

      S(x, y) is true iff x is a sequence of real numbers and y is the sum of the elements of x.

(d) The problem of counting the number of sentences in a document which contain a specified word.

      D = the set of all pairs, <d, w> where d is a document and w is a word whose instances in d are to be counted.

      S(x, y) is true iff x is a pair <d, w> in D and y is the number of instances of w in d.

(e) The problem of finding the Nth even prime number.

      D = the set of all positive integers.

      S(N, y) is true iff N is a positive integer and y is the Nth even prime number.

(f) The problem of determining whether there is an Nth even prime number.

      D = the set of all positive integers.

      S(N, y) is true iff x is a positive integer and ((there is an Nth even prime and y = true (or "Yes")) or (there is no Nth even prime and y = false (or "No"))).

Specifications for a program that solves a problem, <D, S>, can be expressed by preconditions and postconditions, <Pre, Post>, that are related to the problem specifications as follows:

    $X \in D \rightarrow$ Pre and

    $S(x,y) \leftrightarrow Pre(x) \wedge Post(x,y)$.

The elements of D are often called the "valid" inputs for any program that is supposed to solve the problem. Other inputs may be allowed, but they are not "valid" for this problem. This of course is an abuse of the logical term "valid." The desired outputs from such an program are $\{y| \exists x Pre(x) \wedge Post(x, y)\}$.

Definition 1. An program, P, is said to be *partially correct* with respect to a problem just in case if P is run with input from the domain of the problem and P halts, then the output of the program for that input is the solution of the problem for that domain element.

A partially correct program never gives the wrong answer, but in some cases it may give no answer at all. For example, the following program is partially correct with respect to the problem of determining the absolute value of any real number.

```
algorithm partialAbsoluteValue (N)
# Precondition: N is a number.
# Postcondition: Returns the absolute value of N.
      If (N > = 0) then
                abs ← N
      Else
                loop forever
      Endif
      Return abs
Endalgorithm
```

Definition 2. An program, P, is said to be *totally correct* with respect to a problem iff P halts when given any element in the domain of the problem as input and its output is the solution of the problem for that element of its domain.

One reason for distinguishing between partial and total correctness is that proofs of total correctness are often divided into two parts. In one part it is shown that, if P halts with input from the domain of the problem then it gives the correct answer. In the other part it is shown that if P is run with input from the domain of the problem then it must halt. Total correctness = partial correctness + always halts.

Note that if P is totally correct with respect to a problem then P halts for every input from the domain of the problem and its output must be correct in each case. There are no restrictions on what P can do with input that is not in the domain of the problem.

Exercise 1. Suppose a program does nothing but go into an infinite loop no matter what input it is given. For what problems, if any, is a partially correct?

Exercise 2. Suppose a program does nothing but go into an infinite loop no matter what input it is given. For what problems, if any, is it totally correct?

Exercise 3. Show by example that a program may be totally correct with respect to one problem and not totally correct with respect to another. You don't need to write a program, just describe what such a program and problems would be in specific terms.

Exercise 4. Show by example that a program may be partially correct with respect to one problem and totally correct with respect to a different problem. You don't need to write a program, just describe what such a program and problems would be in specific terms.

Definition 3. A program solves a problem iff it is totally correct with respect to that problem.

Definition 4. A decision problem is a problem that asks for a "Yes" or "no" (true or false) answer to a question of the form "Does this element of the domain have some property?" If some specific input has the property in question then the answer to the problem in that case is "Yes" (or true) and if not then the answer is "No" (or false).

A program that solves a decision problem halts with output "Yes" for inputs from the problem domain that have the property and halts with output "No" for inputs from the problem domain that do not have the property. For example, the problem of determining whether a positive integer is a prime number is a decision problem – "yes" N is prime or "No" N is not prime.

Definition 5. A problem is algorithmically solvable iff there is a program which solves it. In particular, *a decision problem is algorithmically solvable* iff there is a program that halts with output "Yes" for every input in the domain of the problem which has the property specified by the problem and halts with output "No" for every input in the domain of the problem which does not have the property specified by the problem.

It comes as a surprise to many people that there are quite reasonable sounding problems of the sort you might think could be solved by means of a computer program which are algorithmically unsolvable. This is a very strong claim, it means that not only is there no known program which solves such a problem, but that there could not possibly ever be a program to solve such a problem, assuming only that our concepts of what a computer is and what a programming language is do not change radically.

You might well ask, how it is possible to show that no one could ever write a program to solve a particular problem. What about newer faster computers and not yet invented programming techniques and languages?

Faster computers will not help. Algorithmic solvability is not a matter of time. If a problem is solvable in any finite length of time it counts as algorithmically solvable. If a solvable problem is not solvable with current technology in a reasonable amount of time, it is currently infeasible, but still solvable.

Newer computer designs will not help. Not even quantum computers, which are discussed briefly in the last chapter. Anything that could rightly be called a computer must have a few characteristics. For example, it would have to generate its output by means of a finite number of steps. Each step must be doable by executing a simple instruction of the sort that can be done by a very simple machine. Each step must work with a finite amount of data. Each step must be doable in a finite amount of time. It turns out that these characteristics alone are all that are needed for there to be algorithmic unsolvability.

Programming techniques and languages not yet invented will not help. As long as they are at least as powerful those that are currently available, problems that are algorithmically unsolvable will be just as unsolvable using those future techniques and languages.

The proof in the next section is an indirect proof. It shows that the halting problem is unsolvable by showing that if it were solvable then a contradictory situation would have to be the case. Since contradictory situations are not possible it is concluded that the problem is not solvable. The halting problem is a decision problem.

18.2 The Halting Problem is Algorithmically Unsolvable

It is not uncommon for one program to have as its input some other program. A program is, after all, just a sequence of characters representing instructions in some programming language. A text editor, for example, can take a program as input and give a modified program as output. A compiler takes a source program as input and gives an object program as output. An interpreter takes a source program and some input for that program as input and gives as output the result of running that source program on that input.

A program may halt for some inputs and not halt for other inputs, instead it might go into an infinite loop for those inputs. The halting problem is: given a syntactically correct program, P, and any finite sequence of symbols, I, to determine whether executing P with input I would or would not halt. This problem would be algorithmically solvable if it were possible to write a program, H, which will take as its input any pair <P, I> (where P is the text of some syntactically correct program and I is any finite sequence of symbols) so that H has output "Yes" if and only if P would halt with input I, and has output "No" if and only if P would not halt with input I. It turns out that the Halting problem is not algorithmically solvable. Here is why.

Definition 6. The halting problem is the problem of determining for any program, P, and any input, I, whether executing P with input I will result in P halting.

Domain: {<P, I> | P is the text of a syntactically correct program in some programming language and I is any finite character string}
Solution Condition: If P halts with input I then the solution is "Yes" and if P never halts with input I then the solution is "No".

Theorem 1. The halting problem is algorithmically unsolvable.

Proof
In the following discussions, the notation P(I), will be used to denote the result of applying program P to input I and H(P, I) to denote the result of applying program H to input <P, I>.

If the halting problem were algorithmically solvable then there would be a program, H, which solved it, i.e.

H(P, I) = "Yes" just in case P(I) halts and
H(P, I) = "No" just in case P(I) does not halt.

Then, building on H, we could define another program S such that S takes the text of syntactically correct programs, P, as its inputs and then S does the following:

1. S calls H(P, P).
2. If H(P, P) halts with output "Yes" then S goes into an infinite loop.
3. If H(P, P) halts with output "No" then S halts.
4. End of definition of S.

Now consider what would happen if S were applied to itself. Clearly, S(S) halts or it does not halt. If S(S) halts then that must happen because of line 3 of the definition of S, hence because H(S, S) halts with output "No". But from the definition of H, if H(S, S) halts with output "No," then S(S) does not halt. This is clearly a contradiction. Hence S(S) cannot halt.

On the other hand, if S(S) does not halt then that must be because of line 2 of the definition of S, hence because H(S, S) halts with output "Yes." But from the definition of H, if H(S, S) halts with output "Yes" then S(S) does not halt. Again this is a contradiction. Hence S(S) halts.

We conclude that there cannot be a program such as S, and hence there cannot be a program such as H, and hence that the halting problem is algorithmically unsolvable.

The overall logical structure of this proof is:

1. If the halting problem were solvable then H would exist.
2. If H existed then S would exist.
3. If S existed then S(S) would halt or S(S) would not halt.
4. If S(S) halted then S(S) would not halt, a contradiction.
5. If S(S) did not halt then S(S) would halt, again a contradiction.
6. Hence S does not exist.
7. Hence H does not exist.
8. Hence the halting problem is not algorithmically solvable.

Notice how general this proof is. It does not depend on what computer or language is or will be used, the proof applies.

18.3   Other Algorithmically Unsolvable Problems

Not only is the halting problem algorithmically unsolvable but so are a number of other problems that are of interest to software developers. The fact that these problems are not algorithmically solvable might be called *programmer employability theorems*. For example, there is the *program equivalence problem*: given any pair of programs, determine whether that pair will always give the same output if given the same input. Another example is *the verification problem*: given a problem and a program, does that program solve that problem?

The algorithmic unsolvability of these and many other interesting problems can be proved by means of a strategy known as reducing one problem to another.

Definition 7. A *problem P is reducible to a problem Q* just in case there is an algorithm for translating any instance of P into an instance of Q in such a way that the solution of that instance of Q can be translated back by an algorithm to a solution of the original instance of P.

Example 2. As you already know, the problem of finding the product of any two positive integers is reducible to the problem of finding the sum of any number of positive integers. Here is how. The problem of finding the product of two positive integers, A and B, can be translated into the problem of finding the sum of B copies of A. The resulting sum is also the product of A and B.

Theorem 2. If problem P is reducible to problem Q and Q is algorithmically solvable then P is algorithmically solvable.

Proof. This is a trivial consequence of Definition 7. To solve any instance of P, translate it into the corresponding instance of Q, use the algorithm of solving that instance of Q, then translate that solution back to the solution to the original instance of P.

Theorem 3. If problem P is reducible to problem Q and P is algorithmically unsolvable then Q is algorithmically unsolvable.

Proof. An algorithmic solution to Q along with the algorithm for translating between instances of P and instances of Q would be an algorithm for solving P. Since P is algorithmically unsolvable there cannot be an algorithm for solving Q either.

Example 3. The halting problem is reducible to the program equivalence problem. Hence the program equivalence problem is algorithmically unsolvable.

Example 4. The halting problem is reducible to the verification problem. Hence by Theorem 3, the verification problem is algorithmically unsolvable.

However, despite the algorithmic unsolvability of a very general problem like the verification problem, there are useful special cases of those problems which are algorithmically solvable.

Chapter 19
Program Correctness Proofs

This chapter shows that despite the general unsolvability of the verification problem, it is possible to prove that individual programs and certain classes of programs are correct. After studying this material you should be able to:

1. Describe the limits of testing as a verification method.
2. Give informal proofs of program correctness expressed in English prose.
3. Use Floyd's method to prove the correctness of some programs.
4. Use rules of inference about assignment and control structures to prove the correctness of some programs.

Outline

19.1   The Limits of Testing

The basic correctness problem is to tell whether a program solves a problem. All programmers know that testing is one strategy for trying to establish correctness. If exhaustive testing is possible then a program can be proved correct by testing. For example, a program that is supposed to take any 8-bit sequence of 0s and 1s as input and give the corresponding even parity bit as output can be exhaustively tested by running all 256 test cases. Problems whose solutions can be obtained by looking up

R. Lover, *Elementary Logic: For Software Development*,
DOI: 10.2007/978-1-84800-082-7, © Springer 2008

the answer in a known list or table can be exhaustively tested. Many problems with only a finite number of different allowed input values can be exhaustively tested. But in general exhaustive testing is not possible, and less than exhaustive testing can not show the absence of errors.

Suppose you wanted a program that took any real number as input and returned the absolute value of that number as output. And suppose someone presented you with the following algorithm as a design for such a program.

```
Algorithm absoluteValue (N)
# Precondition: N is a real number.
# Postcondition: Returns the absolute value of N.
      If (N >= 0) then
                  abs ← N
      Else
                  abs ← -N
      Endif
      Return abs
Endalgorithm
```

What could you do to investigate whether this algorithm solves your problem? Would testing be appropriate? How much testing? Would a lot of testing provide more support than a little testing?

If the algorithm were expressed in a programming language then you should compile the program just to be sure that it is grammatically correct, but aside from concerns about grammatical correctness, testing is really not appropriate for this algorithm because you can "see" that it is correct. What is appropriate here is a correctness proof.

19.2   Proofs Expressed in English Prose

Program verification involves reasoning about the problem and the program. It does not (usually) involve testing. Even if an attempt at verification fails, it may still lead to better understanding of what is wrong with the program (or possibly with the problem). If the attempt succeeds then it provides powerful evidence that the program does solve the problem. In that case we say that we have verified that the program solves the problem, or that we have a proof of correctness of the program (with respect to that problem). Of course human reasoning is error prone, so we can never be absolutely sure that a proof of correctness is itself correct. Errors in proofs themselves can be reduced by making the proofs formal enough that they can be checked by computer programs, assuming that the program that does the checking is itself correct. The least formal, but easiest to make correctness proofs are those expressed in ordinary English, as in the following examples.

Example 1. Let Pr be the problem of finding the sum of any four numbers. Let A be the following algorithm.

```
0        Algorithm sumOfFour(N1, N2, N3, N4)
         # Pre: N1, N2, N3, and N4 are numbers.
         # Post: Returns the sum of N1, N2, N3, and N4.
1            sum12 ← N1 + N2
2            sum34 ← N3 + N4
3            sum ← sum12 + sum34
4            Return sum
         EndAlgorithm
```

Proof of correctness. The proof is almost trivial. After line 1, sum12 is N1 + N2. After line 2, sum34 is N3 + N4. Hence, after line 2, sum12 + sum34 is (N1 + N2) + (N3 + N4). Then, after line 3, sum is sum12 + sum34. Hence, after line 3, sum is (N1 + N2) + (N3 + N4). Finally, after line 4, since sum is returned and sum is (N1 + N2) + (N3 + N4), it follows that the sum of N1, N2, N3, and N4 is returned.

Example 2. Consider again the problem, Pr, of finding the absolute value of any given real number. Let A be the algorithm below.

```
0        Algorithm absoluteValue (N)
         # Precondition: N is a real number.
         # Postcondition: Returns the absolute value of N.
1            If (N >= 0) then
2                    abs ← N
3            Else
4                    abs ← -N
5            Endif
6            Return abs
         EndAlgorithm
```

Proof of correctness. Verifying that A solves Pr is almost trivial, since the argument follows the definition of absolute value so closely. Here is the argument. Suppose N is any real number. Then from our knowledge of arithmetic we know that either N >= 0 or N < 0. If N >= 0 then, by the definition of absolute value, the absolute value of N is N itself. In line 2 of the program, N >= 0 and abs is assigned N. Hence if N>= 0 then at the end of line 2, abs is the absolute value of N. On the other hand, if N < 0 then, again by the definition of absolute value, the absolute value of N is -N. Also, if N < 0 then abs in the program is assigned -N at line 4. So if N < 0 then, at the end of line 4, abs is the absolute value of N. Consequently, regardless of whether N >= 0 or N < 0, after line 5 abs is the absolute value of N. At line 6 abs is returned. Hence the program returns the absolute value of N. Hence A solves Pr.

Example 3. Let Pr be the problem of finding the sum of any nonempty finite sequence of numbers. Let A be the following.

```
0          Algorithm findSum(N)
           # Pre: N is a nonempty finite sequence of numbers.
           # Post: Returns the sum of the elements of N.
1              I ← 0
2              sumSoFar ← N[I]    # Assumes array indices start at 0.
3              I ← 1
4              While (I < length of N) do
5                     sumSoFar ← sumSoFar + N[I]
6                     I ← I + 1
7              Endwhile
8              Return sumSoFar
           EndAlgorithm
```

Proof of correctness. Because a loop is involved, verifying that A solves Pr is a bit harder here than in the previous examples. First notice that after line 3 sumSoFar = N[0] and it is the sum of the first 1 elements of N. Moreover, the only other place that sumSoFar is assigned is at line 5 in the body of the loop. The first time through the loop I = 1 and at the end of line 5 sumSoFar = N[0] + N[1]. The second time through the loop I = 2 and at the end of line 5 sumSoFar = N[0] + N[1] + N[2]. In general, every time through the loop, at the end of line 5 sumSoFar = N[0] + N[1] + ... + N[I], then 1 is added to I, so at the end of line 6 sumSoFar is the sum of the first I elements of N. Finally, when the loop terminates, I = the length of N (i.e. the number of elements of N), so sumSoFar = N[0] + N[1] + ... + N[I - 1], and N[I - 1] is the last element of N. Hence at that point sumSoFar is the sum of all the elements of N. Since line 8 returns sumSoFar, the function returns the sum of all the elements of N.

Some things to notice about these verifications are:

1. The verification process involves a lot of reasoning, as expressed in arguments.
2. The arguments are general, they are not about specific test cases.
3. If the arguments are correct then they do establish with near certainty than the algorithm is correct, i.e. that it solves the problem.
4. A proof of correctness of an algorithm does not show that a program that you believe implements the algorithm is correct and it does not establish that the data your real program has to work with satisfies the preconditions of the algorithm.
5. If an algorithm were complex its verification would be long.
6. Even if the arguments are correct, they can be hard to follow if the verification is more than a few lines long.

Exercise 1. Write proofs of correctness in the style of examples 1 – 3 for each of the following algorithms.

(a)
```
0          Algorithm countZeros(L)
           # Pre: L is a list of numbers.
           # Post: Returns the number of zero elements of L.
```

```
1              count ← 0          # Count is number of zeros found so far.
2              I ← 0              # I is loop control variable
3              While (I < len(L)) do
4                      If (L[I] = 0) then count ← count + 1 Endif
5                      I ← I + 1
               Endwhile
6              Return count
           # EndAlgorithm
```

(b)
```
0          Algorithm countNZP(L)
           # Pre: L is a list of numbers.
           # Post: Returns <number of negative elements of L, number of zero
           #        elements of L, number of positive elements of L>

1                   nCount ← 0    # nCount is number of negatives found so far.
2                   zCount ← 0    # zCount is number of zeros found so far
3                   pCount ← 0    # pCount is number of positives found so far
4                   I ← 0         # I is loop control variable
5                   While (I < len(L)) do
6                   If L[I] < 0 then nCount ← nCount + 1 Endif
7                   If L[I] = 0 then zCount ← zCount + 1 Endif
8                   If L[I] > 0 then pCount ← pCount + 1 Endif
9                   I ← I + 1
           Endwhile
10         Return <nCount, zCount, pCount>
           # EndAlgorithm
```

(c)
```
0          Algorithm isReverseOf(A, B)
           # Pre: A and B are 1-dim arrays of numbers of the same length
           # Post: Returns true if B is reverse of A, else returns false

1                   reply ← true
2                   If (len(A) <> len(B)) then
3                       reply ← false
                   Else
4                       I ← 0
5                       While (I < len(A)) and (reply = true)) do
6                               If (A[I] <> B[len(A) - (1 + I)]) then
7                                       reply ← false
                               Endif
8                       I ← I + 1
                       Endwhile
                   Endif
9              Return reply
           EndAlgorithm
```

(d)

```
0      Algorithm isSorted(A)
       # Pre: A is a nonempty 1-dim array of numbers.
       # Post: Returns "yes" if A is sorted (in either ascending or
       # descending order) and returns "no" otherwise.

       # First determine whether sorted ascending.
1              ASORTED ← "yes"  # Change to "no" if found to be unsorted.
2              I ← 0
3              While (I < Len(A) – 1 and ASORTED = "yes") Do
4                      If (A[I] > A[I + 1]) then
5                              ASORTED ← "no"
                       Endif
6                      I ← I + 1
               Endwhile

       # Then check for sorted descending
7              DSORTED ← "yes"  # Change to "no" if found to be unsorted.
8              I ← Len(A) – 1
9              While (I > 0 and DSORTED = "yes") Do
10                     If (A[I – 1] < A[I]) then
11                             DSORTED ← "no"
                       Endif
12                     I ← I – 1
               Endwhile

13             If (ASORTED = "yes" or DSORTED = "yes") then
14                     return "yes"
               Else
15                     return "no"
               Endif
       EndAlgorithm
```

19.3   Proofs Using Floyd's Method of Invariant Assertions

There are several methods for helping to find and organize correctness proofs other than using informal English. The method described here is based on the work of R. W. Floyd and others. It is called *Floyd's Method* or *the method of invariant assertions*. It consists of annotating some representation of the program with various assertions which, along with justifications for those assertions, will show that the algorithm being discussed is correct. Originally the representation of the algorithm used was a flowchart, but a listing of the program can also be used. The reason why the assertions are called "invariant" assertions is that they are always (invariably) true whenever execution of the program reaches the point to which they are attached.

Example 4. Representing Example 1 above in this way is very easy as it uses only sequential control structure.

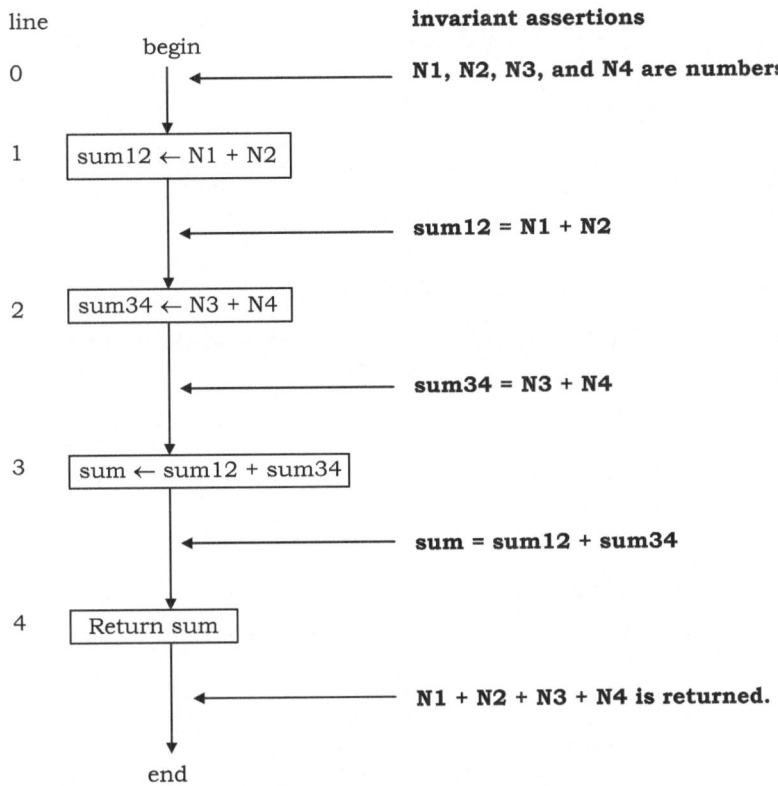

The key features to notice here are:

1. The first invariant assertion is the precondition of the algorithm.
2. The last invariant assertion is the postcondition of the algorithm.
3. There is a "chain" of intermediate assertions on the only path through the program.
4. On a given chain of assertions, each assertion after the first follows logically from previous assertions and the actions described in the corresponding path of the program up to that point on the chain.
5. In this example there are no loops, hence the program will always terminate.
6. To complete the proof, each invariant assertion should be accompanied by the reasons, as given earlier, for why the reader should believe that that assertion is true.
7. This example is misleading in one respect. It has an invariant assertion following each instruction in the algorithm. This is not necessary. There could be many instructions between successive invariant assertions.

Example 5. Consider Example 2 once again. In this example, the control flow is represented graphically by a flowchart.

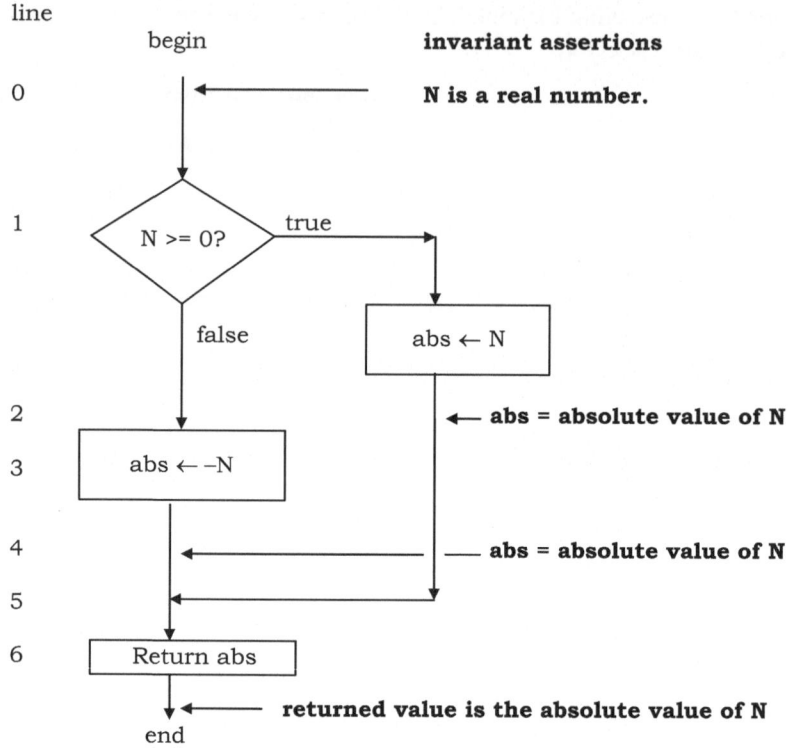

line

begin   **invariant assertions**

0   **N is a real number.**

1   N >= 0?   true

                         false   abs ← N

2   ← **abs = absolute value of N**

3   abs ← –N

4   — **abs = absolute value of N**

5

6   Return abs

                                    ← **returned value is the absolute value of N**
        end

The key features to notice here are:

1. The first invariant assertion is the precondition of the algorithm.
2. The last invariant assertion is the postcondition of the algorithm.
3. There is a "chain" of intermediate assertions on every path through the program.
4. On a given chain of assertions, each assertion after the first follows logically from previous assertions and the actions described in the corresponding path of the program up to that point on the chain.
5. In this example there are no loops, hence no question but what the program will always terminate.
6. To complete the proof, each invariant assertion should be accompanied by the reasons, as given earlier, for why the reader should believe that that assertion is true.
7. Not every instruction is followed immediately by an invariant assertion.

Example 6. Representing Example 3 above requires dealing with a loop,

The new feature to notice here is the loop and the assertion attached to it, called a loop invariant. It is a statement that is true after line 6 is executed, no matter how many times the loop is executed. The method of invariant assertions is named after loop invariants.

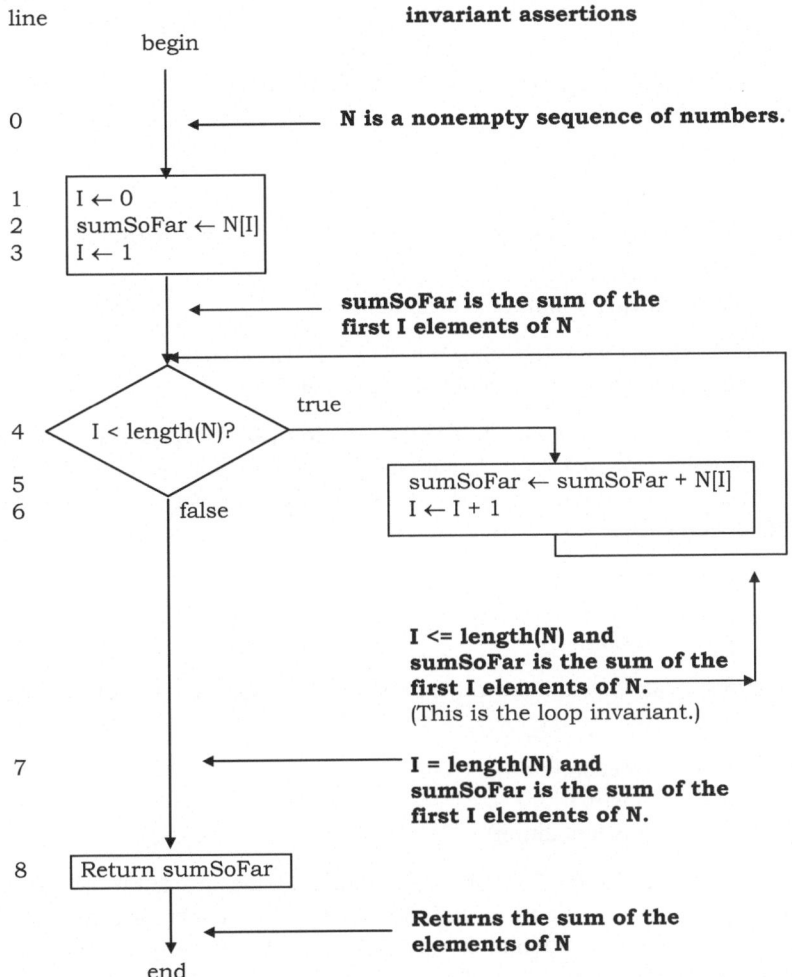

line   **invariant assertions**

begin

0   **N is a nonempty sequence of numbers.**

1 I ← 0
2 sumSoFar ← N[I]
3 I ← 1

sumSoFar is the sum of the first I elements of N

      true
4 I < length(N)?

5   sumSoFar ← sumSoFar + N[I]
6   false I ← I + 1

I <= length(N) and sumSoFar is the sum of the first I elements of N.
(This is the loop invariant.)

7   **I = length(N) and sumSoFar is the sum of the first I elements of N.**

8 Return sumSoFar

Returns the sum of the elements of N

end

Another important point is that we are sure the loop will eventually terminate. This is because I starts out less than length(N) and each time through the loop I is increased by 1. By virtue of the rules of arithmetic, I must eventually = length(N), which causes the loop to terminate. Hence if the loop body is executed then the algorithm will terminate. Moreover, if the loop body does not execute, because length(N) = 1, the algorithm will still terminate, and sumSoFar will still be the sum of all the elements of N.

19.4 Rules of Inference Involving Algorithms

The major problem with using the method of invariant assertions is finding appropriate assertions and reasoning correctly about them. Here logic can help, although it will not do the whole job. The part of logic described in earlier chapters has been known for a long time and is often said to be *classical logic*. The discussion below introduces some new kinds of statements and rules of inference that involve instructions and algorithms. This new part of logic is of recent origin and is sometimes called *Floyd-Hoare logic*.

19.4.1   Notation for Statements Involving Instructions

Consider the following conditional statement:

If (initially) X + 7 were less than Y and then Z was assigned the value of X + 7, then (immediately thereafter) Z would be less than Y.

In the discussion below we will use the notation {A} P {B} to represent conditional expressions of that kind. Notations like {A} P {B} are known as *Hoare triples*, after C. A. R. Hoare. Spacing on a page often makes it more convenient to write them vertically.

{A}   (precondition)
P   (instruction(s))
{B}   (postcondition)

Using this notation, and a few other abbreviations, the statement above could be written:

{X + 7 < Y}   (precondition)
Z ← X + 7   (instruction)
{Z < Y}   (postcondition)

In general the notation {A} P {B} will represent the claim that if the conditions described by the assertion(s) {A} obtained immediately before executing instruction(s) P, then the attempt to execute P would eventually end and, when it did, the conditions described by the assertion(s) {B} would obtain immediately after executing P. The statements of {A} are called preconditions for P and the statements of {B} are called postconditions for P. It is important to notice that the parts of this kind of conditional are joined by "and then" rather that by the simple truth functional "and".

19.4.2   The Assignment Rule

Let P(v) be a condition involving the program variable v and let e be any expression. The assignment rule is: if P(v) is true when expression e is substituted for each instance of v in P(v), and if v is then assigned the value of e, then, after the assignment, P(v) is true. The expression P(e/v) is used to represent the result of replacing each instance of v in P(v) with the expression e. It is read as "P with e in place of v".

The Assignment Rule
$\{P(e/v)\}$
$\underline{v \leftarrow e}$
$\{P(v)\}$

Example 7

$\{2 = 2)$	$P(e/v)$ when $P(v)$ is $v = 2$ and $e = 2$
$v \leftarrow 2$	$v \leftarrow e$
$\{v = 2\}$	$P(v)$
$\{1+1 = 1+1\}$	$P(e/v)$ when $P(v)$ is $v = 2$ and e is $1+1$
$v \leftarrow 1+1$	$v \leftarrow e$
$\{v = 1+1\}$	$P(v)$
$\{X + 7 < Y\}$	$P(e/v)$ when $P(v)$ is $v < Y$ and e is $X + 7$
$v \leftarrow X + 7$	$v \leftarrow e$
$\{v < Y\}$	$P(v)$
$\{10 < x + y < 20\}$	$P(e/z)$ when $P(z)$ is $10 < z < 20$ and e is $x + y$
$z \leftarrow x + y$	$z \leftarrow e$
$\{10 < z < 20\}$	$P(z)$
$\{x + 1 > 1\}$	$P(e/y)$ when $P(y)$ is $y > 1$ and e is $x + 1$
$y \leftarrow x + 1$	
$\{y > 1\}$	
$\{3(x + 1) + 2 > z$	$P(e/x)$ when $P(x)$ is $3x + 2 > z$ and e is $x + 1$
$x \leftarrow x + 1$	
$\{3x + 2 > z\}$	
$2(x + 3) < 5(x + 3)$	$P(e/z)$ when $P(z)$ is $2z < 5z$ and e is $x + 3$
$z \leftarrow x + 3$	
$2z < 5z$	

It is important to be aware that while the examples above are read from top to bottom, when proving programs correct the rule is applied backwards, i.e. $P(e/v)$ is constructed so that $P(v)$ will be true after $v \leftarrow e$ is executed. This will be shown in example proofs below.

Exercise 2. In each case, find $\{P(e/v)\}$ given $v \leftarrow e$ and $\{P(v)$ where v is some variable.

a. $v \leftarrow 5 \ \{v = 5\}$
b. $x \leftarrow z + 4 \ \{3x + 1 > 12$
c. $x \leftarrow x + 5 \ \{x + 5 < z + x\}$
d. $z \leftarrow \min(x, y) \ \{z + \max(x, y) < 0\}$

19.4.3 Rules of Inference about Control Structures

Consider the following argument.

if X were < 3 and then Y was assigned X then Y would be < 3. Moreover if Y were < 3 and then Z was assigned Y then Z would be < 3. Therefore, if X were < 3 and then Y was assigned X and then Z was assigned Y then Z would be < 3.

Expressed symbolically this could be written:

$$\frac{\{X < 3\}\ Y \leftarrow X\ \{Y < 3\}}{\{Y < 3\}\ Z \leftarrow Y\ \{Z < 3\}}$$
$$\overline{\{X < 3\}\ Y \leftarrow X;\ Z \leftarrow Y\ \{Z < 3\}}$$

In general we have:

The Sequence Rule

$$\frac{\{A\}\ P1\ \{B\}}{\{B\}\ P2\ \{C\}}$$
$$\overline{\{A\}\ P1;P2\ \{C\}}$$

In this rule, also called the *rule of composition*, P1 and P2 represent any pair of instructions while P1;P2 represents the single compound instruction whose components are P1 and P2 in that order. The sequence rule can be applied over and over to construct valid arguments about arbitrarily long sequences of instructions.

Notice that the differences among "is", "was" "were", and "would be", are not explicitly indicated in the symbolic notation. However, they are not to be regarded as lost but as implicit in the notation.

There are several rules involving conditional expressions. One of them is a generalization of the following example.

If X were = Y and Y were = Z and then Z was assigned Z + 1, then X would not = Z. Moreover if X were = Y and Y was not = Z then X would not = Z. Consequently, if X were = Y and then the conditional instruction "If Y = Z then Z is assigned Z + 1" was executed then X would not = Z (whether or not Y = Z initially).

Put in symbolic form this becomes:

$$\frac{\{X = Y \text{ and } Y = Z\}\ Z \leftarrow Z + 1\ \{\text{not } X = Z\}}{\text{If } (X = Y \text{ and not } Y = Z) \text{ then not } X = Z}$$
$$\overline{\{X = Y\}\ \text{If } Y = Z \text{ then } Z \leftarrow Z + 1\ \{\text{Not } X = Z\}}$$

More generally we have:

The If Rule

$$\frac{\{A \wedge C\}\ P\ \{B\}}{(A \wedge \sim C) \rightarrow \{B\}}$$
$$\overline{\{A\}\ \text{If } C \text{ then } P\ \{B\}}$$

Here A, B, and C represent conditions (statements), P represents an instruction, and "If C then P" represents the corresponding conditional instruction.

Another rule involving conditional instructions is exemplified by the following argument, in which "NUM(X)" stand for "X is a number" and "ABS(X)" stand for "the absolute value of X".

If X were a number less than 0 and then Y was assigned -X, then Y would = ABS(X). On the other hand, if X were a nonnegative number and then Y were assigned X, then Y would = ABS(X). Therefore, we could conclude that if X were a number and then the conditional instruction 'If X < 0 then Y ← -X else Y ← X' were executed, Y would = ABS(X).

Expressed as an instance of a rule of inference this becomes:

{NUM(X) and X < 0} Y ← -X {Y = ABS(X)}
{NUM(X) and X => 0) Y ← X {Y = ABS(X)}
(NUM(X)} If X < 0 then Y ← -X else Y ←X {Y = ABS(X)}

The general rule is:

The If Else Rule

{A ∧ C} P1 {B}
{A ∧ ~C} P2 {B}
{A} If C then P1 else P2 {B}

Here again A, B, and C represent conditions (statements), P1 and P2 represent instructions, and "If C then P1 else P2" represents the corresponding conditional instruction.

There are also rules involving the various kinds of loops. Here is one example involving While Do. Suppose you want to compute the SUM of the elements in a LIST of N numbers where N > 0. You could do this as follows:

1. COUNT ← 1
2. SUM ← LIST[COUNT]
3.
4. WHILE (COUNT < N) DO
5.   COUNT ← COUNT + 1
6.   SUM ← SUM + LIST[COUNT]
7. END WHILE

The strategy of the algorithm is to accumulate elements of LIST into SUM until SUM is the sum of all of them. More precisely, notice that at line 4 if SUM were the sum of the first COUNT elements of LIST and COUNT were < N and then the body of the loop (lines 5 & 6) were executed once, then SUM would still be the sum of the first COUNT elements of LIST (whether or not COUNT were still < N). The fact that SUM continues to be the sum of the first COUNT elements of LIST is called a loop invariant of that loop. Using I to stand for that loop invariant, using C to abbreviate the claim that COUNT < N, and using P to represent the body of the loop (= the instructions of lines 5 and 6), the next to last statement can be written:

{I ∧ C} P {I}

Since the loop is executed while C is true, i.e. while COUNT < N, at line 8, immediately after the loop execution is completed, we know that I and not C, i.e. SUM is the sum of the first COUNT elements of LIST and not COUNT < N.

Moreover, since during the next to last iteration of the loop COUNT was < N and COUNT is increased by one each time through the loop, COUNT must now = N. Consequently, SUM is the sum of the first N elements of LIST, which is all the elements of LIST. The general rule of which this is an example is:

The While Do Rule
$$\frac{\{\,I \wedge C\,\}\,P\,\{\,I\,\}}{\{\,I\,\}\ \text{WHILE C DO P}\ \{\,I \wedge \sim C\,\}}$$

Here I represents a loop invariant, C represents the loop exit condition, and P represents the loop body.

Other kinds of loops have their own rules. As with classical logic, there are (infinitely) many other rules of inference and several slightly different ways to express them.

19.5   Proofs Using Rules of Inference

Procedure PC: Given the precondition and postcondition for a problem and given an algorithm, to prove that this algorithm solves this problem do the following:

Step 1. Write the algorithm vertically as described below

Algorithm algorithmName(input parameter list)
Pre: Precondition
        First instruction
        Second instruction
        ...
        Last instruction
Post: Postcondition

Step 2. Beginning with the postcondition and working toward the precondition, insert one or more midconditions between each instruction. Each midcondition is a precondition for the instruction following it and a postcondition for the instruction just prior to it. Midconditions must be chosen so that each one can be derived from axioms, definitions, and earlier instructions and conditions by means of rules of inference and previously established results including the theorems of logic, mathematics, and computer science.

Step 3. Indicate which rule of inference justifies each midcondition or postcondition, adding explanatory comments as you think appropriate. Here conditions in Hoare triples are indicated with # as a prefix rather than being enclosed in curly brackets. The result should look like this:

Algorithm algorithmName(input parameter list)
Pre: Precondition
   First instruction
   # Midcondition   justification and comments
   Second instruction
   # Midcondition   justification and comments
   ...
   Last instruction
Post: Postcondition   justification and comments

If the conditions, instructions, justifications, and comments are expressed very informally then the result is an informal correctness proof. If conditions, instructions, and justifications are expressed formally then the result is a formal correctness proof. Formal correctness proofs can be checked for correctness by computer programs but people usually find them long and boring. Informal proofs cannot (yet) be checked for correctness by computer programs, but they are easier for human beings to read and check.

Computer programs can help people generate correctness proofs and people can help computers generate correctness proofs, but except for limited kinds of programs, computers cannot generate error free correctness proofs on their own.

In the examples and exercises given here, instructions will be limited to assignment instructions, if-then and if-then-else instructions, while-do instructions, with nesting of one type of instruction in another allowed. Only simple conditions and mathematical operations will be used.

Example 8. Another proof of Example 1.

0	Algorithm sumOfFour(N1, N2, N3, N4)	
1	# Pre: N1, N2, N3, and N4 are numbers.	
2	# N1 + N2 = N1 + N2	Identity Laws
3	sum12 ← N1 + N2	
4	# sum12 = N1 + N2	Assignment Rule
5	# N3 + N4 = N3 + N4	Identity Laws
6	sum34 ← N3 + N4	
7	# sum34 = N3 + N4	Assignment Rule
8	# sum12 + sum34 = sum12 + sum34	Identity Laws
9	sum ← sum12 + sum34	
10	# sum = sum12 + sum34	Assignment Rule
11	# sum =(N1 + N2) + (N3 + N4)	Substitution Rule
12	# sum = N1 + N2 + N3 + N4	Arithmetic
13	Return sum	
14	# Post: Returns N1 + N2 + N3 + N4	Substitution Rule
	EndAlgorithm	

The proof is constructed from line 14 upwards. Of course, the number of lines and which lines get what numbers is not known until the proof is completed.

Line 14 states the postcondition that should be true immediately after line 13 is executed. Line 12 is constructed so this will be true. Line 11 is constructed so as to conform to the punctuation in line 9. Line 10 is constructed from line 11 by substitution. Line 10 is constructed from line 9 and line 8 is constructed from lines 9 and 10 in anticipation of applying the Assignment rule to lines 8, 9 and 10. To see how this works, recall the Assignment Rule.

$$\frac{\{P(e/v)\}}{v \leftarrow e} \\ \overline{\{P(v)\}}$$

To apply it, line 10 must play the role of $P(v)$ and line 9 must play the role of $v \rightarrow e$ in the Assignment rule. Hence sum corresponds to v and sum12 + sum34 corresponds to e. Hence $P(e/v)$ must be sum12 + sum34 = sum12 + sum34, which is line 8. This is summarized in the following table.

The role of	is played by
$P(v)$	sum = sum12 + sum34
v	sum
e	sum12 + sum34
$v \leftarrow e$	sum $\leftarrow$ sum12 + sum34
$P(e/v)$	sum12 + sum34 = sum12 + sum34

Similarly the Assignment rule is the only rule to use on line 6 and line 3. With this in mind, line 7 is constructed from line 6 and line 5 is constructed from lines 6 and 7 with sum34 as v and N3 + N4 as e. And line 4 comes from line 3 and line 2 comes from lines 3 & 4 with sum12 as v and N1 + N2 as e.

Now that the proof is constructed, it can be read from top to bottom as a proof would normally be read. Line 1 is the precondition, so it needs no other justification. Line 2 is an instance of the Identity laws. Line 3 is an instruction of the algorithm so it needs no justification. Line 4 follows from lines 2 and 3 by the Assignment rule. Line 5 is another instance of the Identity laws, line 6 is another instruction, and line 7 follows from lines 5 and 6 by the Assignment rule. Similarly, line 8 is another instance of the Identity laws, line 9 is an instruction, and line 10 follows from lines 8 and 9 by the Assignment rule. Line 11 follows from lines 4, 7 and 10 by Substitution. Line 12 follows from 11 by the parenthesis dropping conventions of arithmetic. Line 13 is an instruction and line 14 follows from 12 and 13 by substitution.

Another way to view this proof is that it, along with several applications of the sequence rule, shows that the Hoare triple below is true.

{N1, N2, N3, and N4 are numbers.}
sumOfFour(N1, N2, N3, N4)
{Returns N1 + N2 + N3 + N4}

Example 9. Another proof of Example 2.

| 0 | Algorithm absoluteValue (N) | |
| 1 | # Precondition: N is a real number. | |

2	# N >= 0 → N = |N| ∧ ~N >= 0 → -N = |N| Def of |N|	
3	If (N >= 0) then	
4	# N = |N|	If Rule
5	abs ← N	
6	# abs = |N|	Assignment Rule
7	Else	
8	# -N = |N|	If Rule
9	abs ← -N	
10	# abs = |N|	Assignment Rule
	Endif	
11	# abs = |N|	If Rule
12	Return abs	
13	# Postcondition: Returns |N|	Substitution
	EndAlgorithm	

The proof is constructed from line 13 upwards with a view to applying the If Else Rule.

$$\frac{\{A \wedge C\}\ P1\ \{B\} \qquad \{A \wedge \sim C\}\ P2\ \{B\}}{\{A\}\ \text{If}\ C\ \text{then}\ P1\ \text{else}\ P2\ \{B\}}$$

Line 13 which is the postcondition is implied by lines 11 and 12 using substitution. If the following role assignments are made then lines 2 through 11 are an instance of the If Then Rule:

The role of	is played by
A	N >= 0 → N = |N| ∧ ~N >= 0 → -N = |N|
C	N >= 0
P1	abs ← N
~C	~N >= 0
P2	abs ← -N
B	abs = |N|

Finally note that line 2 is implied by the line 1.

Another way to view this proof is that it, along with several applications of the sequence rule, shows that the Hoare triple below is true.

{N is a number.}
absoluteValue(N)
{Returns \|N\|}

Example 10. Another proof of Example 3, with J written in place of I to avoid confusion with the I in the While Do Rule.

Algorithm findSum(N)
Pre: N is a nonempty finite sequence of numbers.
Post: Returns the sum of the elements of N.
        J ← 0
        sumSoFar ← N[J] //Assumes array indices start at 0.
        J ← 1
        While (J < length of N) do
                sumSoFar ← sumSoFar + N[J]
                J ← J + 1
        Endwhile
        Return sumSoFar
EndAlgorithm

This proof is mostly an application of the While Do Rule.

$$\frac{\{\,I \wedge C\}\; P\; \{\,I\,\}}{\{\,I\,\}\; \text{While } C \text{ Do } P\; \{\,I \wedge \sim C\,\}}$$

In order to apply this rule pieces of the algorithm have to be matched to pieces of the rule. Obviously P is the body of the loop and C is the loop control condition. So

The role of	is played by
P	sumSoFar ← sumSoFar + N[J]
	J ← J + 1
C	J ← length of N

The problem is I. What is it doing and how can it be found. I is called a *loop invariant*. It is supposed to be a condition such that if it is true just before the loop body is executed then it will still be true immediately after execution of the loop body ends, no matter how many times the loop body is executed. It may be useful to think of it as "what the loop does", although it is not necessary to characterize it that way. It should also be a condition that aids overall progress of the proof, so it should follow form previously proved conditions. And its truth, along with the truth of ~C, should aid in proving later conditions. There are many conditions which are loop invariants for a given loop but which are probably not useful. For example, any logically true condition. The problem is to find a useful loop invariant. It turns out that finding useful loop invariants cannot be reduced to formal rules. It requires luck or ingenuity. This is why the process of constructing proofs of correct algorithms cannot be automated.

In this case let I be "sumSoFar is the sum of the first J elements of N". Then

The role of	is played by
P	sumSoFar ← sumSoFar + N[J]
	J ← J + 1
C	J < length of N
I	sumSoFar is the sum of the first J elements of N

When the loop is first encountered sumSoFar = N[0], J = 1, and so sumSoFar is the sum of the first J elements of N. If the length of N is 1 then J ← length of N, the loop body will not be executed, and just after the loop I ∧ ~C will be true. On the other hand if N has more elements then the loop body is executed so the value of the next element of N is added to sumSoFar and J is increased by 1. Consequently after the loop body is executed it will still be the case that sumSoFar is the sum of the first J elements of N. Each time J < length of N this process of adding the next element of N to sumSoFar and adding 1 to J will be repeated. And at the end of each execution of the loop body sumSoFar is the sum of the first J elements of N. If the loop halts it will be that J is not < length of N. Moreover, since J increases by 1 each time, when the loop halts J = length of N. Hence sumSoFar will be the sum of all the elements of N. This reasoning is embodied in the proof below.

Algorithm findSum(N)
   # Pre: N is a nonempty finite sequence of numbers.
      # Assumes array indices start at 0.

# 0 = 0	Identity Laws
J ← 0	
# J = 0	Assignment Rule
# N[J] =N[J]	Identity Laws
sumSoFar ← N[J]	
# sumSoFar = N[J]	Assignment Rule
# sumSoFar = N[0]	Substitution
J ← 1	
# sumSoFar is the sum of the first J elements of N	
While (J < length of N) do	
# sumSoFar is the sum of the first J elements of N ∧	
# J ← length of N	
sumSoFar ← sumSoFar + N[J]	
J ← J + 1	
Endwhile	
# sumSoFar is the sum of the first J elements of N ∧	
# J = length of N	Arithmetic and While Do Rule
Return sumSoFar	Substitution

   # Post: Returns the sum of the elements of N.
   EndAlgorithm

Another way to view this proof is that it, along with several applications of the sequence rule, shows that the Hoare triple below is true.

   {N is a nonempty sequence of numbers}
   findSum
   {Returns the sum of the elements of N}

Exercise 3. In each part an incomplete instance of a rule of inference is given. Identify the rule you can apply and fill in the missing conclusion.

(a)

{x and y are integers} z ← x * y {x and y are factors of z}

{x and y are factors of z} w ← z² {x² and y² are factors of w}

?

(b)

{x < 0} y ← x² {y > 0}

{y > 0} z ← -y {z < 0}

?

(c)

{x and y are numbers and x >= y} max ← x {max is the larger of x and y}

{x and y are numbers and ~x >=y} max ← y {max is the larger of x and y}

?

(d)

{a divides b and a divides c} a ← b {a divides b * c}

(a divides b and ~a divides c) → (a divides b * c)

?

(e)

F = J factorial ∧ J < N} J ← J + 1; F ← F * J {F = J factorial}

?

(f)

{P = 2^J ∧ J < N} J ← J + 1; P ← 2 * P {P = 2^J}

?

Exercise 4. Give complete proofs of correctness (supplying midconditions and reasons) for each of the following algorithms.

(a)

Algorithm maxOf2(x, y)

\# Pre: x and y are numbers.

\# Post: Returns the maximum of x and y.

      If (x >= y) then

              max ← x

      Else

              max ← y

      Endif

      Return max

EndAlgorithm

(b)

Algorithm oddFloor(x)

\# Pre: x is an integer.

\# Post: Returns the largest odd integer <= x.

      If (x is odd) then

              rtnVal ← x

```
          Else
                  rtnVal ← x −1
          Endif
          Return rtnVal
  EndAlgorithm
```

(c)
```
Algorithm powerOf2Floor(x)
# Pre: x is a number >=1.
# Post: returns the largest power of 2 < = x
          J ← 0
          While (2^J <= x) Do
                  J ← J + 1
          EndWhile
          Return 2^{J-1}
EndAlgorithm
```

(d)
```
Algorithm countLower(L, B)
# Pre: L is a nonempty list of numbers and B is a number.
# Post: Returns the number of elements of L which are < B.
          bCount ← 0
          J ← 0
          While (J ← len(L)) Do
                  If (L(J) < B then
                          bCount ← bCount + 1
                  Endif
                  J ← J + 1
          EndWhile
          Return bCount
EndAlgorithm
```

Chapter 20
Above and Beyond this Book

This chapter provides information for readers who want to learn more about topics discussed in previous chapters and readers who want to learn about related topics not discussed here. In place of exercises, a few programming challenges are provided.

Both the ACM and the IEEE Computer Society maintain extensive and overlapping digital libraries which can be accessed for a moderate fee. They contain articles on nearly all topics involving the intersection of computing and logic. Your favorite web search engine will get more hits than you have time to look at for any of those topics. I intend to post links to relevant web sites at www.logicforsoftwaredevelopment. com. Listed below are a few books which either go more deeply into topics discussed in this book or discuss related topics not discussed here. The background provided in this book is either helpful or necessary for understanding most of them.

Outline

R. Lover, *Elementary Logic: For Software Development*,
DOI: 10.2007/978-1-84800-082-7, © Springer 2008

20.1   Other Texts on Classical Logic

20.1.1   Standard Texts

Many of the best logic texts are written by philosophers, logicians, and mathematicians with little thought given to computing applications. In addition to the books mentioned in Sources and Bibliography, *Language, Proof and Logic* (Barwise, Etchemendy 2002) is particularly interesting because it includes several programs designed to help the reader learn logic, and it comes with a grading service whereby readers can submit answers to exercises to be graded by a program at Stanford University. Other books worth considering are *Boolean Reasoning: The Logic of Boolean Equations* (Brown 2003), *Methods of Logic* (Quine 1982), *Axiomatic Set Theory* (Suppes 1972), and *Boolean Algebra and Its Applications* (Whitesitt 1995).

20.1.2   Computer Oriented Texts

Proof and Disproof in Formal Logic: An Introduction for Programmers (Bornat 2005), *Logic for Information Technology* (Galton 1990), *Discrete Structures, Logic, and Computability* (Hein 2002), *Logic in Computer Science* (Huth, Ryan 2004), *Logic: A Foundation for Computer Science* (Sperschneider, Antonion 1991), *Logic for Computer Science* (Reeves, Clarke 1990), and *The Deductive Foundations of Computer Programming* (Zohar 1993) are worth examining.

20.2   Extensions of Classical Logic

There are a number of extensions of and rivals to classical logic that are relevant to computer science. A brief survey is contained in *Logics for Artificial Intelligence* (Turner 1984).

20.2.1   Floyd-Hoare Logic

One extension of classical logic, Floyd-Hoare logic, was introduced in Chap. 19. Sources in this tradition include *The Design of Well-Structured and Correct Programs* (Alagic, Arbib 1978), *Proving Programs Correct* (Anderson 1979), *Verification of Sequential and Concurrent Programs* (Apt, Olderolg 1991), *Formal Methods of Program Verification and Specification* (Berg, Boebert, Franta, Moher1982), *A Discipline of Programming* (Dijkstra 1976), *Program Verification* (Francez 1992), *The Science of Programming* (Gries 1981), and *Programming Logics: An Introduction to Verification and Semantics* (Gumb 1989).

20.2.2   Temporal, Modal, and Dynamic Logics

Other extensions of classical logic include temporal logic, modal logic, and dynamic logic. *Logics of Time and Computation* (Goldblatt 1992) is a survey of these. *Logic in Computer Science: Modelling and Reasoning about Systems* (Huth, Ryan 2000) extends classical logic in several ways and is very readable. Dynamic logic is covered in great detail in *Dynamic Logic* (Harel, Kozen, Tiuryn 2000).

20.3   Rivals to Classical Logic

Rivals to classical logic include multi-valued logic, intuitionistic logic, and fuzzy logic. *Logics for Artificial Intelligence* (Turner 1984) discusses both of these. *Deviant Logic Fuzzy Logic: Beyond the Formalism* (Haack 1996) discusses several rivals to classical logic from the perspective of philosophy rather than computer science. Perhaps the most interesting rival to classical logic is quantum logic, as is now being developed for quantum computers and quantum computer programming, discussed below.

20.4   Applications of Logic to Computing or Computing to Logic

20.4.1   Logic Circuits

Truth functional logic is central to the design of logic circuits for computers. Discussions of this can be found in most introductory computer science books, e.g. *Foundations of Computer Science* (Aho, Ullman 2004).

20.4.2   3-Valued Logic and SQL

SQL statements involving relational databases with null data fields seem to violate the law of excluded middle. One way to deal with this is to use 3-valued logic, as described in *A Guide to the SQL Standard* (Date 1997) and *SQL Clearly Explained* (Harrington 1998).

20.4.3   More on Expressing and Using Specifications

Using logic in aid of writing problem and program specifications and using these in aid of writing provably correct programs is discussed in *Software Specification: A Comparison of Formal Methods* (Gannon, Purtilo, Zelkowitz 1994), *The Way of Z:*

Practical Programming with Formal Methods (Jacky 1997), S*pecifying Systems:
The TLA + Language and Tools for Hardware and Software Engineers* (Lamport
2003) and *Software Blueprints: Lightweight Uses of Logic in Conceptual Modelling*
(Robertson, Agusti 1999). The process of making "correct by construction" pro-
grams is described in *Program Construction: Calculating Implementations from
Specifications* (Backhouse 2003).

20.4.4   *Logic Testing of Software*

Many introductory programming books have a chapter on testing that often includes
discussion of various logic based "coverages." Most texts on software testing discuss logic based testing procedures. Several of these are discussed in Boris Beizer's
classic *Software Testing Techniques* (Beizer 1990).

20.4.5   *Computability and Algorithmic Unsolvability*

The question of what can and what cannot be computed by means of a computer
program is a fundamental issue in computer science. Among many interesting
books on this topic are *Solvable Cases of the Decision Problem* (Ackermann 1962),
Computability and Logic (Boolos, Jeffrey 1989), *Computability and Unsolvability*
(Davis 1973), *Mathematical Theory of Computation* (Manna 1974), and *Introduction
to Languages, Machines and Logic: Computable Languages, Abstract Machines
and Formal Logic* (Parkes 2002). For readers who want to read original sources,
*The Undecidable: Basic Papers on Undecidable Propositions, Unsolvable Problems
and Computable Functions* (Davis 2004) is a collection of classic papers.

20.4.6   *AI and Computer Aided Reasoning*

Various computer reasoning programs have been written, mostly in the Prolog
(programming in logic) and Lisp (list processing) programming languages. They
vary from artificial intelligence programs designed to mimic human reasoning
without interaction with humans to computer aided reasoning systems designed to
help people reason better. Early expectations of spectacular success with such programs were disappointed. Automated natural language translation, for example,
turned out to be much harder than originally anticipated. However, expert systems
that were confined to very narrow problems and often included some interaction
with humans have been usefully deployed for many years. Moreover, slow but
steady progress has been made on the hard problems so, for example, it is now
possible to buy a natural language translation program for a few hundred dollars
that does a moderately good job.

More interesting perhaps are computer aided reasoning systems such as the ACL2 system described in *Computer-Aided Reasoning: An Approach* and *Computer-Aided Reasoning: ACL2 Case Studies* (Kaufmann, Manolios, Moore 2002a, 2002b). This is a system which helps people state and prove theorems whose proofs are mechanically verifiable.

The Art of Prolog (Sterling 1994) is a classic Prolog text. *Expert Systems: Principles and Programming* (Giarrantano 2005) is a wide-ranging discussion of AI programming which includes a free AI programming language, CLIPS, and has a nice appendix on "Software Resources.". *Probabilistic Reasoning in Intelligent Systems: Networks and Plausible Inference* (Pearl 1988) has a good discussion of reasoning under uncertainty.

20.4.7   Quantum Computing and Programming

Quantum computing is a very rapidly developing field even by computer industry standards. Hardly a week goes by without an announcement of some new development in the search for ways to make practical quantum computers. Interesting new algorithms appear much less frequently. However, several recently developed quantum programming languages may help people develop new algorithms.

General background in quantum physics that should be accessible to readers of this book can be found in *The Odd Quantum* (Treiman 2002) and *Paradox Lost: Images of the Quantum* (Wallace 1996).

Among interesting popularizations of quantum computing are *Minds, Machines, and the Multiverse* (Brown 2002), *A Shortcut Through Time* (Johnson 2003), *Entangled World: The Fascination of Quantum Information and Computation* (Jurgen 2006), and *Programming the Universe* (Lloyd 2006).

Seriously technical but still "introductory" are *Principles of Quantum Computation and Information, Volume I: Introductory Concepts* (Benenti, Casati, Strini 2005) and the very widely cited *Quantum Computation and Quantum Information* (Nielsen, Chuang 2000).

20.5   Programming Challenges

For software developers, writing software to implement logical procedures described in some parts of this book should be an interesting and instructive challenge. Listed below are some programming challenges (PCs) you might consider, along with a few remarks about them. Assume that each of the PC statements below begins with "Write a program in your favorite programming language that"

PC1. Given a statement expressed in English as input, will give a correct logical English abbreviation of it as output.

This is an extremely hard problem. Because English is so complicated and subtle I would strongly advise you against trying to write such a program, although you might learn a lot while trying and failing. However, especially if you are interested in natural languages, you might try to define a sufficiently small subset of English vocabulary and grammar in which users could express statements to be used as input to your program. Your program should give correct logical English abbreviations of them as output. Using restricted subsets of English to write instructions in something resembling English was part of the idea behind COBOL and SQL, which at one point was called "structured English Query Language"." The challenge here is to express statements, not instructions. Suggestion: start with an extremely limited subset of English with no logical variables and no quantifiers.

PC2. Given a character string, determine whether it is a tff . This and the next challenge are closely related.

PC3. Given a tff, identify its parts, i.e. identify its name symbols, predicate symbols, variables, logical functions, etc.

PC4. Given a tff and an assignment of truth values for its elementary statements, determine the truth value of the statement.

PC5. Given a tff, make and display a truth table for it.

PC6. Given a tff, determine whether it is TF-true, TF-false, or TF-contingent.

PC7. Given the tffs of an argument, determine whether the argument is TF-valid, TF-inconsistent, or TF-contingent.

PC8. Given two tffs and a rule of inference, determine whether the second tff follows from the first by means of that rule of inference.

PC9. Given a small set of tffs and a small set of rules of inference, apply those rules of inference to generate a small set of new correct logical consequence tffs.

PC10. Given a set of tffs, determine whether it is redundant and enumerate each tff that is redundant with respect to the others.

PC11. Given a proof expressed in some standard form and given a set of axioms and rules of inference, determine whether that proof is correct.

PC12. Given an argument, determine whether it is or is not TF-valid, i.e. find a decision procedure for truth functional validity.

PC13. Given an argument find a formal proof (using rules of inference) that the argument form is TF-valid valid or find a truth functional interpretation in which all the premises are true and the conclusion is false.

All the challenges above had to do with truth functional logic. The next few have to do with quantificational logic. You will need to use information not covered in this book to do some parts of them. PC14, 15 and 16 are much harder than PC1 –13 and some parts of PC16 are impossible.

PC14. See how far you can get repeating PC1–PC13 with syllogisms and substituting logical concepts such as L-true, L-false, L-contingent, L-valid, etc. where appropriate. This is a special case of PC15. Syllogisms are discussed in many introductory logic texts, e.g. (Copi, Cohen 2005).

PC15. See how far you can get repeating PC1–PC13 with expressions involving logical variables, predicates, and quantifiers but in which only 1-place predicates are allowed (the monadic predicate calculus) and substituting logical concepts such as L-true, L-false, L-contingent, L-valid, etc. where appropriate.

PC16. See how far you can get repeating PC1—PC13 with expressions involving logical variables, predicates of any degree, and quantifiers and substituting logical concepts such as L-true, L-false, L-contingent, L-valid, etc. where appropriate.

Solutions to Selected Exercises

Chapter 1

Exercise 1. For a–d, use the logical English abbreviations described below to transform the English statements into logical English

Grammatical category	English	Logical English
Name	Bob	b
Name	Alice	a
1-place predicate	…is tall	$T_1(...)$
2-place predicate	is taller than…	$T_2(..., ...)$
(a) Atomic statement	Alice is tall	$T_1(a)$
(c) Atomic statement	Alice is taller than Bob	$T_2(a, b)$

Exercise 2. For a–d, use the logical English abbreviations described below to transform the English statements into logical English

Grammatical category	English	Logical English
Name	Samuel Clemens	a
Name	Mark Twain	b
2-place predicate	…is identical to…	$... = ...$
(a) Atomic statement	Mark Twain is Samuel Clemens	$b = a$
(c) Atomic statement	Mark Twain is Mark Twain	$b = b$

Exercise 3. For a–h, use the logical English abbreviations described below to transform the English statements into logical English

Grammatical category	English	Logical English
Name	Alice	a
Name	Bob	b
Name	2	c_2
Name	3	c_3
Name	5	c_5
1-place predicate	…is tall	$T_1(...)$
2-place predicate	…is taller than…	$I(..., ...)$

R. Lover, *Elementary Logic: For Software Development*,
DOI: 10.2007/978-1-84800-082-7, © Springer 2008

Grammatical category	English	Logical English
2-place predicate	...is identical to...	... = ...
2-place predicate	...is larger than...	$L(..., ...)$
(a) Atomic statement	Alice is taller than Bob	$I(a, b)$
(c) Atomic statement	Alice is identical to Alice	$a = a$
(e) Atomic statement	2 is larger than 3	$L(c_2, c_3)$
(g) Atomic statement	3 is larger than 5	$L(c_3, c_5)$
(h) Atomic statement	5 is larger than 3	$L(c_5, c_3)$

Exercise 4. For a– q, use the logical English abbreviations described below to transform the English statements into logical English. When using "f" and "g" for addition and multiplication, use prefix notation. When using " + "and "*" for addition and multiplication, use infix notation.

Grammatical category	English	Logical English
Name	Bob	b
Name	Alice	a
Name	Sam	s
Name	Mark	d
1-place predicate	...is tall	$T_{1(...)}$
2-place predicate	...is taller than...	$T_2(..., ...)$
2-place predicate	...is identical to...	... = ...
2-place predicate	...is the father of...	fatherOf(..., ...)
Name	2	2
Name	3	3
Name	5	5
Math function name	Plus	f
Math function name	Times	g
(a) Atomic statement	Alice is Alice	$a = a$
(c) Atomic statement	Bob is taller than Mark	$T_2(b, d)$
(e) Atomic statement	Sam is tall	$T_1(s)$
(g) Def. description	3 plus 2	$f(3, 2)$
(i) Def. description	2 plus (3 plus 5)	$f(2, f(3,5))$
(k) Atomic statement	2 plus (3 times 3) is identical to (2 plus 3) times 3	$f(2,g(3, 3) = g(f(2, 3), 3)$
(m) Def. description	(2 plus 3) times 3	$g(f(2, 3), 3)$
(o) Def. description	3 + 5	$f(3, 5)$
(q) Atomic statement	2 + (3 * 5) = (3 + 2) * 5	$f(2, g(3, 5)) = g(f(3, 2), 5)$

Chapter 2

Exercise 1. For each part, identify the missing grammatical category and use the logic notation described below to transform the English statements into logical English.

Grammatical category	English	Logical English
Statement	a = 3	A
Statement	b = 5	B
Statement	a + b = 8	C
(a) Negation	not (a = 3)	(~A)
(c) Conjunction	a = 3 and b = 5	(A ∧ B)
(e) Conditional	If a = 3 then b = 5	(A → B)
(g) Conditional	If a = 3 or b = 5 then a + b = 8	((A ∨ B) → C)
(i) Conditional	If a not = 3 and b not = 5 then a + b not = 8	(((~A) ∧ (~B))→ (~C))

Exercise 2. Fully restore parentheses to the following logical English notations. Suggestion: work from the inside out.

(a) P ∨ Q ∧ R
    P ∨ (Q ∧ R) ∧ has higher precedence than ∨
    (P ∨ (Q ∧ R)) Restore outer parentheses

(c) P → Q ∨ R
    P → (Q ∨ R) ∨ has higher precedence than →
    (P → (Q ∨ R)) Restore outer parentheses

(e) (p ∨ q) ∨ r
    ((p ∨ q) ∨ r) restore outer parentheses

(g) ~P → ~Q ∨ R
    (~P) → (~Q) ∨ R ~ has highest precedence
    (~P) → ((~Q) ∨ R) ∨ higher than →
    ((~P) → ((~Q) ∨ R)) Restore outer parentheses

(i) ~P ∧ Q ∨ R → S ↔ T
    (~P) ∧ Q ∨ R → S ↔ T ~ has highest precedence
    ((~P) ∧ Q) ∨ R → S ↔ T ∧ has next highest
    (((~P) ∧ Q) ∨ R) → S ↔ T ∨ is next
    ((((~P) ∧ Q) ∨ R) → S) ↔ T → is next
    (((((~P) ∧ Q) ∨ R) → S) ↔ T) Restore outer parens.

Exercise 3. Use the following statement letters to transform each of the English statements below into logical English. Use parenthesis dropping.

English	English logical
The program compiled correctly	P
The file was sorted	S
The file was corrupted	C
There was an error in the sort routine	E
The program ran correctly	R
The error flag was set at line 4,008	F
a < b	L

(a) If the program ran correctly then the file was sorted.

$$R \rightarrow S$$

(c) If the error flag was set at line 4,008 then the file was corrupted.

$$F \rightarrow C$$

(e) A sufficient condition for the file being corrupted is that the error flag was set at line 4,008.

$$F \rightarrow C$$

(g) A necessary and sufficient condition for the file being corrupted is that the error flag was set at line 4,008.

$$F \leftrightarrow C$$

(i) If the program compiled correctly and the file was sorted then the program ran correctly or a < b.

$$P \wedge S \rightarrow R \vee L$$

(k) If a < b and the file was sorted correctly then the program ran correctly if and only if there was not an error in the sort routine.

$$L \wedge S \rightarrow (R \leftrightarrow \sim E)$$

Exercise 4. Use the following statement letters to transform each of the logical English statements below into English.

Logical English	English
P	The program compiled correctly
S	The file was sorted
C	The file was corrupted
E	There was an error in the sort routine
R	The program ran correctly
F	The error flag was set at line 4,008
L	a < b
(a) R → P	If the program ran correctly then it compiled correctly
(c) ~P → ~R	If the program did not compile correctly then it did not run correctly
(e) C ∨ E →	~P If the file was corrupted or there was an error in the sort routine then the program did not compile correctly

Exercise 5. Use the following statement letters to transform each of the English statements below into logical English.

English	Logical English
6 is a domain value of the problem	S
1 is a domain value of the problem	O
0 is the solution value of the problem	N
The domain data is sorted small to large	A
The domain data is sorted large to small	D

(a) If 1 is a domain value of the problem then the domain data is not sorted small to large or large to small.

$$O \rightarrow \sim(A \vee D)$$
$$\text{or } O \rightarrow \sim A \wedge \sim D$$

(c) If a domain value of the problem is not 6 and is not 1 then the domain data is not sorted.

$$\sim S \wedge \sim O \rightarrow \sim A \wedge \sim D$$
$$\text{or } \sim S \wedge \sim O \rightarrow \sim(A \vee D)$$

(e) If the domain data is sorted large to small or small to large then the solution value of the problem is 0.

$$3A \vee D \rightarrow N$$

(g) A sufficient condition for the solution value of the problem to be 0 is that a domain value of the problem is 6 if and only if the domain data is sorted small to large.

$$(S \leftrightarrow A) \rightarrow N$$

Exercise 6. Use the following statement letters to transform each of the English statements below into logical English.

Logical English	English
S	6 is a domain value of the problem
O	1 is a domain value of the problem
N	0 is the solution value of the problem
A	The domain data is sorted small to large
D	The domain data is sorted large to small
(a) N ∨ ~N	0 is the solution value of the problem or 0 is not the solution value of the problem
(c) S → ~O	If 6 is a domain value of the problem then 1 is not a domain value of the problem
(e) N → S ∨ O	If 0 is a solution value of the problem then 6 is a domain value of the problem or 1 is a domain value of the problem

Chapter 3

Exercise 1. Identify the variables in the following statements and conditions.

Statement or condition	Variables
(a) In general, if it looks like a duck and walks like a duck then it is a duck	It (twice) (Note that "a duck" is an indefinite description)
(c) $3 < 5 + x$	X
(e) He who hesitates is lost	He, "He who hesitates" is a description
(g) $x < 5$	X
(i) $c = a + z$	Z

Exercise 2. Determine which of the following are conditions and which are not. Explain why your answer is correct. If an expression is a condition tell whether it is true of single things, pairs of things, triples of things, or what.

(a) $a = a$	Not a condition
(c) $x = x$	Condition, true of individual things
(e) $A(x, x)$	Condition, true of individual things
(g) $A(x, b, z)$	Condition, true of pairs of things
(i) $x > y \lor y > z$	Condition, true of triples of things

Exercise 3. For each of the following statements create two different conditions by replacing one or more names or descriptions with variables.

Statement	Conditions
(a) $a < 3 \lor a = 3 \lor a > 3$	$x < 3 \lor x = 3 \lor x > 3$
	$z < 3 \lor a = 3 \lor a > 3$
(c) Jack and Jill went up the hill	Jack and x went up the hill
	x and Jill went up the hill
(e) $3 + 5 = 5 + 3$	$3 + x = x + 3$
	$x + y = y + x$

Exercise 4. For each of the following conditions, create two different statements by replacing all variables with names or descriptions. Assume that a and b are names.

Condition	Statements
(a) $x = y \land y = x$	$1 + 2 = 3 \land 3 = 1 + 2$
	$a = b \land b = a$
(c) _____ was absent	Jack was absent
	Jill was absent
(e) $x > 99 \lor z < 5$	$100 > 99 \lor 14 - b < 5$
	$a > 99 \lor 1 < b$

Exercise 5. For each description below, make two different open descriptions.

Description	Open descriptions
(a) The present king of France	The present king of _____ The present king of x
(c) 3 + 5	x + 5 3 + x
(e) A person in this room	A _____ in this room a person in this _____
(g) Some record from file 77	Some record from x Some record from y

Exercise 6. For each of the following open descriptions, create two different descriptions by replacing all the variables with names or descriptions. Remember that all instances of a given variable should be replaced by the same name or description.

(a) y + x   3 + 2   1 + 33
(c) $(x^2)^3$ $(3^2)^3$ $(77^2)^3$

Exercise 7. Using P(x) to abbreviate "x is a program" and B(x) to abbreviate "x has bugs" go through the transformation process described above using "All programs have bugs." in place of "All humans are mortal."

English	Logical English
All programs have bugs	$\forall x$(If x is a program then x has bugs) $\forall x$(If P(x) then B(x)) $\forall x$(P(x) $\rightarrow$ B(x))

Exercise 9. Using the same abbreviations, write logical English for the following statements.

English	Logical English
(a) Something is useful	$\exists x$(U(x))
(c) Something is bigger than a	$\exists x$(B(x, a))
(e) Everything is bigger than something	$\forall x \exists y$(B(x, y))
(g) A is bigger than everything or a is bigger than nothing	$\forall x$(B(a, x)) $\vee$ $\forall x$(~B(a, x)) or $\forall x$(B(a x)) $\vee$ ~$\exists x$(B(a, x))
(i) If some program is useful then all programs are useful	$\exists x$(P(x) $\wedge$ U(x)) $\rightarrow$ $\forall x$(P(x) $\rightarrow$ U(x)) or P(a) $\wedge$ U(a) $\rightarrow$ $\forall x$(P(x) $\rightarrow$ U(x))
(k) If a is a program and a is not useful then not all programs are useful	P(a) $\wedge$ ~U(a) $\rightarrow$ ~$\forall x$(P(x) $\rightarrow$ U(x)) or P(a) $\wedge$ ~U(a) $\rightarrow$ $\exists x$(P(x) $\wedge$ ~U(x))

Exercise 10. Using the abbreviations as above transform the following logical English notation into English.

Logical English	English
(a) ~∃x(U(x)) → ∃x(~U(x))	If nothing is useful then there is something which is not useful
(c) ∃x(B(x, b)) ∧ B(a, b)	Something is bigger than b and a is bigger than b
(e) ~∃x(U(x)) → ∀x(~U(x))	If there is nothing useful then everything is not useful

Chapter 4

Exercise 1. For each passage below, analyze the passage in the way Examples 7–12 were analyzed. Give reasons for your claims.

(a) If today is Friday then today is payday.

Analysis: This is not an argument, it is a conditional statement.

(c) If x were 5 at line 20 then the program would have crashed, and it did. So, probably, x was 5 at line 20.

Analysis: An inductive argument, with "so" as conclusion indicator. It is inductive because the conclusion is asserted to only "probably" follow from the premises.

> P_1: If x were 5 at line 20 then the program would have crashed.
> P_2: It did (crash).
> C: (Probably) x was 5 at line 20.

(d) If the program was run yesterday then a run log entry for it would have been made. No run log entry for it was made. Moreover, if the program was not run yesterday the records in it are not current.
Hence the records in it are not current.

Analysis: This is a complex deductive argument with "hence" as a conclusion indicator. It has an implicit conclusion which is an implicit premise for another argument.

> P_1: If the program was run yesterday then a run log entry for it would have been made.
> P_2: No run log entry for it was made.
> C_1: (implicit) The program was not run yesterday.
> P_3: (implicit) The program was not run yesterday.
> P_4: If the program was not run yesterday then the records in it are not current.
> C_2: The records in it are not current.

Exercise 2. Use logical English to express the structure of each of the arguments below. If the argument is simple then use the format shown in Examples 13 and 14. If the argument is compound then use the tree structure shown in Example 16.

(a) Since today is Monday, tomorrow must be Tuesday.

> MonToday
> ‾‾‾‾‾‾‾‾‾
> TueTomorrow

(c) It will probably rain here soon, since the sky is dark and it is raining just west of here.

> DarkSky $\wedge$ RainWest
> ‾‾‾‾‾‾‾‾‾‾‾‾‾‾‾‾‾‾‾‾
> ProbRain

(e) Since the file is sorted, it must be in ascending or descending order. It is not in ascending order. Hence it is in descending order.

Fsorted
Asc ∨ Dsc ~ Asc
_____
Dsc

(g) I have tested this program with hundreds of test cases and it worked correctly in each case. Hence, this program is correct.

PTested ∧ PWorked
_____
PCorrect

(i) a*b > 0 because either a > 0 and b > 0 or else a < 0 and b < 0. Since c < 0 and a*b > 0, it follows that c*a*b < 0. And since d is also < 0, d*c*a*b must be > 0.

$$\frac{\frac{(a>0 \wedge b>0) \vee (a<0 \wedge b<0)}{a*b>0} \quad\quad c<0}{\frac{c*a*b<0 \quad\quad d<0}{d*c*b*a > 0}}$$

Chapter 5

Exercise 1. Suppose A = {2, 4, 6, 8}, B = {1, 3, 5, 7}, and C = {1, 2. 3}.
Use set notation to express the result of performing the following operations.

(a) A ∪ B = {1, 2, 3, 4, 5, 6, 7, 8}
(c) A ∩ C = {2}
(e) A – C = {4, 6, 8}
(g) C × A = {<1, 2>,<1, 4>, <1, 6>, <1, 8>, <2, 2>, <2, 4>, <2, 6>, <2, 8> ,<3,
          2>, <3, 4>, <3, 6>, <3, 8>}

Exercise 2. Write each of the following using logical English notation. Use I(x) to
abbreviate the condition that x is an integer, P(x) abbreviate the condition that x is a
positive integer, and so on.

(a) The set of all integers.
     {x | I(x)}

(c) b is an element of C.
     b ∈ C

(e) The ordered pair <b, c> is an element of the product of sets F and G.
     <b, c> ∈ F × G

Exercise 3. Use English to express interpretations of the following expressions of
set theory.

(a) b ∈ G b is an element of G.
(c) B = C ↔ (B ⊂ C) ∧ (C ⊂ B) B equals c if and only if B is a subset of C and C
     is a subset of B.
(e) <a, b> ∈ B × C The ordered pair <a, b> is an element of the product of B and C.

Exercise 4. For each pair of sequences below determine whether they are identical
considered as sequences, as bags, and as sets.

		Sequence	Bag	Set
(a) <1, 1 + 1, 1 + 1 + 1>	<1, 2, 3>	Yes	Yes	Yes
(c) <1, 1 + 1, 1 + 1 + 1>	<1, 2, 2, 3>	No	No	Yes
(e) <1, 2, 3>	<3, 2, 1>	No	Yes	Yes

Exercise 5. For each of the following determine whether the statement is true or
false, and say why.

(a) <3, 5> ∈ <   True, 3 < 5
(c) <3, 3> ∈ <   False, 3 ~ < 3
(e) <1, 1 + 1> ∈ <   True, 1 < 1 + 1

Exercise 6. For each of the following, determine the domain and range of the relation, and express each using logical English. Use I(x) to represent the property of being an integer, R(x) to represent the property of being a rational number, and P(x) to represent the property of being a person. Invent and explain your own notation for the less than relation, the parent of relation, and so on.

(a) The less than relation between integers (positive, zero, and negative).

Domain = {x | I(x) ∧ ∃y(I(y) ∧ x < y} = the set of all integers

Range = {y | I(y) ∧ ∃x(I(x) ∧ x < y} = the set of all integers.

(c) The "is a parent of" relation between people.

Domain = {x | P(x) ∧ ∃y(P(y) ∧ x is the parent of ẏ}

    = {all parents}

Range = {y | P(y) ∧ ∃x(P(x) ∧ x is a parent of y}

    = {all children}

    = {all people}

(e) The "likes" relation between people

Domain = {x | P(x) ∧ ∃y(P(y) ∧ x likes y)}

    = {all people who like someone}

Range = {y | P(y) ∧ ∃x(P(x) ∧ x likes y)}

    = {all people who are liked by someone}

(g) The "is taller than" relation among basketball players.

Domain = {x | BBP(y) ∧ ∃y(BBP(y) ∧ x is taller than y)}

    = {all people who are taller than someone}

    = {all but the shortest people}

Range = {y | BBP(x) ∧ ∃x(BBP(x) ∧ x is taller than y)}

    = {all people who are shorter than someone}

    = {all but the tallest people}

Exercise 7. For each of the following relations, determine its domain and its range. Then determine whether it is a functional relation.

(a) The relation R(x, y) such that x and y are people and y is a (biological) child of x.

Domain is set of all people who are parents.

Range is set of all people, since every person is a child.

Not functional, since specifying a parent does not uniquely determine a child.

(c) The relation R(x, y) such that x and y are people and y is the current husband of x in a monogamous society.

Domain is set of all current wives.

Range is set of all current husbands.

Is functional since in a monogamous society specifying a wife uniquely
    determines a husband.

(e) The relation R(x, y) such that x and y are positive integers and y is a factor of x.
   Domain is set of all positive integers, since all positive integers have 1 and
       themselves as factors.
   Range is set of all positive integers, since all positive integers are factors
       of some positive integer, e.g. themselves.
   Not relational, since all positive integers have more than one factor.

(g) The relation R(<x, y>, z) with x, y, and z integers and z = x or z = y.
   Domain is set of all pairs of integers.
   Range is set of all integers.
   Not functional since specifying <x, y> does not uniquely determine z.

Chapter 6

Exercise 1. Describe the domain and range for each of the following problem specifications. Tell how many elements are in the domain and in the range. Say what a program that solved the problem would do.

(a) The problem of alphabetizing a specific list of English words.
>   Domain = the set whose only element is that list of words.
>   Range = the set whose only element is that list of words in alphabetic order.
>   Domain and range have one element each.
>   A program that solved this problem would take the specified list of English words as input and give that list, in alphabetic order, as output.

(c) The problem of eliminating duplicates from a specific list of numbers.
>   Domain = the set whose only element is that list of numbers.
>   Range = the set whose only element is that list of numbers with duplicates removed.
>   Domain and range have one element each.
>   A program that solved this problem would take the specified list of numbers as input and give that list, with duplicates removed, as output.

Exercise 3. Look for examples of vagueness and ambiguity in the problem specifications described in Sect. 1 above.

Note: Correct answers may differ.

The problem of finding the square root of any positive integer might be said to be functionally ambiguous, since each positive integer has two square roots, e.g. 2 and −2 are both sometimes called square roots of 4. However, in most contexts, the expression "the square root" of a number is intended to refer to the positive square root of that number, so no ambiguity would be involved. Another possible difficulty is that the number of digits required to be shown for a square root is not specified. The square root of 2 for example has infinitely many decimal digits, any finite number of digits is only an approximation. This could be viewed as a vagueness in the specification or an incompleteness in the specification.

There is no defect with the problem of finding the smallest positive integer larger than 7.

There is a bit of ambiguity in the specification of the problem of sorting a specific list of names. Presumably this means sorted in alphabetic order but in some contexts, sorting on length might be what is intended. Another ambiguity is that the specification does not say whether the names are to be sorted on last name then the rest of the name, or are they to be sorted first name and the rest of the name, e.g. which comes first "Adam Zimmer" or "Zbignew Abernathy". There is also some vagueness in saying exactly what counts as alphabetic order, for example in the case of names

with nonstandard symbols in them. There are probably some standard ways of specifying this, but how many specifiers or programmers know what it is, or even where
to find them. If there is more than one, which one should be used. Perhaps the order
to use is that specified by Unicode numeric codes, but perhaps not.

The problem of sorting arbitrary lists of names has much the same problems as
the problem of sorting a specified list of names.

The problem of finding the larger of any ordered pair of numbers is very clear,
although nothing is said explicitly about what to do if the two numbers of the pair
are the same. Are both "larger" or is there no "larger" one?

There is little to complain about in the specification of the problem of finding a
customer record from a specific file, except perhaps to say how the record is to be
organized and formatted for output. This could be viewed as an example of
incompleteness.

The problems of Exercise 1 are largely free of defects.

Exercise 5. Write the corresponding expression for MAX3.

$$w = \text{MAX3}(x, y, z) \leftrightarrow (w = x \lor w = y \lor w = z)$$
$$\land w >= x \land w >= y \land w >= z$$

Exercise 7. Express the following problem using logic notation. Determine what
class a student belongs to as a function of the number of semester hours of credit
earned where a student with <=30 credits is a freshman, 31–60 credits is a sophomore,
61–90 credits is a junior, and >90 credits is a senior. There is no upper limit on the
number of credits a student can earn. Use the abbreviations from the previous
examples.

$$\text{DOM}(x) \leftrightarrow I(x) \land 0 <= x$$

$$\text{SOL}(x, y) \leftrightarrow ((x > 90 \lor y = \text{"senior"})$$
$$\lor (61 <= x \land x <= 90 \land y = \text{"junior"})$$
$$\lor (31 <= x \land x <= 60 \land y = \text{"sophomore"})$$
$$\lor (x <= 30 \land y = \text{"freshman"}))$$

Exercise 8. Express the following problem specifications using logic notation. Use
the following abbreviations. Invent others if you need them.

DOM(x)	x is in the domain of the problem
SOL(x, y)	y is the solution of the problem for domain element x
NUMSEQ(z)	z is a finite sequence of numbers
MIN(y, z)	y is the minimum of the elements of sequence of numbers z
ASORT(y)	y is sorted in ascending order
DSORT(y)	y is sorted in descending order

(a) The problem of finding the minimum of a finite sequence of numbers.

$$\text{DOM}(x) \leftrightarrow \text{NUMSEQ}(x)$$
$$\text{SOL}(x, y) \leftrightarrow \text{MIN}(y, z)$$

(c) The problem of determining whether one finite sequence of numbers is longer than another finite sequence of numbers.

Let $\text{LEN}(x)$ represent the length of sequence x. Then the problem can be represented by:

$$\text{DOM}(x) \leftrightarrow x = <x_1, x_2> \wedge \text{NUMSEQ}(x_1) \wedge \text{NUMSEQ}(x_2)$$
$$\text{SOL}(x, y) \leftrightarrow (y = \text{``yes''} \wedge \sim(\text{LEN}(x_1) = \text{LEN}(x_2)))$$
$$\vee(y = \text{``no''} \wedge (\text{LEN}(x_1) = \text{LEN}(x_2)))$$

Chapter 7

Exercise 1. Write pseudocode for each of the following algorithms expressed in English. Note your solutions do not have to be exactly the same as the given solutions, but they should be similar and equivalent.

(a) To find the smallest of three integers first find the smaller of the first two then find the smaller of that and the third.

Algorithm smallestOf3(a, b, c)
Pre: a, b, and c are integers.
Post: Returns the smallest of a, b, and c.

    If (a < b) then
        smaller ← a
    else
        smaller ← b
    endif
    If (c < smaller) then
        Return c
    else
        Return smaller
    endif

endAlgorithm

(c) To find the smallest of a nonempty list of integers, examine the integers in order from beginning to end, keeping track of the smallest integer examined so far. At the end it will be the smallest in the list.

Algorithm findMin(L)
Pre: L is a nonempty list of integers, L[0], L[1], ...
Post: Returns the smallest element of L.

    smallest < L[0]   # Initially L[0] is smallest so far.
    len ← length of L
    I ← 1
    While (I ← len) do
        If (L[I] < smallest) then
            smallest ← L[I]
        endif
        I ← I + 1
    endwhile
    Return smallest
endAlgorithm

(e) To determine whether a nonempty list of numbers is sorted small to large look for pairs of numbers in the list which are out of order, i.e. larger first and smaller second. If no such pairs are found then the list is sorted from small to large.

Algorithm aSorted(L)
Pre: L is a nonempty list of numbers.
Post: Returns true if L is sorted in ascending order, false otherwise.
Assumes a list of length 1 is in ascending order.

    len ← length of L
    If (len = 1) then
          Return true
    else
        I ← 0
        While (I < len − 1) do
            If (L[I] > L[I + 1]) then
                Return false
            endif
        I ← I + 1
        endwhile
        Return true
    endif
endAlgorithm

(g) To determine whether x is in the interval [a, b] or in [c, d] but not in the intersection of the two intervals, first determine whether x is in [a, b] then determine whether x is in [c, d]. If x is in either or both intervals then the condition is false, otherwise the condition is true.

Algorithm symmetricDifference(x, a, b, c, d)
Pre: x, a, b, c, and d are real numbers with a < = b and c < = d.
Post: Returns true if x is in [a, b] or in [c, d] but not in both.

    If (((a < = x) and (x < = b)) or ((c < = x) and (x < = d))) and
    not((a < = x) and (x < = b)) and ((c < = x) and (x < = d)))) then
        Return true
    else
        Return false
    endif
endAlgorithm

Chapter 8

Exercise 1. Determine which of the statements below are materially equivalent. Explain your answers. Hint: first determine which statements are true and which are false. Assume the numbers referred to here are all nonnegative integers.

(a) There are odd numbers.
(c) If a number is even and prime than it is not odd.
(e) Every number is odd.
(g) Every number identical to 3 is prime.
(i)   The smallest prime number is 2.

Since a, c, g, and I are all true, they are all materially equivalent to each other.

Exercise 2. Assume that P is true and Q, is false. For each pair of statements below determine whether the one on the left is materially equivalent to the one on the right. Note that in each case this requires only a simple truth value calculation, not the construction of a whole truth table.

(a) P   Q   No
(c) P and Q   Q   Yes

Exercise 3. Determine which of the statements below materially imply which others. Explain your solution.

(a) There are odd numbers.
(c) If a number is even and prime than it is not odd.
(e) Every number is odd.
(g) Every number identical to 3 is prime.
(i)   The smallest prime number is 2.

Since a, c, g, and i are all true, each of them materially implies all those in that list, but none of them materially implies e. Since e is false, it materially implies all of them.

Exercise 4. Assume that P is true and Q, is false. For each pair of statements below determine whether the one on the left materially implies the one on the right. Then determine whether the one on the right materially implies the one on the left. Then determine whether the two statements are materially equivalent. Note that in each case this requires only a simple truth value calculation, not the construction of a whole truth table.

a. P   Q
   T   F   no, yes, no
c. P or Q   Q
        T   F   no, yes, no

Exercise 5. Use the definitions above to determine which of the statements below are materially true and which are materially false.

(a) There are odd numbers.
(c) If a number is even and prime than it is not odd.
(e) Every number is odd.
(g) Every number identical to 3 is prime.
(i) The smallest prime number is 2.

In this case, using the definitions amounts to thinking about examples.
Materially true: a, c, g, i
Materially false: e

Exercise 6. In each case, say whether the statement is true of a finite or an infinite number of things. If it is true of a finite number of things then write the statement as a conjunction or disjunction. Assume that S = {2, 3, 4, 5}

(a) All prime numbers are odd.
        Infinite
(c) Some prime numbers are odd.
        Infinite
(e) All elements of S are prime numbers.
        Finite: 2 is prime ∧ 3 is prime ∧ 4 is prime ∧ 5 is prime
(g) All prime numbers in S are odd.
        Finite: if 2 is prime then 2 is odd ∧ if 3 is prime then 3 is odd ∧ if 4 is
            prime then 4 is odd ∧ if 5 is prime then 5 is odd
(i) All even numbers in S are prime.
        Infinite

Exercise 7. There are many possible solutions. Here is one.

> # Line 02 generates error message if ordinary evaluation of "or" is
> # used. Prints "Shortcut used" and does not generate error
> # message if shortcut evaluation is used.

```
01   x ← 1
02   If ((x = 1) or (x/0 = 5))
03        Print "x/0 = 5 should generate error message"
04   Else
05        Print "Shortcut used"
06   Endif
```

Exercise 9. Do the following bitwise calculations.

(a)   not 11010110
          00101001

(c)   11010110
       or 01100101
           11110111

Chapter 9

Exercise 1. Do a similar calculation assuming that P, Q, and R are all true.

1. "not P": not true is false.
3. "R and (not P)": true and false is false.
4. "(not Q) or (R and (not P))": false or false is false.

Exercise 3. Write expressions like Expressions 2, 3, and 4 above for each of the following statements. If the English is ambiguous about connectives, pick some reasonable order of evaluation and forge ahead.

(a) Today is Wednesday and it is raining and it is hot.
   (W and R) and H
   $(W \wedge R) \wedge H$
   $W \wedge R \wedge H$

(c) Today is not Wednesday and it is not raining and it is not hot.
   ((not W) and (not R)) and (not H)
   $((\sim W) \wedge (\sim R)) \wedge (\sim H)$
   $\sim W \wedge \sim R \wedge \sim H$

(e) Today is Wednesday and either it is not raining or it is not hot.
   W and ((not R) or (not H))
   $W \wedge ((\sim R) \vee (\sim H))$
   $W \wedge (\sim R \vee \sim H)$

(g) Today is Wednesday and it is not the case that it is raining or it is hot.
   W and (not (R or H))
   $W \wedge (\sim(R \vee H))$
   $W \wedge \sim(R \vee H)$

Exercise 4. Finish the table below by inserting parentheses so that the connectives are evaluated in the order specified. Do not change the order of the connectives or the elementary statements.

	order			statement	
	not	and	or	using precedence rule	not using precedence rule
a.	1	2	3	not P and Q or R	((not P and Q) or P)
c.	2	1	3	not (P and Q) or R	(not (P and Q)) or R
e.	3	1	2	not ((P and Q) or R)	not ((P and Q) or R)

Exercise 5. Make a truth table for each complex statement below. Indicate which is the final column.

(a) ~(~P)

$$
\begin{array}{c|c}
P & \sim(\sim P) \\
\hline
T & T \\
F & F \\
\end{array}
$$
   * main column

(c) P ∨ (P ∧ Q)

$$
\begin{array}{cc|cc}
P & Q & P \vee & (P\wedge Q) \\
\hline
T & T & T & T \\
T & F & T & F \\
F & T & F & F \\
F & F & F & F \\
\end{array}
$$
   * main column

(e) (P ∨ Q) ∧ ~P

$$
\begin{array}{cc|ccc}
P & Q & (P \vee Q) & \wedge & \sim P \\
\hline
T & T & T & F & F \\
T & F & T & F & F \\
F & T & T & T & T \\
F & F & F & F & F \\
\end{array}
$$
   *main column

(g) Q ∨ (~Q)

$$
\begin{array}{c|ccc}
Q & Q & \vee & (\sim Q) \\
\hline
T & T & T & F \\
F & F & T & T \\
\end{array}
$$
   *main column

(i) P ∧ (~P)

$$
\begin{array}{c|ccc}
P & P & \wedge & (\sim P) \\
\hline
T & T & F & F \\
F & F & F & T \\
\end{array}
$$
   *main column

Exercise 6. For each of the following, try to determine what you can about the truth values of the component statements in case the compound statement is true. Then check your answers by finding or constructing a truth table for each one.

(a) ~(~P) If ~(~P) is true then ~P must be false, so P must be true.

$$
\begin{array}{c|ccc}
P & \sim & (\sim P) \\
\hline
T & T & F & T \\
F & F & T & F \\
\end{array}
$$

(c) P ∨ (P ∧ Q) If P ∨ (P ∧ Q) is true then either P is true or P ∧ Q is true. If P were false, neither part would be true. So P must be true. Q can be true or false.

P	Q	P ∨ (P ∧ Q)	
T	T	T	T
T	F	T	F
F	T	F	F
F	F	F	F

(e) (P ∨ Q) ∧ ~P If (P ∨ Q) ∧ ~P is true than (P ∨ Q) must be true and ~P must be true. Hence P must be false. But if P is false and (P ∨ Q) is true then Q must be true.

P	Q	(P ∨ Q)	∧	~ P	
T	T	T	F	F	
T	F	T	F	F	
F	T	T	T	T	
F	F	F	F	T	

(g) (Q ∨ (~Q)) If (Q ∨ (~Q)) is true than Q is true or ~Q is true, but this is the case no matter what. So (Q ∨ (~Q)) is true no matter whether Q is true or false.

Q	Q ∨ ~ Q	
T	T	F
F	T	T

(i) (Q ∨ ~P) ∧ P If (Q ∨ ~P) ∧ P is true then (Q ∨ ~P) must be true and P must be true. So P must be false. Hence in order for (Q ∨ ~P) to be true Q must be true.

P	Q	(Q ∨ ~ P)	∧	P
T	T	T F	T	
T	F	F F	F	
F	T	T T	F	
F	F	T T	F	

(k) (Q ∨ ~P) ∧ ~Q If (Q ∨ ~P) ∧ ~Q is true then (Q ∨ ~P) and ~Q must be true. Hence Q must be false. But if Q is false and (Q ∨ ~P) is true then ~P must be true, hence P must be false.

P	Q	(Q ∨ ~P)	∧	~ Q	
T	T	T F	F	F	
T	F	F F	F	T	
F	T	T T	F	F	
F	F	T T	T	T	

Exercise 7. For each of the following, try to determine what you can about the truth values of the component statements in case the compound statement is false. Then check your answers by finding or constructing a truth table for each one.

(a) ~(~P) If ~(~P) is false then ~P must be true and hence P must be false.

P	~ (~ P)
T	T F T
F	F T F

(c) P ∨ (P ∧ Q) If P ∨ (P ∧ Q) is false then P must be false and (P ∧ Q) must also be false. But if P is false then (P ∧ Q) will be false no matter what truth value Q has.

P Q	P ∨ (P ∧ Q)
T T	T T
T F	T F
F T	F F
F F	F F

(e) (P ∨ Q) ∧ ~P If (P ∨ Q) ∧ ~P is false then ~P is false (and P true) or (P ∨ Q) is false. And if P is true than (P ∨ Q) must be true. So if P is true, then (P ∨ Q) ∧ ~P is false no matter the truth value of Q. While if P is false then Q must also be false.

P Q	(P ∨ Q) ∧ ~Q
T T	T F F
T F	T F F
F T	T T T
F F	F F T

(g) (Q ∨ (~Q)) If (Q ∨ (~Q)) is false then Q must be false and ~Q must be false. But this is impossible.

Q	Q ∨ ~Q
T	T F
F	T T

(i) (Q ∨ ~P) ∧ P If (Q ∨ ~P) ∧ P is false then either P is false or (Q ∨ ~P) is false. If P is true then the only way to make (Q ∨ ~P) false is for Q to be false.

P Q	(Q ∨ ~P) ∧ P
T T	T F T
T F	F F F
F T	T T F
F F	T T F

(k) (Q ∨ ~P) ∧ ~Q if (Q ∨ ~P) ∧ ~Q is false then either Q must be true or (Q ∨~P) must be false. If Q is true then the truth value of P is irrelevant. If Q is false then P must be true in order for (Q ∨ ~P) to be false

P Q	(Q ∨ ~P) ∧ ~Q
T T	T F F F
T F	F F F T
F T	T T F F
F F	T T T T

Chapter 10

Exercise 1. Do a value trace table of just P and MIN for the following algorithm, with LIST = <7, 3, 5, 1>.

```
0    Algorithm FindMin(LIST,N)
        # Preconditons: LIST is a list of N numbers with N >= 1.
        # Postcondition: MIN is the smallest element of LIST.
1.         P ← 1                    # P points to the next element of LIST
2.         MIN ← LIST[P]
3.         While P < = N DO
4.             If LIST[P] < MIN Then MIN ← LIST[P] EndIf
5.                 P ← P + 1
6.         Repeat
7.         Return MIN
      EndAlgorithm
```

With LIST = <7, 3, 5, 1> and N = 4, trace P and MIN for FindMin.

line	P	MIN	Comments
0	?	?	Both are initially unassigned
1	1		
2	1	7	
3			1 < = 4, so enter loop
4			LIST[1] = 7 which is not < 7, so skip assignment
5	2		
3			2 < = 4
4		3	LIST[2] = 3 < 7, so do the assignment
5	3		
3			3 < = 4
4			LIST[3] = 5 which is not < 3, so skip assignment
5	4		
3			4 < = 4
4		1	LIST[4] = 1 < 3, so do the assignment
5	5		
3			5 is not < = 4, so exit loop
7			Done, so return

Exercise 3. Finish the trace table above.

line	x	y	z	output	comments
initially	3	5	7		
1	3	6	7		~(2 * 3 > 7), so y ← y + 1
2	13	6	7		
3	13	6	7	This is silly	7 < 3 * 5 ∧ 13 > 6
4	13	6	7		13 < 3 * 6, so repeat.
5	18	6	7		
6	18	7	7		
7	18	7	7	18 7 7	
4					18 < 3 * 7, so repeat.
5	23				
6	8				
7				23 8 7	
4					23 < 3 * 8, so repeat.
5	28				
6		9			
7				28 9 7	
4					28 not < 3 * 9 and ~x = y, so exit loop. Continue program.

Exercise 5. Do a similar trace table but with x = 7, y = 5, z = 3

line	x	y	z	output	comments
initially	7	5	3		
1					2 * 7 > 3, no assignment
2	8				
3				This is silly	3 < 7 + 5 and 7 > 5
4					8 < 3 * 5, so repeat
5	13				
6		6			
7				13 6 3	
4					13 < 3 * 15, so repeat
5	18				
6		7			
7				18 7 3	
4					18 < 3 * 7, so repeat
5	23				
6		8			
7				23 8 3	
4					23 < 3 * 8, so repeat
5	28				
6		9			
7				28 9 3	
4					~28 < 3 * 9, so exit and continue program

Exercise 7.

> If $(((a = 0)$ and not$(b = 0))$ or $(b = 0$ and not$(a = 0)))$ then
>> Print "yes"
>
> else
>> Print "no"
>
> endif

(a) If a and b are both $= 0$ before I, what will I print? Why?
(b) If a and b are both $= 1$ before I, what will I print? Why?
(c) If $a = 0$ and $b = 7$ before I, what will I print? Why?
(d) If $a = 0$ before I and I prints "no" then what can you tell about the value of b before I? Explain.

(a)
1. Before I, if $a = b = 0$ then not$(b = 0)$ is false
2. Hence $((a = 0)$ and not $(b = 0))$ is false.
3. Similarly, if $a = b = 0$ then not$(a = 0)$ is false.
4. Hence $((b = 0)$ and not$(a = 0))$ is false.
5. Hence $(((a = 0)$ and not $(b = 0))$ or $((b = 0)$ and not$(a = 0)))$ is false.
6. Hence I's condition is false.
7. Hence I will print "no".

(c)
1. Before I, if $a = 0$ and $b = 7$ then $(a = 0)$ is true and not$(b = 0)$ is true.
2. Hence $((a = 0)$ and not$(b = 0))$ is true.
3. Hence $(((a = 0)$ and not $(b = 0))$ or $((b = 0)$ and not$(a = 0)))$ is true.
4. Hence I's condition is true.
5. Hence I will print "yes".

Exercise 8.

> If (not$(a = 0$ and $b <> 0)$ and (not$(b = 0$ and $c <> 0)$ and $(c = 0))$ then
>> Print "yes"
>
> else
>> Print "no"
>
> endif

(a) If $a = b = c = 0$ before I, what will I print? Why?
(b) If I prints "yes" what can you say about the values of a, b, and c? Why?
(c) If I prints "no" what can you say about the values of a, b, and c? Why?
(d) If $a > b > c = 0$ before I, what will I print? Why?

(a)
1. $a = b = 0$ before I implies (not$(a = 0)$ and $b <> 0)$ is true.
2. $b = c = 0$ before I implies (not$(b = 0)$ and $c <> 0)$ is true.
3. 1 and 2 above with $c = 0$ implies the I's condition is true.
4. Hence I will print "yes"

(c)
1. If I prints "no" then its condition must be false.
2. Hence at least one of its conjuncts must be false.
3. So either $c <> 0$, or $b = 0$ and $c <> 0$, or $a = 0$ and $b <> 0$ or any consistent combination of these conditions. For example, if $c = 0$ then $a = 0$ and $b <> 0$.

Exercise 9

I_1:   If not($a = 0$ and $b <> 0$) then

$c \leftarrow 0$

else

$c \leftarrow 3$

endif

I_2:   If not($b = 0$ and $c <> 0$) then

$d \leftarrow 2$

else

$d \leftarrow 4$

endif

Let A represent the condition $a = 0$ and B represent the condition $b = 0$. For each of the four possible pairs of truth values for A and B, what can you say about the numeric values of c and d? Why?

(a) A and B both true.
(b) A true, B false
(c) A false, B true
(d) A and B both false.

(a)
1. Both true implies $a = 0$ and $b = 0$.
2. Hence I_1's condition is true.
3. Hence $c = 0$ after I_1 and before I_2.
4. $b = 0$ and $c = 0$ imply that I_2's condition is true.
5. Hence $d = 2$ after I_2.
6. So $c = 0$ and $d = 2$.

(c)
1. A false and B true imply $a <> 0$ and $b = 0$.
2. So I_1's condition is true.
3. So $c = 0$ after I_1 and before I_2.
4. Hence I_2's condition is true.
5. So $d = 2$ after I_2.
6. So $c = 0$ and $d = 2$.

Exercise 10. Given the following instructions from the middle of a program and assuming that a, b, and c have been assigned values before I_1.

I_1:   if $a = 0$ then $b \leftarrow 1$ else $b \leftarrow 0$ endif # So $b = 0$ or $b = 1$
I_2:   if $b <> 0$ then $c \leftarrow 0$ else $c \leftarrow 1$ endif # So $c = 0$ or $c = 1$

(a) If $c = 0$ after I_2
1. Then $b = 1$ before I_2 since if $b = 0$ before I_2 then $c \leftarrow 1$ by I_2.
2. Since $b = 1$ before I_2, $a = 0$ before I_1, since if $a <> 0$ before I_1 then $b \leftarrow 0$ by I_1.
3. However, b could have any value before I_1 since whatever value it had is wiped out by the assignments of I_1.
4. So If $c = 0$ after I_2 then $a = 0$ and b could have any value before I_1.

Chapter 11

Exercise 1
For each of the following, determine whether it is TF-true, TF-false, or TF-contingent. Hint, find or make a truth table for each. Then examine its final column.

(a) P ∧ ~P

P	P ∧ ~P
T	F
F	F

TF-False

(c) P ↔ P

P	P ↔ P
T	T
F	T

TF-true

(e) P ↔ ~~P

P	P ↔ ~~P
T	T
F	T

TF-true

(g) P → Q ∨ P → ~Q

P Q	P → Q ∨ P → ~Q
T T	T T F
T F	F T T
F T	T T T
F F	T T T

TF-true

(i) P → Q ∨ Q → P

P Q	P → Q ∨ P → Q
T T	T T T
T F	F T T
F T	T T F
F F	T T T

TF-true

(k) ~(P ∧ Q) ↔ ~P ∧ ~Q

P Q	~(P ∧ Q) ↔ ~P ∧ ~Q
T T	F T F
T F	T F F
F T	T F F
F F	T T T

TF-contingent

Exercise 2. Use Procedure TFL to try to determine the logical status of each of the English statements below. First find logical English for each statement, then find an appropriate tff. Then do the truth table for that tff. Then apply Procedure TFL.

(a) Today is Monday and today is not Monday.
  logical English: Mon ∨ ~ Mon
  tff: M ∨ ~ M

M	M ∧ ~M
T	T T F T
F	F T T F

TFL: Since there are all Ts in the final column, the original statement is a TF-true.

(c) If Today is Monday and today is not Monday then the Sun is cold.
  logical English: Mon ∧ ~ Mon → Cold
  tff: M ∧ ~ M → C

M	S	M ∧ ~ M → C
T	T	F T
T	F	F T
F	T	F T
F	F	F T

TFL: Since there are all Ts in the final column, the original statement is TF-true.

(e) If everything is blue then nothing is blue.
  logical English: ∀xBlue(x) → ~∃xBlue(x)
  tff: B → C

B	C	B → C
T	T	T
T	F	F
F	T	T
F	F	T

TFL: Since the final column has some Ts and some Fs, the original statement is truth functionally contingent, but the original statement has some quantifiers, so TFL fails to classify it.

(g) (If today is Monday then the Moon is blue) just in case (if the Moon is not blue then today is not Monday).
logical English: (Mon → Blue) ↔ (~Blue → ~Mon)
tfl: (M → B) ↔ (~B → ~ M)

B	M	(M → B)	↔	(~B → ~ M)
T	T	F	T	T
T	F	F	T	T
F	T	F	T	T
F	F	F	T	T

TFL: Since the final column is all Ts, the original statement is TF-true.

(i) If it is not raining or it is not snowing and, moreover, it is raining, then it is not snowing.
Logical English: ((~Rain ∨ ~Snow) ∧ Rain) → ~Snow
tfl: ((~R ∨ ~S) ∧ R) → ~S

R	S	(~ (R ∨ ~ S) ∧ R)	→	~ S
T	T	F	F	T
T	F	T	T	T
F	T	T	F	T
F	F	T	F	T

TFL: Since the final column is all Ts, the original statement is TF-true.

(k) It is not the case that today is Friday and that today is payday if and only if today is not Friday or today is not payday.
Logical English: ~(Fri ∧ Pay) ↔ (~Fri ∨ ~Pay)
tff: ~(F ∧ P) ↔ (~F ∨ ~P)

F	P	(~(F ∧ P)	↔	(~F ∨ ~P)
T	T	F	T	F
T	F	F	T	T
F	T	F	T	T
F	F	F	T	T

TFL: Since the final column is all Ts, the original statement is TF-true.

Exercise 3. Use your knowledge of truth tables, TF-truth, and TF-falsity to simplify the following instructions. Note that in some cases there may be no way to simplify an instruction.

(a) If (x = 0) then
      If not (x = 0) then
           Print 'Hello'
      Endif
           Print 'Goodby'
    Endif

Since the inner condition contradicts the outer condition, "Hello" will never be printed. The simplified instruction is

    If (x = 0) then Print "Goodby" Endif

(c) While (x = 0)
      While not (x = 0)
        x ← x − 1
        Print x
      Endwhile
    Endwhile

If not (x = 0) initially then the loop is bypassed, doing nothing. If x = 0 initially then the inner loop does not execute, so again nothing happens. The simplified instruction is no instruction at all.

(e) If (x > y and not y < 0 or not x > y and y < 0 or not y < 0 or x > y)
    then Print "This is a mess" Endif

Here the condition is complicated enough to be interesting. Let P stand for "x > y" and Q stand for "y < 0". Then the following is a truth table for the condition in this instruction.

P	Q	$P \wedge \sim Q$	$\vee$	$\sim P \wedge Q$	$\vee$	$\sim Q$	$\vee$	P
T	T	F		F	F	F		T
T	F	T		T	F	T		T
F	T	F		T	T	T		T
F	F	F		F	F	T		T

order of evaluation   4   1   6   2   5   7   3   8*main column

This analysis shows That the condition is a tautology, so it will always be true, so it can be eliminated and the instruction can be simplified to just

    Print "This is a mess."

Chapter 12

Exercise 1. Make a decision table for the following specifications for calculating weekly pay for salespeople.

Everyone gets a base salary no matter what. Trainees get an additional $100 per week. Experienced salespeople in established territories are expected to sell at least $2,000 per week. If they do not then they get only their base salary. Anyone who sells more than $2,000 in a week gets a 10% commission on the amount over $2,000. Anyone selling in a new territory gets an additional 15% commission on the amount over $2,000.

		R1	R2	R3	R4	R5	R6	R7	R8
C1	Experienced	T	T	T	T	F	F	F	F
C2	Est. territory	T	T	F	F	T	T	F	F
C3	Sold > 2,000/week	T	F	T	F	T	F	T	F
A1	sal←base	Y	Y	Y	Y	Y	Y	Y	Y
A2	sal←sal + .10* (sales-2,000)	Y	N	Y	N	Y	N	Y	N
A3	sal←sal + 100	N	N	N	N	Y	Y	Y	Y
A4	sal←sal + .15*(sales-2,000)	N	N	Y	N	N	N	Y	N

Exercise 3. Try to simplify the result of Exercise 2. No further simplification is possible.

Exercise 5. Determine the number of Rules (columns) needed for a complete decision table for processing records where the transaction type can be "add", "change", or "delete", and the transaction code can be "FR", "SO", "JR", "SR", or "SP". Assume that each combination of transaction type and code requires different processing. What are the moduli of the two conditions?

The modulus of transaction type is 3.
The modulus of transaction code is 45
So the number of rules needed is 3*5 = 15.

Exercise 7a. Construct a pair of decision tables for calculating insurance origination fees according to the following specifications. Make your tables compact by using "don't care" condition entries, extended condition entries, and extended action entries as appropriate. Have one table for each kind of insurance.

At one time The North Carolina consumer loan laws allowed lenders to charge insurance origination fees for the life insurance and for the accident and health insurance they may offer borrowers. Borrowers are not required to buy either kind of insurance. For each of the two kinds of insurance the origination fee is: $0 if the amount of indebtedness is less than $250, $1 if the amount is between $250 and $500, and $2 if the amount is greater than $500. Borrowers occasionally renew their loans, i.e. borrow more before the original loan is completely repaid. In that case they can again choose none, one, or both kinds of insurance and another loan origination fee can be charged for each kind of insurance except that no more than two origination fees for each type of insurance can be charged in any one year period. Your decision tables should assign the appropriate fee for each of the two kinds of insurance, i.e. your action entries should specify what insurance origination fee to assign under various circumstances for each of the two kinds of insurance.

Insurance amounts in $100s

	1	2	3	4	5	6	7	8	9	10	11	12
Wants insurance	T	T	T	T	T	T	F	F	F	F	F	F
>1 fees charged	T	T	T	F	F	F	T	T	T	F	F	F
Amount of insurance	<2.5	2.5–5	>5	<2.5	2.5–5	>5	<2.5	2.5–5	>5	<2.5	2.5–5	>5
Fee ←	0	0	0	0	1	2	0	0	0	0	0	0

Note that this can be simplified.

Insurance amounts in $100s

	123	4	5	6	7–12
Wants insurance	T	T	T	T	F
>1 fees charged	T	F	F	F	–
Amount of insurance	–	<2.5	2.5–5	>5	–
Fee ←	0	0	1	2	0

Exercise 9. Make a decision table for the following specifications. The subroutine is to delete new record from a sequential access file. It is to do this by opening the master file, creating a new master file, and copying records from the master file to the new master file until it has read the record to be deleted. It does not copy that record to the new master file. Then it copies the remaining records from the master file to the new master file, closes both files, and returns to the calling program.

It is assumed that each record has a KEY field and that the subroutine is given the key value of the record to be deleted.

	R1	R2	R3	R4
Master file closed	T	F	F	F
At end of master file	–	T	F	F
Delete key = record key	–	–	T	F
Open master file	Y	N	N	N
Create new file	Y	N	N	N
Read record from master file	N	N	Y	Y
Write record to new file	N	N	N	Y
Close master file and new file	N	Y	N	N
Repeat	Y	N	Y	Y

Chapter 13

Exercise 1. Identify the scope of each quantifier and the free and bound instances of each variable in the wffs below. Tell which wffs are closed and which are open.

(a) ∀xPx ∧ ∃yPy The scope of ∀x is Px, scope of ∃y is Py, x is bound by ∀x and y is bound by ∃y.

(c) ∀z(Pz → Rzb) The scope of ∀z is (Pz → Rzb), and all instances of z are bound by ∀z.

(e) ∀x(Pxy ↔ ∃y(Qxy ∨ Rx)) The scope of ∀x is (Pxy ↔ ∃y(Qxy ∨ Rx)), the scope of ∃y is (Qxy ∨ Rx), x is bound by ∀x and y is bound by ∃y

Exercise 2. Using the interpretation described in Example 3, determine the truth value of each of the following wffs in I. Explain your reasoning.

(a) Pc → Qc is true in I because Pc is true in I and Qc is true in I.

(c) ∃x∀yBxy is false in I since ∀yBxy is not true in any extension I_x of I. To see this note that if ∀yBxy were true in I_x then Bxy would have to be true in every extension I_{xy} of I_x, i.e. there would have to be some assignment to x such that for any assignment to y, Bxy would be true, but there is no way to make such an assignment.

Exercise 3. Show that each of the following wffs are L-true

(a) ~∀xPx → ∃x~Px, i.e. if it is not the case that everything has property P then there is something which does not have property P.

The only way for ~∀xPx → ∃x~Px to be false in any interpretation is for ~∀xPx to be true and ∃x~Px to be false. Suppose I were such an interpretation. Then in I ∀xPx would be false. That would mean that not every extension I_x of I to x would have Px true in I_x. But if this were the case then Px would be false in that I_x. Hence ~Px would be true in I_x. Hence ∃x~Px would be true in I. This contradicts the hypothesis that ∃x~Px is false in I. Hence ~∀xPx → ∃x~Px cannot be false in any interpretation. Hence it is true in all its interpretations. Hence it is L-true.

(c) Pa → ∃xPx, i.e if a has property P then something has property P.

The only way for Pa → ∃xPx to be false in any interpretation is for Pa to be true and ∃xPx to be false. Suppose I were such an interpretation. Then in I Pa would be true. So Px would be true in any extension of I to x in which x were interpreted as a. Hence ∃xPx would be true in I. This contradicts the hypothesis that ∃xPx is false in I. Hence there can be no such interpretation as I. Hence Pa → ∃xPx cannot be false in any interpretation. Hence it is true in all its interpretation. Hence it is L-true.

Exercise 4. Show that each of the following wffs are L-false.

(a) ∀x(Px ↔ ~Px), i.e. everything has property P if and only if it does not have property P.

Suppose there were an interpretation, I, of ∀x(Px ↔ ~Px) it which it were true. Then in I Px ↔ ~Px would be true in every extension of I to x. Suppose I$_x$ were such an extension. Then Px and ~Px would have to have the same truth values in I$_x$. But this is not possible, if one is true the other must be false and vice versa. So there cannot be such an extension and hence there cannot be such a thing as I. Hence ∃x(Px ↔ ~Px) is false in all its interpretations. Hence it is L-false.

(c) ∃xPx ∧ ∀y~Py, i.e. there is something with property P and everything is such that it does not have property P.

Suppose there were an interpretation, I, of ∃xPx ∧ ∀y~Py in which it were true. Then both ∃xPx and ∀y~Py would be true in I. If ∃xPx were true in I then there would be an extension, I$_x$, of I to x in which Px would be true. On the other hand, if ∀y~Py were true in I then ~Px would be true in every extension I$_x$ of I to x. Hence, no matter how x was interpreted, Px would be false. This contradicts the earlier conclusion that there would be an extension, I$_x$, of I to x in which Px would be true. Hence there is no such I. Hence ∃xPx ∧ ∀y~Py if false in all of its interpretations. Hence ∃xPx ∧ ∀y~Py is L-false.

Exercise 5. For each of the following L-contingent wffs, try to find an interpretation in which it is true and an interpretation in which it is false.

(a) ∀xPx. An interpretation, I$_1$, in which ∀xPx is true is <D, V> where D is the set of all integers and V(P) is also the set of all integers, i.e. P is interpreted as the property of being an integer. The wff is true in I$_1$ because every extension of I to x must assign some integer to x, so Px will be true in that extension. Hence ∀xPx is true in I$_1$.

An interpretation I$_2$ in which ∀xPx false is <D, V> where D is the set of all integers and V(P) is the set of positive integers, i.e. P is interpreted as the property of being a positive integer. Any extension of I$_2$ to x in which x is interpreted as a negative integer is one in which Px is false. Hence ∀xPx is false in I$_2$.

(c) ∀xEy(Rxy ∧ Ryx). If D = {1, 2} and V(R) = {<1, 1>, <1, 2>, <2, 1>, <2,2>} then the wff is true in I. To see this notice that ∀xEy(Rxy ∧ Ryx) is true in I just in case Ey(Rxy ∧ Ryx) is true in I$_x$ for every extension of I to x. Suppose I$_x$ is any such extension, then Ey(Rxy ∧ Ryx) is true in I$_x$ just in case there is an extension of it, I$_{xy}$ in which Rxy ∧ Ryx is true. Moreover, Rxy ∧ Ryx will be true in I$_{xy}$ if and only if Rxy is true in I$_{xy}$ and Ryx is true in I$_{xy}$. To show that this is so, consider that any extension of I to x and then to y will interpret x as either 1 or 2 and will interpret y as either 1 or 2. Hence <x, y> will be interpreted as <1, 1>,<1, 2>, <2, 1>, or <2, 2>. Since all four of these ordered pairs are in $V(P)$, whichever one is the interpretation of $<x, y>$ in I_{xy} will be in $V(R)$. Hence Rxy will be true in I_{xy}. A similar argument shows that Ryx will also be true in I_{xy}. Hence Rxy $\wedge$ Ryx will also be true in I_{xy}. Hence Ey(Rxy $\wedge$ Ryx) will be true in I_x. Since the choice of I_x was completely general, this shows that $\forall x Ey(Rxy \wedge Ryx)$ is true in I.

On the other hand, if I is any interpretation in which $D = \{1, 2\}$ and $V(R) = \{<1,1>, <2,2>\}$ then any extension of I in which x and y are interpreted as different, such x as 1 and y as 2 will be an interpretation in which Rxy $\wedge$ Ryx will be false. Hence $\forall x Ey(Rxy \wedge Ryx)$ is false in I.

Exercise 6. Apply Procedure QL to each of the following statements. Hint: you can use the lists of L-true, L-false, and L-contingent wffs given in Examples 6, 7, and 8. Explain your reasoning.

(a) All programs have bugs. This statement has the form $\forall x(Px \rightarrow Qx)$ where Px in interpreted as "x is a program" and Qx is interpreted as "x has bugs." This wff is one of Examples 6, so the original statement is logically contingent.

(c) If all men are mortal and Socrates in a man then Socrates is mortal. This statement has the form $(\forall x(Px \rightarrow Qx) \wedge P(a)) \rightarrow Q(a)$, with Px representing "x is a man", Qx representing "x is mortal", and a naming Socrates. Since the wff is among Examples 4, it is L-true, so the original statement is L-true.

Chapter 14

Exercise 1

Determine whether each pair of statement forms shown in Examples 1 are logically equivalent by using truth tables.

(a) P   ~~P

P	P	↔	~	~	P
T	T	**T**	T	F	T
F	F	**T**	F	T	F

The equivalence is a tautology, so they are truth functionally equivalent.

(c) P ∧ Q   Q ∧ P

P	Q	P ∧ Q ↔ Q ∧ P		
T	T	T	**T**	F
T	F	F	**T**	T
F	T	T	**T**	T
F	F	T	**T**	T

The equivalence is a tautology, so they are truth functionally equivalent.

(e) P ∨ Q   Q ∨ P

P	Q	P ∨ Q ↔ Q ∨ P		
T	T	T	**T**	F
T	F	F	**T**	T
F	T	T	**T**	T
F	F	T	**T**	T

The equivalence is a tautology, so they are truth functionally equivalent.

(g) P ∧ (Q ∨ R)   (P ∧ Q) ∨ (P ∧ R)

P	Q	R	P ∧ (Q ∨ R) ↔ (P ∧ Q) ∨ (P ∧ R)					
T	T	T	T	T	**T**	T	T	T
T	T	F	T	T	**T**	T	T	F
T	F	T	T	T	**T**	T	T	T
F	T	T	F	F	**T**	F	F	F
F	T	F	F	T	**T**	F	F	F
F	F	T	F	T	**T**	F	F	F
F	F	F	F	F	**T**	F	F	F

The equivalence is a tautology, so they are truth functionally equivalent.

(i) P ∨ Q   ~(~P ∧ ~Q)

P	Q	P ∧ Q	↔	~(~P ∧ ~Q)
T	T	T	**T T**	F
T	F	T	**T T**	F
F	T	T	**T T**	F
F	F	F	**T F**	T

The equivalence is a tautology, so they are truth functionally equivalent.

(j) ~(P ∧ Q)   ~P ∧ ~Q

P	Q	~(P ∧ Q)	↔	~P ∧ ~Q
T	T	F T	**T**	F
T	F	T F	**F**	F
F	T	T F	**F**	F
F	F	T F	**T**	T

The equivalence is not a tautology, so they are not truth Functionally equivalent.

(l) P ∧ Q ∨ ~P ∧ ~Q   P ↔ Q

P	Q	(P ∧ Q ∨ ~P ∧ ~Q)			↔	(P ↔ Q)
T	T	T	T	F	**T**	T
T	F	F	F	F	**T**	F
F	T	F	F	F	**T**	T
F	F	F	T	T	**T**	T

The equivalence is a tautology, so they are truth functionally equivalent.

Exercise 2. Use truth tables to determine which of the following pairs of programming language instructions are equivalent. In case they are not equivalent specify the conditions under which they will give rise to different behaviors. Assume that short cut evaluation is not used.

(a) If x > 0 and (y < x or z < y) then Print "Hello" Endif

   If (x > 0 and y < x) or z < y) then Print "Hello" Endif

Let "P" represent "x > 0", "Q" represent "y < x", and "R" represent "z < y". Then the truth table for the equivalence is.

P	Q	R	P ∧ (Q ∨ R) ↔ (P ∧ Q) ∨ R				
T	T	T	T	T	**T**	T	T
T	T	F	T	T	**T**	T	T
_T_	_F_	_T_	F	T	**F**	F	T
T	F	F	F	F	**T**	F	F
_F_	_T_	_T_	F	T	**F**	F	T
F	T	F	F	T	**T**	F	F
F	F	T	F	F	**F**	F	T
F	F	F	F	F	**T**	F	F

The underlined truth value assignments indicate the circumstances under which the two instructions could give rise to different behaviors.

(c) If not (x > 0 and z < y) then Print "Hello" Endif

> If not z < y or not x > 0 then Print "Hello" Endif

Let "P" represent "x > 0" and "Q" represent "z < y". Then the truth table for the equivalence is:

P	Q	~(P ∧ Q) ↔ ~Q ∧ ~P			
T	T	F	T	**T**	F
_T_	_F_	T	F	**F**	F
_T_	_T_	T	F	**F**	F
F	F	T	F	**T**	T

The underlined truth value assignments indicate the circumstances under which the two instructions could give rise to different behaviors.

(e) While (not(x > 0 and y < z))
> print(x, y)
> x ← x − y
endwhile

While (not y < z and x > 0)
> print(x, y)
> x ← x − y
endwhile

P	Q	~(P ∧ Q) ↔ ~Q ∧ P				
T	T	F	T	**T**	F	F
T	F	T	F	**F**	T	T
F	T	T	F	**T**	F	F
F	F	T	F	**T**	T	F

when x > 0 and not y < z the two loops will behave differently.

Exercise 3. Use truth tables to determine which of the following pairs of SQL instructions are TF-equivalent. In case they are not, specify the conditions under which they could give rise to different reports. Do not assume anything about what data is in the tables, the data may be entirely different from the date in the tables used earlier. Do assume that there are no nulls in the data tables.

(a) SELECT supplier, item_number
     FROM suppliers
     WHERE not (unit_price = 3.00 and qty100_price > 500.00)

     SELECT supplier, item_number
     FROM suppliers
     WHERE not (unit_price = 3.00) and not (qty100_price > 500.00)

Let "P" represent "unit_price = 3.00" and "Q" represent "qty100_price > 500.00". Then the truth tables for the equivalence is:

P	Q	~(P ∧ Q)	↔	~P ∧ ~Q
T	T	F	**T**	F
T	F	T	**F**	F
F	T	T	**T**	T
F	F	T	**T**	T

The underlined truth value assignments indicate the circumstances under which the two statements could give different results, depending of course on the actual data in the tables.

(c) SELECT item_number, sell_price
     FROM items
     WHERE color = "blue" and on_hand < 100 or on_order = 0

     SELECT item_number, sell_price
     FROM items
     WHERE (color = "blue" or on_hand < 100) and (color = "blue" or on_order = 0)

Let "P" represent "color = blue", "Q" represent "on_hand < 100", and "R" represent "on_order = 0". Then the truth tables for the equivalence is:

P	Q	R	(P ∧ Q)	∨	R	↔	(P ∨ Q)	∧	R
T	T	T	T	T	**T**	T	T		
T	T	F	T	T	**F**	T	F		
T	F	T	F	T	**T**	T	T		
T	F	F	F	F	**T**	T	F		
F	T	T	F	T	**T**	T	T		
F	T	F	F	T	**T**	T	F		
F	F	T	F	F	**F**	F	F		
F	F	F	F	T	**T**	F	F		

The underlined truth value assignments indicate the circumstances under which the two statements could give different results, depending of course on the actual data in the tables.

Exercise 4. Explain why the following logical equivalence claims are true.

(a) $\forall xPx \equiv \forall yPy$ Suppose I is any interpretation of $\forall xPx \leftrightarrow \forall yPy$ and $\forall xPx$ is true in I, then Px is true of every element in the domain of I. But Py will also be true of every element of I. Hence $\forall yPy$ will be true in I. On the other hand, suppose $\forall xPx$ is false in I. Then there is some element, d, of the domain of I of which Px is false. But in that case Py will also be false of d. Hence $\forall yPy$ will be false in I. Since this argument applies to any interpretation it follows that $\forall xPx \equiv \forall yPy$.

(c) $\exists xPx \equiv \sim\forall x\sim Px$ Suppose I is any interpretation of $\exists xPx \leftrightarrow \sim\forall x\sim Px$ and $\forall xPx$ is true in I. Then there is an element, d, of the domain of I of which Px is true. Hence $\forall x\sim Px$ is false in I. Hence $\sim\forall x\sim Px$ is true in I. On the other hand, suppose $\exists xPx$ is false in I. Then there is no element, d, of the domain of I of which Px is true. Hence $\sim Px$ is true of all elements of the domain of I. Hence $\forall x\sim Px$ is true in I. Hence $\sim\forall x\sim Px$ is false in I. Since this argument applies to any interpretation it follows that $\forall xPx \equiv \sim\forall y\sim Py$.

Exercise 5. For each of the pairs of wffs below, find an interpretation in which one of them is true and the other is false. Hint for item c the fact that every pen in my desk has either red ink or black ink is not the same as every pen in my desk having red ink or every pen in my desk having black ink.

(a) P $\sim$P

Let I be any interpretation in which P is true. then $\sim$P is false in I.

(c) $\forall x(Px \vee Qx)$ $\forall xPx \vee \forall xQx$

Let I be an interpretation in which P is the property of being a pen on my desk with red ink and Q is the property of being a pen on my desk with blue ink. Suppose that there are three pens on my desk, one with red ink and two with blue ink. Then $\forall x(Px \vee Qx)$ is true in I but $\forall xPx \vee \forall xQx$ is false in I.

(e) $\forall x\exists yQxy$ $\exists y\forall xQxy$

Let I be the interpretation with D = the set of integers and let V(Q) be the greater than relation between integers. Then $\forall x\exists yQxy$ is true in I since for every integer there is an integer which it is greater than. But $\exists y\forall xQxy$ is false in I since there is no integer which is less than every integer.

Exercise 6. Determine whether the statement on the right is truth functionally redundant relative to the set of statements on the left.

Set of statements   Statement

(a) {P}   Q ∨ (~Q) redundant

P	Q	P	P ∧ (Q ∨ (~Q))	
T	T	T	T	T
T	F	T	T	T
F	T	F	F	T
F	F	F	F	T

(c) {P ∨ Q, Q ∨ R, ~Q}   R ∧ P redundant

P	Q	R	((P ∨ Q) ∧ (Q ∨ R))			∧~Q	(∧ S)	∧(R∧P)	
T	T	T	T	T	T	F	F	F	T
T	T	F	T	T	T	F	F	F	F
T	F	T	T	T	T	T	T	T	T
T	F	F	T	F	F	F	F	F	F
F	T	T	T	T	T	F	F	F	F
F	T	F	T	T	T	F	F	F	F
F	F	T	F	F	F	F	F	F	F
F	F	F	F	F	F	F	F	F	F

Exercise 7. Determine which of the following sets of statements are TF-redundant and which are not. Note that showing that a set of statements is not redundant requires separately investigating what happens when each element of S is removed, e.g. by removing each component of the original set S in turn and, for each of them, comparing the truth table for (∧S) with the truth table for (∧S) with that element of S removed. You might also find some shortcut in particular cases.

(a) {P, ~P, ~~P} redundant: P and ~~P are equivalent, so ~~P is redundant with respect to the rest of the set.

(c) {P∧Q, P, Q} redundant: any element can be removed without changing the truth table of the conjunction of the remaining elements.

Chapter 15

Exercise 1. Suppose you could establish that an argument was valid but that its conclusion was false. What could you tell about its premises?

Its premises are not all true, since if they were all true and the argument were valid, its conclusion would have to be true.

Exercise 2. For each of the remaining rows of the table, do an analysis as was done in the examples above. This is not as laborious a task as it may seem. You can eliminate several rows at a time, for example an argument cannot be sound and invalid, so rows 3, 7, 11, 15, 19, and 23 can all be treated at once. The hard part will be coming up with example arguments for some of the rows that are possible.

Rows 1, 2, 8, 9, 10, and 22 are discussed in the examples. Rows 3, 7, 11, 15, 19, and 23 are treated in the discussion of this exercise. Rows 13, 17, and 21 are not possible because all the premises of a sound argument must be true. Rows 5 and 6 are not possible because a valid argument with all true premises must have a true conclusion. This accounts for all but rows 4, 12, 14, 16, 18, 20, and 24. Each of these is possible, as is shown by the examples below.

Row 4: Pick any true statement as the premise. Pick any other true statement that has nothing to do with the first as the conclusion. As long as the premise has nothing to do with the conclusion the argument will be invalid and hence unsound. For example:

P: 3 > 5.
C: Snow is generally colder than steam.

Row 14: Pick any valid argument and add a false premise having nothing to do with the argument and you have an example for this row.

P1: All men are mortal.
P2: Socrates is a man.
P3: Mount Everest is a small mountain.
C: Socrates is mortal.

Row 18: The example for Row 22 showed that a valid argument can lead from all false premises to a false conclusion. The example below shows that a valid argument can lead from all false premises to a true conclusion. Together they illustrate the fact that validity is not much good in the search for truth if you don't use true premises.

P1: All mammals are green.
P2: All green things have hearts.
C: All mammals have hearts.

Row 24: Just replace the conclusion of the example for Row 20 with an unrelated false statement and we have an example for this row.

P: All mammals are green.
C: 5 < 3.

Exercise 3. Write the conditional corresponding to the following argument, as was done in the Example 9.

For every number there is a number such that their sum = 0.
c is a number.
_____
There is a number such that it plus c = 0.

(If for every number there is a number such that their sum = 0 and c is a number) then there is a number such that it plus c = 0.

Exercise 5. Use informal methods. If the argument is valid, explain why. If it is invalid, give a counterexample.

(a) Today is Monday
_____
    tomorrow must be Tuesday.

Valid. By definition, the day after Monday is Tuesday and the day after today is tomorrow.

(c) The rest of the program works perfectly.
_____
    If there is a problem with the program it must be in the new procedure.

Invalid. For example, the problem with the program could be user error.

(e) If x were 5 at line 2,020 then the program would have crashed.
    It did crash.
    _____
    So probably x was 5 at line 2,020.

Invalid. First this is an inductive argument, so validity is not an issue. Second, it is invalid even without the word probably in the conclusion. It could be that if x were any value other than zero at line 2,020 the program would have crashed.

(g) If the program was run yesterday then a run log entry for it would
    have been made.
    No run log entry for it was made.
    Moreover, if the program was not run yesterday then the records in
    it are not current.
    _____
    Hence the records in it are not current.

Valid if reconstructed as follows.

If the program was run yesterday then a run log entry for it would
   have been made.
<u>No run log entry for it was made.</u>
The program was not run yesterday.
Moreover, if the program was not run yesterday then the records in
   <u>it are not current.</u>
Hence the records in it are not current.

This is a compound argument with "The program was not run yesterday" as an
implicit conclusion of the first argument. If the first two premises are true then the
first premise is a true conditional with false consequent. Hence its antecedent is
false. Hence the implicit conclusion is true. If the second premise of the second
argument is true then it is a true conditional with true antecedent. The only way for
this to happen if for the consequent to be true also.

Exercise 7. Apply the truth table test to each of the following argument forms.

(a) <u>~(P ∧ Q), R ↔ ~P, P → ~R, Q</u>
    P

P	Q	R	((((~P ∧ Q) ∧ (R ↔ ~P)) ∧ (P →~R)) ∧ Q) → P							
T	T	T	F	T	F	F	F	F	F	T
T	T	F	F	T	F	T	F	T	F	T
T	F	T	T	F	F	F	F	F	F	T
T	F	F	T	F	T	T	T	T	F	T
F	T	T	T	F	T	T	T	T	T	F
F	T	F	T	F	F	F	F	T	F	T
F	F	T	T	F	T	T	T	T	F	T
F	F	F	T	F	F	F	F	T	F	T

Since the conditional is contingent, the test fails.

(c) <u>P → ~(Q ∧ R), ~P ∨ Q</u>
    ~R

P	Q	R	(((P → ~ (Q ∧ R)) ∧ (~P ∨ Q) → ~R					
T	T	T	F	T	F	F	F	F
T	T	F	F	T	F	F	F	T
T	F	T	T	F	F	T	F	F
T	F	F	T	F	F	F	F	T
F	T	T	T	T	T	F	T	T
F	T	F						
F	F	T						
F	F	F						

Since the conditional is TF-contingent, the test fails.

(e) $\dfrac{\sim(P \vee Q), \sim(P \wedge \sim Q)}{P \leftrightarrow Q}$

P	Q	($\sim$(P $\vee$ Q)$\wedge$ $\sim$(P $\wedge$ Q)) $\rightarrow$ (P $\leftrightarrow$ Q)
T	T	F T F T F T T
T	F	F T F F T T F
F	T	F T F T F T F
F	F	T F T T F T T

Since the conditional is a tautology, the argument form is valid.

Exercise 8. Use an informal approach to showing the validity or invalidity of each of the following arguments.

(a) All birds are bipeds., Chalky is not a biped.
    Chalky is not a bird.

Valid. If the premises were true the conclusion could not be false. If Chalky were a bird then by the first premise, Chalky would be a biped. But this contradicts the second premise. Hence Chalky is not a bird.

(c) All birds are bipeds., Everything is a biped.
    Everything is a bird.

Invalid. Suppose there were only birds and people. them both premises would be true, but the conclusion would be false.

(e) Tweety is a bird.
    Everything is a bird.

Invalid. The world we live in is one is which Tweety (the cartoon character) is a bird but not everything is a bird.

(g) Everything is a bird.
    My cat is a bird.

Valid. If everything is a bird then my cat, being something, would have to be a bird.

Exercise 9. Determine which of the following argument forms are valid and which are not valid. If an argument form is valid explain why it is valid, i.e. explain why the corresponding conditional must be true in all of its interpretations. If it is invalid, give a counterexample, i.e. give an interpretation in which all the premises are true and the conclusion is false.

(a) $\dfrac{\forall x(Px \rightarrow Qx), \sim Qa}{\sim Pa}$

All arguments of this form are valid. The idea is that everything that has property P also has property Q, but a does not have property Q, then a cannot have property P either.

The corresponding conditional wff is $(\forall x(Px \rightarrow Qx) \wedge {\sim}Qa) \rightarrow {\sim}Pa$. If the argument form were not valid then there would be an interpretation, I, of the conditional in which it is false. In that case $(\forall x(Px \rightarrow Qx) \wedge {\sim}Qa)$ would be true in I and ${\sim}Pa$ would be false in I. Hence both $\forall x(Px \rightarrow Qx)$ and ${\sim}Qa$ would have to be true in I and Pa would be true in I as well. Since $\forall x(Px \rightarrow Qx)$ is true in I, $Px \rightarrow Qx$ must be true in every extension of I to x. In particular it must be true in any extension to x in which x is interpreted as a. Hence $Pa \rightarrow Qa$ is true in that extension. Combined with the fact that Pa is true in I it follows that Qa is true in that extension of I. But Qa is false in I, so it is false in this extension of I. So Qa is true and Qa is false in that extension. This is contrary to the law of noncontradiction. Hence the assumption the argument form is not valid is false. Hence it is valid.

(c) $\underline{\forall x(Px \rightarrow Qx), \forall xQx}$
$\quad \forall xPx$

This is not a valid argument form. Let I be an interpretation in which the domain is the set of positive integers, Px means "x is a prime number" and Qx means "x is an integer." Then $\forall x(Px \rightarrow Qx)$ is true in I, since all prime numbers are positive integers. But $\forall xPx$ is false in I, since not every positive integer is a prime number.

(e) $\underline{Pa}$
$\quad \forall xPx$

This is an invalid form. Let I be the interpretation in which the domain is the set of animals, Px is interpreted as "x is a cat", and a is interpreted as my cat, Chalky. Then Pa is true in I because Chalky is a cat. But $\forall xPx$ is not true in I because not all animals are cats.

(g) $\underline{\forall xPx}$
$\quad Pa$

This is a valid form. Let I be any interpretation in which $\forall xPx$ is true. Then Px is true in every extension of I to x. No matter how a is interpreted, Px will be true of a in those extensions of I to x in which x is identified with a. Hence Pa is true in I.

Chapter 16

Exercise 1. Identify one correct rule of inference that could be used to justify each of the following inferences. If no single correct rule can justify the inference, say so.

(a) If the file were sorted in ascending order the Adams record would be first. Moreover, the file is sorted in ascending order. Hence the Adams record is first.

Solution: *modus ponens* (also known as affirming the antecedent and as →-elimination))

(c) Today is Tuesday and it is raining here now. Hence today is Tuesday.

Solution: simplification (also know as ∧-elimination)

(e) If $x = 5$ then $y = 7$. Also, if $a > 0$ then $b < 0$. Moreover, $x = 5$ or $a > 0$. Consequently, $y = 7$ or $b < 0$.

Solution: constructive dilemma

(g) $(x = 3) \leftrightarrow (y < 0)$

   $\overline{\phantom{(x = 3) \leftrightarrow (y < 0)}}$

   $(y < 0) \leftrightarrow (x = 3)$

Solution: ↔ is commutative

(i) $S \to (T \vee Q)$

   $\overline{}$

   $S \to (S \wedge (T \vee Q))$

Solution: No one rule given will justify this, although it is correct.

(k) $S \leftrightarrow (R \wedge (\sim Q))$, $(R \wedge S) \leftrightarrow (T \vee S)$

   $\overline{}$

   $(R \wedge S) \leftrightarrow (T \vee (R \wedge (\sim Q)))$

Solution: substitution rule 2 (also know as sub2) by substituting $R \wedge (\sim Q)$ for the second instance of S in $(R \wedge S) \leftrightarrow (T \vee S)$.

Exercise 3. Given the following three premises, apply valid rules of inference to them to arrive at four conclusions that differ from the premises and from the example given below. For each of the four inferences you may use any of the three given premises or any of the conclusions you have from previous inferences. For each inference, tell what inference you are making and give a name of rule you are applying.

Premises: $A \wedge (B \vee C)$, $B \to \sim D$, $\sim \sim D$

Solution: Correct answers will differ.

1. Infer D from ~~D using ~~-elimination.
2. Infer A from A ∧ (B ∨ C) using ∧-elimination
3. infer ~B from B → ~D and ~~D using *modus tollens*
4. Infer A ∧ ~B from the given premises and the conclusion above using ∧-introduction.

Exercise 4. For each of the incorrect rules above, give a counterexample that shows that the rule is incorrect.

(a) $\dfrac{P \rightarrow Q, Q}{P}$ (affirming the consequent)

If today is the last day of class then there is a test today.
There is a test today
Therefore today is the last day of class.

In any class in which there is a mid term test not on the last day of class and a test on the last day of class, this argument would have true premises and a false conclusion on the day of the mid term test.

(c) $\dfrac{P \rightarrow Q}{Q \rightarrow P}$ (converting a consequent)

If today is Friday then there is a test today.
If there is a test today then today is Friday.

In any class in which there was a test on every Friday and occasionally on other days, this argument would have a true premise and false conclusion on any test day that is not a Friday.

Chapter 17

Exercise 1. Fill in columns 2 and 4 for the following (formal) proof of the correctness of the argument form

A → (B ∧ C), ~C / ~A

Proof:

1.	1	A → (B ∧ C)	premise
2.	2	~C / ~A	premise / conclusion
3.	2	(~B) ∨ (~C)	∨ introduction 2
4.	2	~(B ∧ C)	de Morgan 2
7.	1,2	~A	modus tollens 6, 1

Exercise 3. If A is replaced by "x > 0", B is replaced by "y = 1", and C is replaced by "z = 5" then what specific argument does the proof of Exercise 1 show to be valid?

P1: If x > 0 then y = 1 and z = 5.
P2: not z = 5.
C: Not x > 0.

Exercise 4
Use conditional proof to prove the following. Hint, in some cases you may have to use the rule of conditional proof more than once in a single proof.

a. A → C, B → D / (A ∧ B) → (C ∧ D)

1.	1	A → C	premise
2.	2	B → D / (A ∧ B) → (C ∧ D)	premise / conclusion
3.	3	A ∧ B	assume for CP
4.	3	A	∧ elim. 3
5.	1,3	C	→ elim. 1,3
6.	3	B	∧ elim. 3
7.	2,3	D	→ elim. 2,6
8.	1,2,3	C ∧ D	∧ intro. 5, 7
9.	1,2	(A ∧ B) → (C ∧ D)	→ intro. 3, 8

c. A → (B → C) / (A ∧ B) → C

1.		A → (B → C) / (A ∧ B) → C	premise/conclusion
2.	2	A ∧ B	assume for CP
3.	2	A	∧ elim. 2
4.	1,3	B → C	→ elim. 1, 3
5.	1,2,3	B	∧ elim. 2
6.	2	C	→ elim. 4, 5
7.	1	(A ∧ B) → C	→ intro. 2, 6

Exercise 5. Use indirect proof to prove the following

a. P ∨ Q, P ∨ ~Q / P

1.	1	P ∨ Q	premise
2.	2	P ∨ ~Q / P	premise / conclusion
3.	3	~P	assume for indirect proof (IP)
4.	1,3	~Q	disjunctive syllogism 1, 3
5.	2,3	~~Q	disjunctive syllogism 2, 3
6.	2,3	Q	~~ elim. 5
7.	1,2,3	Q ∧ ~Q	∧ intro. 6, 4
8.	1,2	P	~ elim. 3, 7

c. (S ∧ T) ∨ Q, (S ∧ T) ∨ R, R → ~Q / (S ∧ T)

1.	1	(S ∧ T) ∨ Q	premise
2.	2	(S ∧ T) ∨ R	premise
3.	3	R → ~Q / S ∧ T	premise / conclusion
4.	4	~(S ∧ T)	assume for IP
5.	1,4	Q	disj. syll. 1, 4
6.	2,4	R	disj. syll. 2, 4
7.	2,3,4	~Q	→ elim. 3, 6
8.	1,2,3,4	Q ∧ ~Q	∧ intro. 5, 7
9.	1,2,3	S ∧ T	~ elim. 4, 8

Exercise 6. For each of the following, either construct a formal proof of it or show a counterexample to it. Note: a counterexample to an allegedly valid argument form could be given by specifying an assignment of truth values of the elementary statements involved which made all the premises true and the conclusion false. A counterexample to an allegedly valid argument form could also be given by showing an instance of that form with obviously true premises and a false conclusion.

a. P → Q, Q → R, R → S, S → T, T → U, ~U / ~P

1.	1	P → Q	premise
2.	2	Q → R	premise
3.	3	R → S	premise
4.	4	S → T	premise
5.	5	T → U	premise
6.	6	~U / ~P	premise / conclusion
7.	5,6	~T	modus tollens 5, 6
8.	4,5,6	~S	modus tollens 4, 7
9.	3,4,5,6	~R	modus tollens 3, 8
10.	2,3,4,5,6	~Q	modus tollens 2, 9
11.	1,2,3,4,5,6	~P	modus tollens 1, 10

c. $(P \rightarrow (Q \rightarrow R)) / ((P \rightarrow Q) \rightarrow R)$

In case P, Q, and R are all false, the premise will be true and the conclusion false, so this is not a theorem.

e. $((P \wedge Q) \rightarrow R) / (P \rightarrow (Q \rightarrow R))$

1.	1	$((P \wedge Q) \rightarrow R) / (P \rightarrow (Q \rightarrow R))$	premise / conclusion
2.	2	P	assume for CP
3.	3	Q	assume for CP
4.	2,3	$P \wedge Q$	$\wedge$ intro 2, 3
5.	1,2,3	R	$\rightarrow$ elim 1, 4
6.	1,2	$Q \rightarrow R$	$\rightarrow$ intro 3, 5
7.	1	$P \rightarrow (Q \rightarrow R)$	$\rightarrow$ intro 2, 6

g. $((P \rightarrow R) / (P \wedge Q) \rightarrow R$

1.	1	$((P \rightarrow R) / (P \wedge Q) \rightarrow R$	premise / conclusion
2.	2	$P \wedge R$	assume for CP
3.	2	P	$\wedge$ elim 2
4.	1,2	R	$\rightarrow$ elim 1, 4
5.	1	$(P \wedge Q) \rightarrow R$	$\rightarrow$ intro 2, 4

Exercise 7. For each of the following alleged theorems of logic (tautologies), either construct a formal proof of it or show a counterexample to it. Note: a counterexample to an alleged tautology could either be an assignment of truth values which was not all ts in its final column or an instance of the statement form which is false.

a. $((P \vee Q) \rightarrow R) \rightarrow ((P \rightarrow R) \vee (Q \rightarrow R))$

Theorem: $((P \vee Q) \rightarrow R) \rightarrow ((P \rightarrow R) \vee (Q \rightarrow R))$
Proof:

1.	1	$(P \vee Q) \rightarrow R$	assume for CP
2.	2	$P \vee Q$	assume for CP
3.	1,2	R	$\rightarrow$ elim 1, 2
4.	4	P	assume for CP
5.	1,2	$P \rightarrow R$	$\rightarrow$ intro 3, 4
6.	1,2	$(P \rightarrow R) \vee (Q \rightarrow R)$	$\vee$ intro 5
7.		$((P \vee Q) \rightarrow R) \rightarrow ((P \rightarrow R) \vee (Q \rightarrow R))$	$\rightarrow$ intro 2, 6

c. $((P \rightarrow R) \vee (Q \rightarrow R) \rightarrow ((P \vee Q) \rightarrow R)$

Theorem: $((P \rightarrow R) \vee (Q \rightarrow R) \rightarrow ((P \vee Q) \rightarrow R)$
Proof:

1.	1	$((P \rightarrow R) \vee (Q \rightarrow R)$	assume for CP
2.	1	$P \rightarrow R$	$\wedge$ elim 1
3.	3	$P \wedge Q$	assume for CP
4.	3	$P \wedge$	elim 3
5.	1,3	$R \rightarrow$	elim 2, 4
6.	1	$(P \wedge Q) \rightarrow R$	$\rightarrow$ intro 3, 5
7.		$((P \rightarrow R) \wedge (Q \rightarrow R) \rightarrow ((P \wedge Q) \rightarrow R)$	$\rightarrow$ intro 1, 6

e. ~(P ∨ Q) ↔ (~P ∧ ~Q)

Theorem: ~(P ∨ Q) ↔ (~P ∧ ~Q)
Proof:

1.	1	~P ∧ ~Q	assume for CP
2.	1	~P	∧ elim 1
3.	1	~Q	∧ elim 1
4.	4	P ∨ Q	assume for IP
5.	1,4	Q	disj. syll. 2, 4
6.	1,4	Q ∧ ~Q	∧ intro 3, 5
7.	1	~(P ∨ Q)	~ intro 3, 6 (dis. 4)
8.		(~P ∧ ~Q) → ~(P ∨ Q)	→ intro 1, 7 (dis. 1)

This is the end of first part of the proof.

9.	9	~(P ∨ Q)	assume for CP
10.	10	P	assume for IP
11.	10	P ∨ Q	∨ intro 10
12.	9,10	(P ∨ Q) ∧ ~(P ∨ Q)	∧ intro 9, 11
13.	9	~P	~ intro 10, 12 (dis. 10)
14.	14	Q	assume for IP
15.	14	P ∨ Q	∧ intro 14
16.	9,14	(P ∨ Q) ∧ ~(P ∧ Q)	→ intro 9, 15
17.	9	~Q	~ intro 14, 16 (dis. 14)
18.	9	~P ∧ ~Q	→ intro 13, 17
19.		~(P ∨ Q) → ~P ∧ ~Q	→ intro 9, 18 (dis. 9)

This is the end of the second part of the proof.

| 20. | | ~(P ∨ Q) ↔ (~P ∧ ~Q) | ↔ intro 8, 19 |

g. ((P ∧ Q) ∨ (P ∧ ~Q)) This is not a tautology. Let P be false and Q be either value.

Exercise 8. In each of the following, write the instance of the general proof that results if P is replaced by "Today is Tuesday", Q is replaced by "We have a meeting today", R is replaced by "It is raining", S is replaced by "It is snowing", and T is replaced by "Today is Thursday".

(a) The proof in Example 4.
(b) The proof in Example 5.
(c) The proof in Example 6.
(d) The proof in Example 7.

(a) Instance of Example 4.

1.	1	If today is not Tuesday then we have a meeting today and it is raining	premise
2.	2	It is not raining.	premise
		Therefore today is Tuesday	conclusion
3.	3	Today is not Tuesday	assume (for IP)
4.	1,3	We have a meeting today and it is raining	$\to$ elim. 1,3 (or MP 1,3)
5.	1,3	It is raining.	$\wedge$ elim. 4
6.	1,2,3	It is raining and it is not raining	$\wedge$ intro. 5,2 (a contradiction)
7.	1,2	Today is Tuesday	~ elim 3,6 (assumption in 3 is discharged)

(c) Instance of Example 6.

1.	1	If it is raining or we have a meeting today then today is Tuesday	premise
2.	2	If today is Tuesday then it is snowing and today is Thursday	premise
3.	3	It is not snowing or today is not Thursday	premise
		Hence, It is not the case that it is raining or we have a meeting today.	conclusion
4.	4	It is raining or we have a meeting today	assume (for IP)
5.	1,4	Today is Tuesday	$\to$ elim. 1,4
6.	1,2,4	It is snowing and today is Thursday	$\to$ elim. 2,5
7.	3	It is not the case that it is snowing and today is Thursday	de Morgan 3
8.	1,2,3,4	It is snowing and today is Thursday and it is not the case that both it is snowing and today is Thursday.	$\wedge$ intro. 6, 7
11.	1,2,3	It is not the case that it is raining or we have a meeting today.	~ intro. 4, 8

Exercise 9. Using the style of Example 9, construct proofs of the following theorems. Suggestion: Use the fact that $(x = 0) \vee ((x < 0) \vee (x > 0))$ and $(y = 0) \vee ((y < 0) \vee (y > 0))$ and $(z = 5) \vee ((z < 5) \vee (z > 5))$. Note: your proofs may differ and still be correct.

a.

Theorem: $(x = 0 \rightarrow \sim z = 5) \wedge \sim(z < 5 \vee z > 5) \rightarrow \sim x = 0$.

Proof:

1.	1	$(x = 0 \rightarrow z = 5) \wedge \sim(z < 5 \vee z > 5)$	assume for CP
2.	1	$x = 0 \rightarrow z = 5$	$\wedge$ elim. 1
3.	1	$\sim(z < 5 \vee z > 5)$	$\wedge$ elim. 1
4.	1	$\sim z < 5 \vee \sim z > 5$	de Morgan 3
5.	1	$\sim z < 5$	$\wedge$ elim 4
6.	1	$\sim z > 5$	$\wedge$ elim 4
7.	1	$z < 5 \vee (z = 5 \vee z > 5)$	arithmetic
8.	1	$z = 5 \vee z > 5$	disjunctive syllogism 7, 5
9.	1	$z > 5 \vee z = 5$	$\vee$ is communicative
10.	1	$z = 5$	disjunctive syllogism 9, 6
11.	1	$\sim \sim z = 5$	$\sim \sim$ intro 10
12.	1	$\sim x = 0$	modus tollens 2,
13.		$(x = 0 \rightarrow \sim z = 5) \wedge \sim(z < 5 \vee z > 5)$ $\rightarrow \sim x = 0.$	$\rightarrow$ intro 1, 6

c.

Theorem: $(((y = 1 \rightarrow (z = 5 \wedge x = 0)) \wedge \sim z = 5) \rightarrow \sim y = 1$

Proof:

1.	1	$(((y = 1 \rightarrow (z = 5 \wedge x = 0)) \wedge \sim z = 5)$	assume for CP
2.	1	$(((y = 1 \rightarrow (z = 5 \wedge x = 0))$	$\wedge$ elim 1
3.	1	$\sim z = 5$	$\wedge$ elim 1
4.	1	$\sim z = 5 \vee \sim x = 0$	$\vee$ intro 3
5.	1	$\sim(z = 5 \wedge x = 0)$	de Morgan 4
6.	1	$\sim y = 1$	modus tollens 1, 5
7.		$(((y = 1 \rightarrow (z = 5 \wedge x = 0)) \wedge \sim z = 5)$ $\rightarrow \sim y = 1$	$\rightarrow$ intro 1, 6

Chapter 18

Exercise 1. Suppose a program does nothing but go into an infinite loop no matter what input it is given. For what problems, if any, is a partially correct?

It is partially correct for every problem since there are no cases where it halts with the wrong answer.

Exercise 3. Show by example that an program may be totally correct with respect to one problem and not totally correct with respect to another. You don't need to write a program, just describe what such a program and problems would be in specific terms.

Obviously, answers will vary. An algorithm that correctly calculates the sum of any positive integers and gives output −1 for inputs that are not positive integers is totally correct for the problem of finding the sum of any two positive integers but is not totally correct for the problem of finding the sum of any two integers.

Chapter 19

Exercise 1. Write proofs of correctness in the style of examples 1–3 for each of the following algorithms.

(a)
```
0        Algorithm countZeros(L)
         # Pre: L is a list of numbers.
         # Post: Returns the number of zero elements of L.

1                count ← 0        # Count is number of zeros found so far.
2                I ← 0            # I is loop control variable
3                While I < len(L) do
4                        If L[I] = 0 then count ← count + 1 Endif
5                        I ← I + 1
                 Endwhile
6                Return count
         EndAlgorithm
```

Proof of Correctness: Count is supposed to be the number of zeros found so far in L. The loop invariant is that count is the number of zeros in L found so far. Initially no zeros have been found and initially count is assigned zero at line 1. If the list is empty the loop terminates immediately and the algorithm returns 0 at line 6. If the list is not empty then setting I to zero in line 2 causes the loop at line 3 to start by examining the first element of L. If it is zero then count is incremented by 1 and if not then count stays as it was. Line 5 increases I by 1. Consequently, after one iteration of the loop count is still the number of zeros in L found so far. Each time through the loop count is increased by 1 if a new zero is found and left as it was otherwise. If the loop terminates, all the elements of L have been examined and count is the number of zeros in L found so far. And this is the total number of zeros in L, since all of L has been examined. Hence countZeros(L) returns the number of zeros in L. Moreover, the loop must terminate since I begins at zero and increases by 1 each time through the loop. Eventually I must become = or > the length of L. At that point the loop is exited.

c.
```
0        Algorithm isReverseOf(A, B)
         # Pre: A and B are 1-dim arrays of numbers of the same length
         # Post: Returns true if B is reverse of A, else returns false

1                reply ← true
2                If len(A) < > len(B) then
3                        reply ← false
                 Else
4                I ← 0
5                While (I < len(A)) and (reply = true)) do
6                        If A[I] < > B[len(A) - (1 + I)) then
7                                reply ← false
```

                      Endif
8   I ← I + 1
                 Endwhile
            Endif
9   Return reply
        EndAlgorithm

Proof of Correctness: Initially reply is assigned true and it remains true unless the element at position I of A does not match the element at position Len(A) – (1 + I) of B. In this case reply is set to false and the loop is immediately exited. A useful loop invariant is that the first I elements of A have been compared with the last I elements of B and that corresponding elements of A and B are the same, i.e. the first element if A = the last element of B, the second element of A = the next to last element of B, and so on. Initially I is set to zero at line 4 and the loop invariant is (vacuously) true, i.e. the first 0 elements of A have been compared with the last 0 elements of B and corresponding elements of A and B are the same. If A is empty then the loop body is skipped, control passes to line 9 and true is returned, as it should be. If len(A) > 0 then the loop body is executed for the first time and A[0] is compared with B[len(A) – (1 + I)] which is the last element of B. If they are different B is not the reverse of A, reply is assigned false, and the loop terminates with control passing immediately to line 9 where false is returned. If the two list elements are the same then reply remains true, I is increased by 1, and the loop invariant remains true. This process is repeated each time the loop body is executed. If the loop is terminated prematurely it is because corresponding elements of A and B have been found which are not the same, B is not the reverse of A, reply is assigned false, control passes to line 9, and false is returned. If the loop exits normally, with I = len(A) then corresponding elements of A and B are the same for the length of A (and B), B is the reverse of A, reply is still true, and control passes to line 9 where true is returned. The loop must eventually exit, and the program halt, because I starts at 0 and increases by 1 each time the loop body is executed, so eventually I = > len(A). Hence isReverseOf(A, B) returns true if B is reverse of A, and returns false otherwise.

Exercise 2. In each case, find {P(e/v)} given v ← e and {P(v) where v is some variable.

(a) v ← 5 {v = 5} e must be 5 and P(e/v) must be P(v) with every instance of v replaced by 5, so P(e/v) must be 5 = 5.

(c) x ← x + 5 {x + 5 < z + x} e must be x + 5 and v must be x. So P(e/v) must be (x + 5) + 5 < (x + 5).

Exercise 3. In each part an incomplete instance of a rule of inference is given. Identify the rule you can apply and fill in the missing conclusion.

(a) An instance of the Sequence Rule

$$\frac{\{x \text{ and } y \text{ are integers}\} \ z \leftarrow x * y \ \{x \text{ and } y \text{ are factors of } z\}}{\{x \text{ and } y \text{ are factors of } z\} \ w \leftarrow z^2 \ \{x^2 \text{ and } y^2 \text{ are factors of } w\}}$$
$$\{x \text{ and } y \text{ are integers}\} \ z \leftarrow x * y; \ w \leftarrow z^2 \ \{x^2 \text{ and } y^2 \text{ are factors of } w\}$$

(c) An instance of the If Else Rule

{x and y are numbers and x >= y} max ← x {max is the larger of x and y}
{x and y are numbers and ~x ≥= y} max ← y {max is the larger of x and y}
_____
{x and y are numbers}
If x > = y} max ← x else max ← y
{max is the larger of x and y}

(e) An instance of the While Do Rule

{F = J factorial ∧ J < N} J ← J Î 1; F ← F * J {F = J factorial}
_____
{F = J factorial}
While (J < N) Do
        J ← J + 1; F ← F * J
Endwhile
{F = J factorial ∧ ~J < N}

Exercise 4

Give complete proofs of correctness (supplying midconditions and reasons) for each of the following algorithms.

(a) Algorithm maxOf2(x, y)
        # Pre: x and y are numbers.
        # Post: Returns the maximum of x and y.

                If (x > = y) then
                        max ← x
                Else
                        max ← y
                Endif
                Return max
        EndAlgorithm

Proof:
Algorithm maxOf2(x, y)
# Pre: x and y are numbers.
# Post: Returns the maximum of x and y.
# ((x > = y) ← x is the maximum of x and y) ∧
# (~x > = y) ← y is the maximum of x and y   Arithmetic
        If (x > = y) then
                # x = x   Identity Laws
                max ← x
                # max = x
# x > = y ← max is the maximum of x and y   Substitution
        Else
                # y = y   Identity Laws
                max ← y
                # max = y   Assignment Rule
~x > = y → max is the maximum of x and y   Endif

max is the maximum of x and y   If Then Rule
    Return max
Returns the maximum of x and y.
EndAlgorithm

(c)
Algorithm powerOf2Floor(x)
Pre: x is a number $>= 1$.
Post: returns the largest power of $2 <= x$

       $J \leftarrow 0$
       While ($2^J <= x$) Do
            $J \leftarrow J + 1$
       EndWhile
       Return 2^{J-1}
EndAlgorithm

Proof:
Algorithm powerOf2Floor(x)
Pre: x is a number $>= 1$.
$(2^J <= x \land \sim 2^{J+1} <= x) \rightarrow 2^J$ is the largest power of $2 <= x$ Arithmetic
$0 = 0$ Identity Rule
    $J \leftarrow 0$
# $J = 0$ Assignment Rule
# $2^J = 1$ Arithmetic
# 2^J is a power of 2 and $2^J <= x$ Arithmetic
    While ($2^J <= x$) Do
# $J + 1 = J + 1$ Identity Laws
        $J \leftarrow J + 1$
        # $J = J$ Assignment Rule
    EndWhile
#
2J-1 is the largest power of $2 <= c$.   While Do Rule
    Return 2J-1
Post: returns the largest power of $2 <= x$
EndAlgorithm

Sources and Bibliography

Sources

Aside from the selection and arrangement of topics, some perhaps novel errors, and a few personal stories this book consists of paraphrases of standard material that can be found in many previously published books.

The strictly logical material can be found in many introductory logic texts. The most widely use of these is *Introduction to Logic (Copi & Cohen, 2005)*. It has a good coverage of the subtleties involved in formalizing ordinary informal English. Another very readable classic text is *Introduction to Logic (Suppes, 1999)*. It includes a careful treatment of definitions. An especially concise treatment is found in *Logic Primer* (Allen & Hand, 2001). More advanced, but still readable, accounts of logic are found in *Language, Proof, and Logic (Barwise & Etchemendy, 2002)*, *Mathematical Logic (Kleene, 2002)*, *Introduction to Mathematical Logic (Mendelson, 1997)*, *First-Order Logic (Smullyan, 1995)*, *Elementary Logic Revised Edition (Quine, 1980)*, *Methods of Logic (Quine, 1982)*, *Introduction to Logic (Gensler, 2002)*, and many others.

The material on decision tables is based on *Decision Tables in Software Engineering (Hurley, 1983)*. The discussion of algorithmic unsolvability is based on *Algorithmics the Spirit of Computing (Harel, 2004)* and *Introduction to Automata (Nelson 1968)*. The discussion of program correctness proofs is based on *Proving Programs Correct (Anderson, 1979)*, *The Design of Well-Structured and Correct Programs (Alagic & Arbib, 1978)*, *Formal Methods of Program Verification (Berg et al., 1982)*, and *Program Verification (Francez, 1992)*. Finally, I have benefited from many of the books described in the following bibliography.

Bibliography

The books listed below all contain material at or near the intersection of logic with computer science. In several cases the books listed here are out of print classics. Where I knew of a modern reprint that is the edition described.

Ackermann, W., (1962), *Solvable Cases of the Decision Problem*, North-Holland, Amsterdam.

Aho, Alfred V., and Jeffrey D. Ullman, (1994), *Foundations of Computer Science*, New York, NY, Computer Science Press.

Alagic, Suad, and Michael A. Arbib, (1978), *The Design of Well-Structured and Correct Programs*, Berlin Heidelberg New York, Springer.

Allen, Colin, and Michael Hand, (1991), *Logic Primer*, 2nd edn, Cambridge, MA, The MIT Press.

Anderson, Robert B., (1979), *Proving Programs Correct*, London, Wiley.

Apt, Krzysztof R., and Ernst-Rudinger Olderog (1991), *Verification of Sequential and Concurrent Programs*, Berlin Heidelberg New York, Springer.

Backhouse, Roland, (2003), *Program Construction: Calculating Implementations from Specifications*, London, Wiley.

Barwise, Jon, and John Etchemendy, (2002), *Language, Proof, and Logic*, Stanford, CA, Center for the Study of Language and Information.

Beizer, Boris, (1990), *Software Testing Techniques*, 2nd edn, New York, Van Nostrand Reinhold.

Benenti, Guiliano, Guilio Casati, and Guiliano Strini, (2004), *Principles of Quantum Computation and Information, Volume 1: Basic Concepts*, New Jersey, World Scientific Publishing Co.

Beizer, Boris, (1990), *Software Testing Techniques*, New York, Van Nostrand Reinhold.

Berg, H. K., W. E. Boebert, W. R. Franta, and T. G. Moher, (1982), *Formal Methods of Program Verification and Specification*, EngleWood Cliffs, NJ, Prentice-Hall.

Boolos, George S., and Richard Jeffrey, (1989), *Computability and Logic*, 3rd edn, Cambridge, UK, Cambridge University Press.

Bornat, Richard, (2005), *Proof and Disproof in Formal Logic: An introduction for Programmers*, Oxford, Oxford University Press.

Brown, Julian, (2002), *Minds, Machines, and the Multiverse: The Quest for the Quantum Computer*, New York, Simon & Schuster.

Brown, Frank Markham, (2003), *Boolean Reasoning: The Logic of Boolean Equations*, Mineola, New York, Dover Publications.

Copi, Irving M., and Carl Cohen, (2005), *Introduction to Logic*, 12th edn, Englewood Cliffs, NJ, Prentice Hall.

Date, C. J. and Hugh Darwen, (1997), *A Guide to the SQL Standard*, Reading, MA, Addison-Wesley.

Davis, Alan M., (1990), *Software Requirements Analysis and Specification*, Englewood, Cliffs, NJ, Prentice Hall.

Davis, Martin, (1982), *Computability and Unsolvability*, New York, Dover Publications.

Davis, Martin, (Ed.), (2004), *The Undecidable: Basic Papers on Undecidable Propositions, Unsolvable Problems and Computable Functions*, NY, USA, Raven Press.

Dijkstra, Edsger W., (1976), *A Discipline of Programming*, Englewood, Cliffs, NJ, Prentice-Hall.

Francez, Nissim, (1992), *Program Verification*, Reading, MA, Addison-Wesley.

Gallier, Jean H., (1986), *Logic for Computer Science: Foundations of Automatic Theorem Proving*, New York, Harper & Row.

Galton, Antony, (1990), *Logic for Information Technology*, New York, Wiley.

Gardner, Martin, (1958), *Logic Machines and Diagrams*, New York, McGraw-Hill.

Genesereth, Michael R. and Nils J. Nilsson, (1987), *Logical Foundations of Artificial Intelligence*, Los Altos, CA, Morgan Kaufmann Publishers.

Gensler, Harry J., (2002), *Introduction to Logic*, London, Routledge.

Giarrantano, Joseph C., and Gary D. Riley, (2005), *Expert Systems: Principles and Programming*, Boston, MA, Course Technology.

Goldblatt, Robert, (1992), *Logics of Time and Computation,* 2nd edn, Revised and Expanded, Stanford, Center for the Study of Language and Information.

Gries, David, (1981), *The Science of Programming*, Berlin Heidelberg New York, Springer.

Gumb, Raymond D., (1989), *Programming Logics: An Introduction to Verification Semantics*, New York, Wiley.

Haak, Susan, (1996), *Deviant Logic, Fuzzy Logic: Beyond the Formalism*, Chicago, London, The University of Chicago Press.

Halmos, Paul R., (1998), *Naïve Set Theory*, Berlin Heidelberg New York, Springer.

Harel, David, Dexter Kozen, and Jerzy Tiuryn, (2000), *Dynamic Logic*, Cambridge, MA, The MIT Press.

Harel, David, (2004), *Algorithmics the Spirit of Computing*, 3rd edn, Reading, MA, Addison-Wesley.

Harrington, Jan L. (1998), *SQL Clearly Explained*, Morgan Kaufmann

Hein, James L., (2002), *Discrete Structures, Logic, and Computability*, 2nd edn, Jones and Bartlett

Hurley, Richard B., (1983), *Decision Tables in Software Engineering*, New York, Van Nostrand Reinhold.

Huth, Michael R. A. and Mark D. Ryan, (2004), *Logic in Computer Science: Modelling and Reasoning about Systems,* 2nd edn, New York, NY, Cambridge University Press.

Jackson, Daniel, (2006), *Software Abstractions: Logic, Language, and Analysis*, Cambridge, MA, The MIT Press.

Johnson, George, (2003), *A Shortcut Through Time: The Path to the Quantum Computer*, New York, Alfred A. Knopf,.

Jurgen, Audretsch, (Ed.), (2006), *Entangled World: The Fascination of Quantum Information and Computation*, New York, Wiley-VTH.

Kaufmann, Matt, Panagiotis Manolios, and J. Strother Moore, *Computer-Aided Reasoning: An Approach*, (2002a), hardback version published in 2000 by Kluwer Academic Publishers.

Kaufmann, Matt, Panagiotis Manolios, and J. Strother Moore, *Computer-Aided Reasoning: ACL2 Case Studies*, (2002b), hardback version published in 2000 by Kluwer Academic Publishers.

Kleene, Stephen Cole, (2002), *Mathematical Logic*, New York, Dover Publications.

Lloyd, Seth, (2006), *Programming the Universe: A Quantum Computer Scientist Takes On the Cosmos*, New York, Alfred A. Knopf.

Manna, Zohar, (1974), *Mathematical Theory of Computation*, New York, Dover Publications.

Manna, Zohar, (1980), *Lectures on the Logic of Computer Programming*, Philadelphia, PA, Society for Industrial and Applied Mathematics.

Manna, Zohar, and Richard Waldinger, (1993), *The Deductive Foundations of Computer Programming*, Reading, MA, Addison-Wesley.

Mead, Jerud J., and Anil M. Shende, (2001), *Persuasive Programming*, Wilsonville, OR, Franklin, Beedle & Associates.

Mendelson, Elliott, (1997), *Introduction to Mathematical Logic,* 4th edn, London. Chapman & Hall/CRC.

Moschovakis, Y. N. (Ed.), (1992), *Logic from Computer Science*, Berlin Heidelberg New York, Springer.

Neilson, Michael A., and Isaac L. Chaung, (2002), *Quantum Computation and Quantum Information*, Cambridge, MA, Cambridge University Press.

Nelson, R. J., (1968), *Introduction to Automata*, New York, Wiley.

Nielson, Hanne Riis, and Flemming Nielson, (2007), *Semantics with Applications: An Appetizer*, Berlin Heidelberg New York, Springer.

O'Donnell, John, Cordelia Hall, and Rex Page, (2006), *Discrete Mathematics Using a Computer*, Berlin Heidelberg New York, Springer.

Quine, Willard VanOrman, (1980), *Elementary Logic Revised Edition*, Cambridge, MA, Harvard University Press.

Quine, Willard VanOrman, (1982), *Methods of Logic*, Cambridge, MA, Harvard University Press.

Parkes, Alan P., (2002), *Introduction to Languages, Machines, and Logic: Computable Languages, Abstract Machines, and Formal Logic*, Berlin Heidelberg New York, Springer.

Pearl, Judea, (1988), *Probabilistic Reasoning in Intelligent Systems: Networks of Plausible Inference*, Revised Second Printing, San Mateo, CA, Morgan Kaufmann Publishers.

Reeves, Steve, and Michael Clarke, (1990), *Logic for Computer Science*, Reading, MA, Addison-Wesley Publishing Co.

Robertson, David, and Jaume Agusti, (1999), *Software Blueprints: Lightweight Uses of Logic in Conceptual Modelling*, New York, ACM Press.

Schagrin, Morton L., William J. Rapaport, and Randall R. Dipert, (1985), *Logic: a Computer Approach*, New York, McGraw-Hill.

Smullyan, Raymond M., (1995), *First-Order Logic*, New York, Dover Publications.

Sperschneider, V., and G. Antoniou, (1991), *Logic A Foundation for Computer Science*, Reading, MA, Addison-Wesley Publishing Co.

Sturling, Leon, and Ehud Shapiro, (1994), *The Art of Prolog*, 2nd edn, Cambridge, MA, The MIT Press.

Suppes, Patrick, (1972), *Axiomatic Set Theory*, New York, Dover Publications.

Suppes, Patrick, (1999), *Introduction to Logic*, New York, Dover Publications.

Torasso, Pietro, and Luca Console (1989), *Diagnostic Problem Solving: Combining Heuristic, Approximate, and Causal Reasoning*, New York, Van Nostrand Reinhold.

Treiman, Sam, (2002), *The Odd Quantum*, Princeton University Press.

Tucker, Allen B., W. James Bradley, Robert D. Cupper, and David K. Garnick, (1992), *Fundamentals of Computing I: Logic Problem Solving Programs and Computers*, New York, McGraw-Hill.

Turner, Raymond, (1984), *Logics for Artificial Intelligence*, Chichester, Ellis Harwood Limited.

Walker, Henry M., (1994), *The Limits of Computing*, Boston, MA, Jones and Bartlett.

Wallace, Phillip R., (1996), *Paradox Lost: Images of the Quantum*, Berlin Heidelberg New York, Springer

Whitesitt, J. Eldon, (1995), *Boolean Algebra and Its Applications*, New York, Dover Publications.

Index